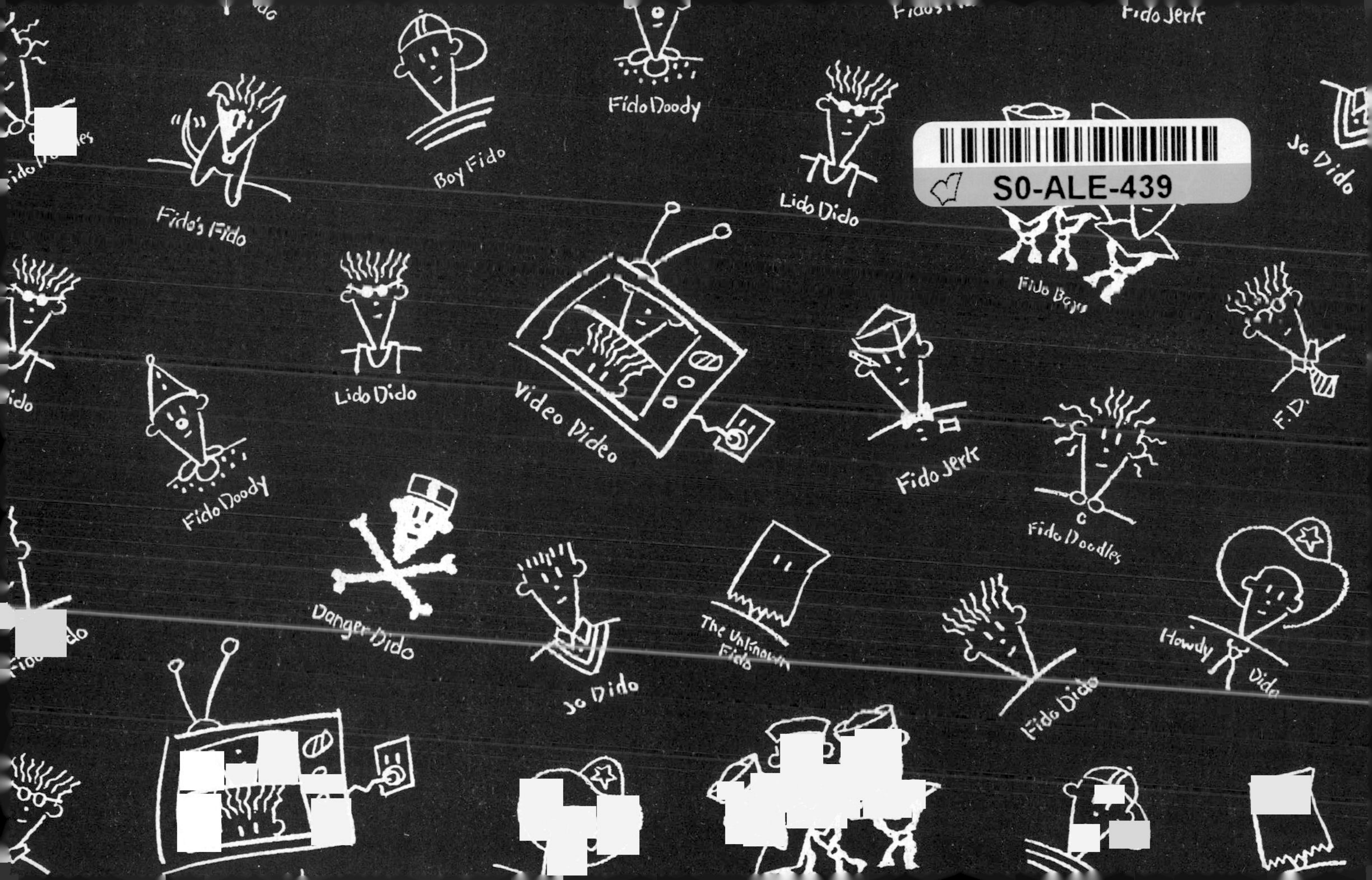

Fido Doody
Boy Fido
Fido's Fido
Lido Dido
Jo Dido
Fido Boys
Video Dido
Lido Dido
Fido Jerk
F.D.
Fido Doody
Fido Doodles
Danger Dido
Jo Dido
The Unknown Fido
Howdy Dido
Fido Dido

This book is black + white.

In this book, nobody's
grass is greener.

Any resemblance to people
living or barely scraping by
is purely on purpose.

This book is dedicated to whoever owns it.

----
your name here.

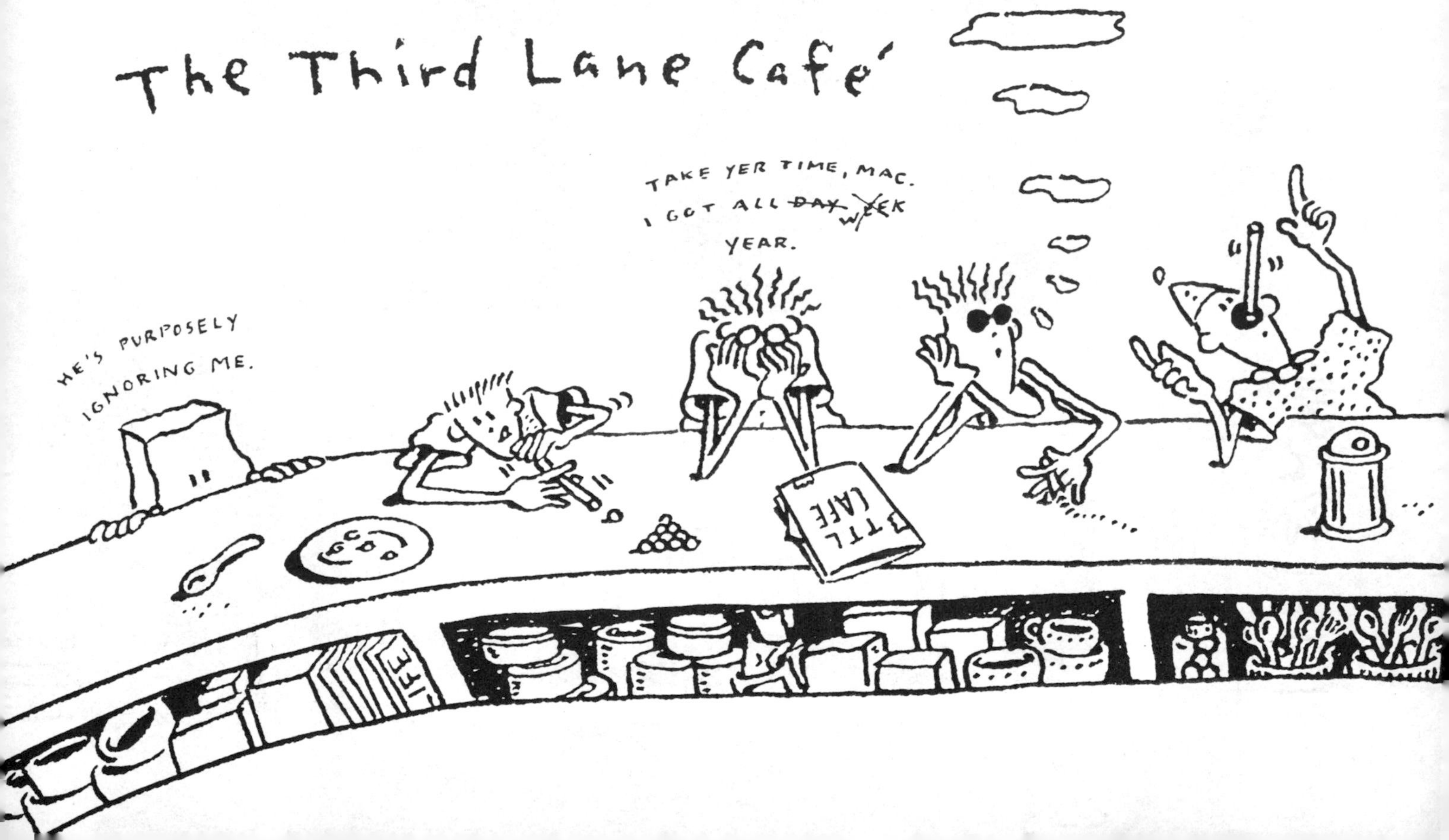
The Third Lane Café
HE'S PURPOSELY IGNORING ME.
TAKE YER TIME, MAC. I GOT ALL ~~DAY~~ ~~WEEK~~ YEAR.
TTL CAFE

what's yer specialty?
same day service.
MAY I AT LEAST HAVE SOME WATER?
HAVE I ORDERED YET?
ZZZZZZZZ

Fido is for Fido.
Fido is against no one.
Fido is Youth.
Fido has no age.
Fido sees everything.
Fido judges nothing.
Fido is Innocent.
Fido is Powerful.
Fido comes from the past.
Fido is the future.

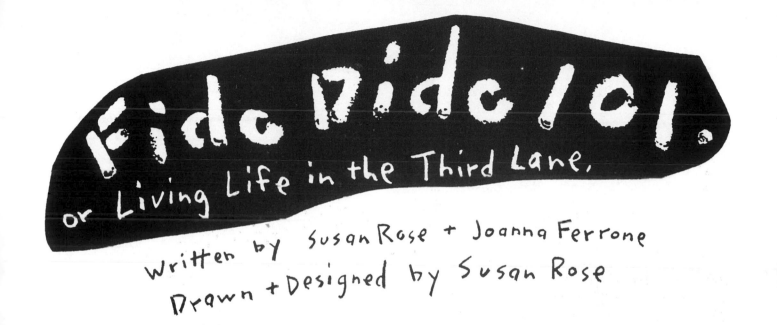

Fido Dido 101,
or Living Life in the Third Lane,

Written by Susan Rose + Joanna Ferrone

Drawn + Designed by Susan Rose

TOPPER BOOKS
AN IMPRINT OF PHAROS BOOKS • A SCRIPPS HOWARD COMPANY
NEW YORK

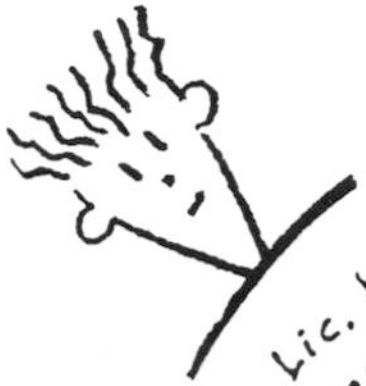

First published in 1988
Paperback edition distributed in the
United States by Ballantine Books, a
division of Random House, Inc. and in
Canada by Random House of Canada, Ltd.
Library of Congress Catalog Card Number: 87-71942
Pharos ISBN: 0-88687-331-2
Ballantine Books ISBN: 0-345-35227-0
Printed in United States of America
Topper Books
An Imprint of Pharos Books
A Scripps Howard Company
200 Park Avenue
New York, NY 10166
10 9 8 7 6 5 4 3 2 1

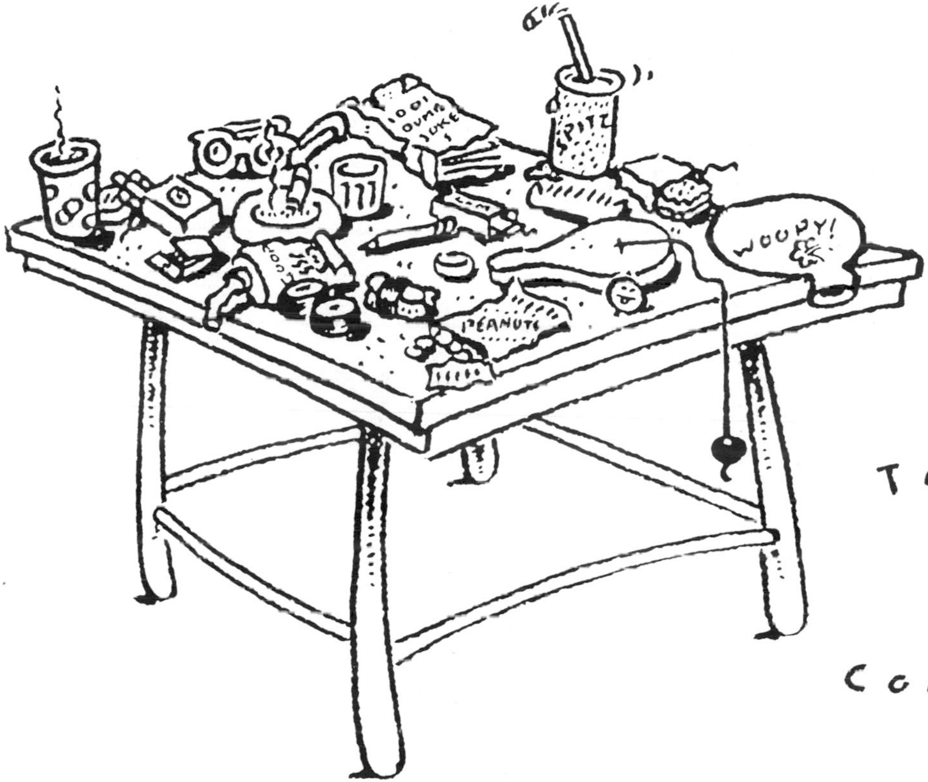
SPITZ
WOOPY!

Table of Contents

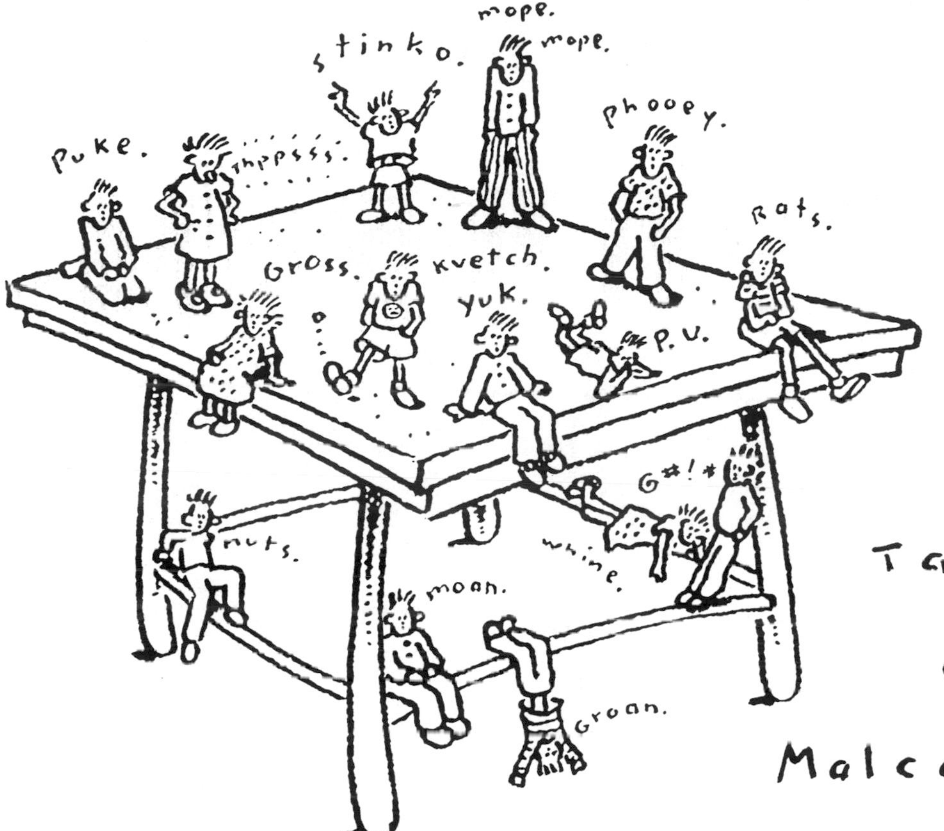
mope.
mope.
stinko.
puke.
thppsss.
phooey.
Rats.
Gross.
kvetch.
yuk.
P.U.
G#!*
nuts.
whine.
moan.
Groan.

Table of Malcontents

HERE'S YER HANDY DANDY
Fido Dido Cast O' characters
REFERENCE GUIDE

With some hints to help answer that nagging question:
"How can I tell a Fido from a Dido and vice versa?"

This is Fido Dido.

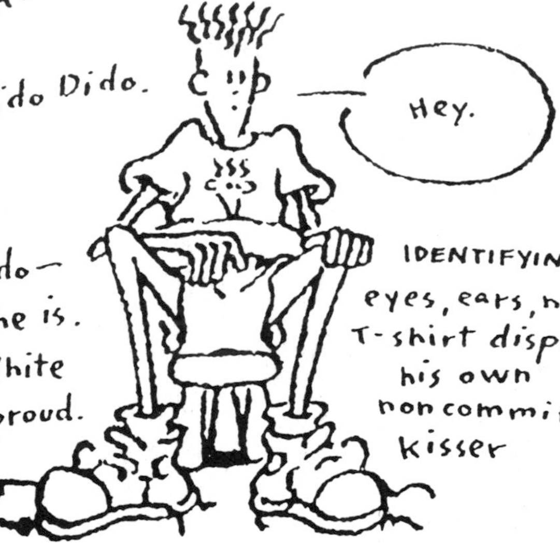

Yer basic Fido—
he is what he is.
Black + White
and he's proud.

IDENTIFYING MARKS:
eyes, ears, nose, hair—
T-shirt displaying
his own
noncommittal
kisser

Fido Dido and Fido's Fido
are room mates.
The I'm Odd—Yer Odd Couple.

This is
Fido's Fido.

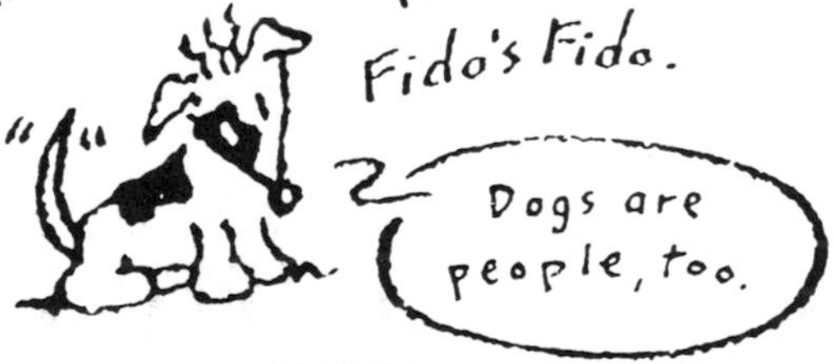

IDENTIFYING MARKS:
one black eye — one white eye
100% pure mutt

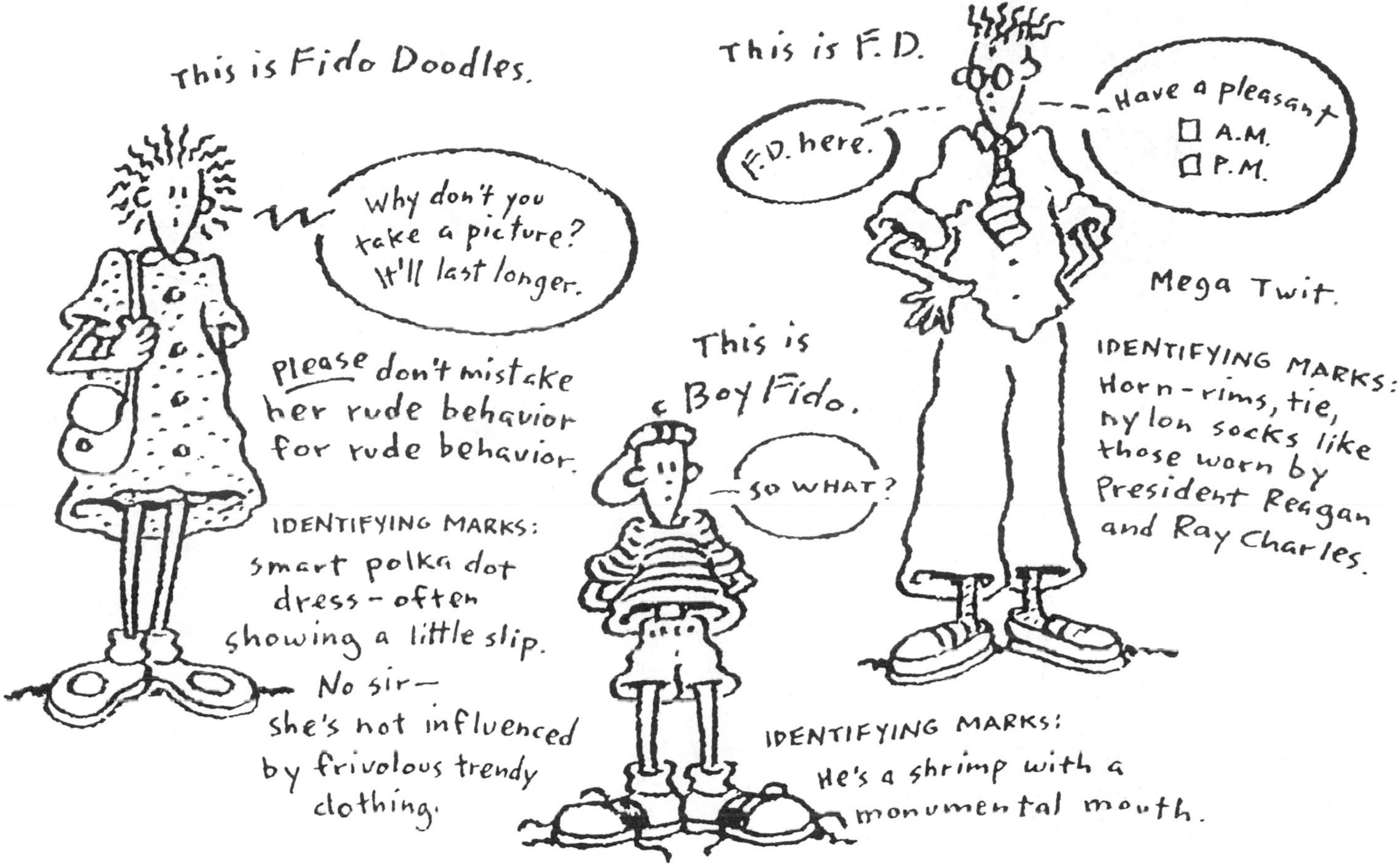

This is Fido Doodles.
Why don't you take a picture? It'll last longer.
please don't mistake her rude behavior for rude behavior.
IDENTIFYING MARKS:
smart polka dot dress - often showing a little slip.
No sir— she's not influenced by frivolous trendy clothing.
This is a Boy Fido.
SO WHAT?
IDENTIFYING MARKS:
He's a shrimp with a monumental mouth.
This is F.D.
F.D. here.
Have a pleasant
☐ A.M.
☐ P.M.
Mega Twit.
IDENTIFYING MARKS:
Horn-rims, tie, nylon socks like those worn by President Reagan and Ray Charles.

This is Lido Dido.

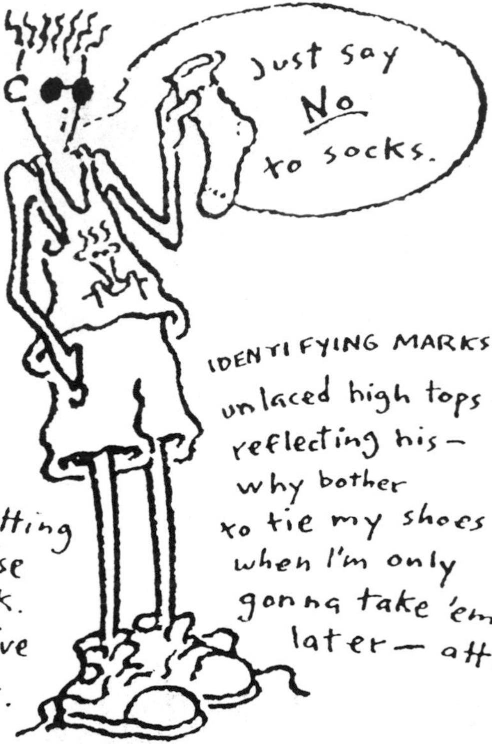

Lido sez:
Hey look—
If I got a job
I might be putting
somebody else
out of work.
I couldn't live
with that.

IDENTIFYING MARKS:
unlaced high tops—
reflecting his—
why bother
to tie my shoes
when I'm only
gonna take 'em off
later—attitude.

Meet Dribble Dido.

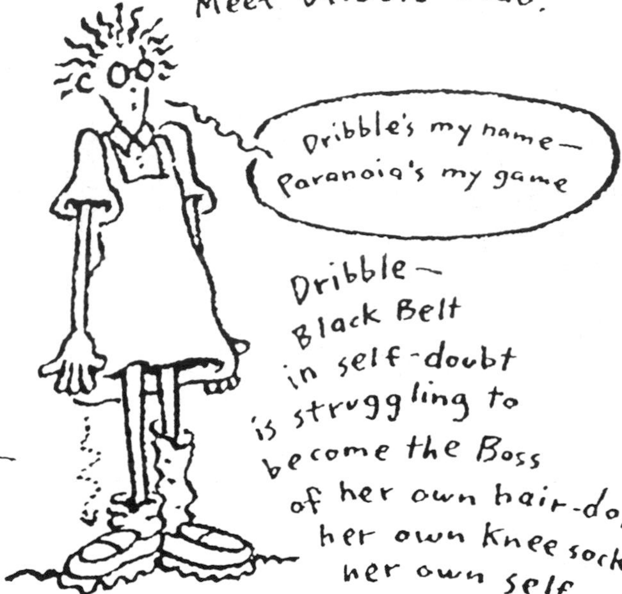

Dribble—
Black Belt
in self-doubt
is struggling to
become the Boss
of her own hair-do,
her own knee socks,
her own self.

IDENTIFYING MARKS: a jumper which
resembles a Catholic School Uniform
but is actually an expensive
Japanese design and eye glasses

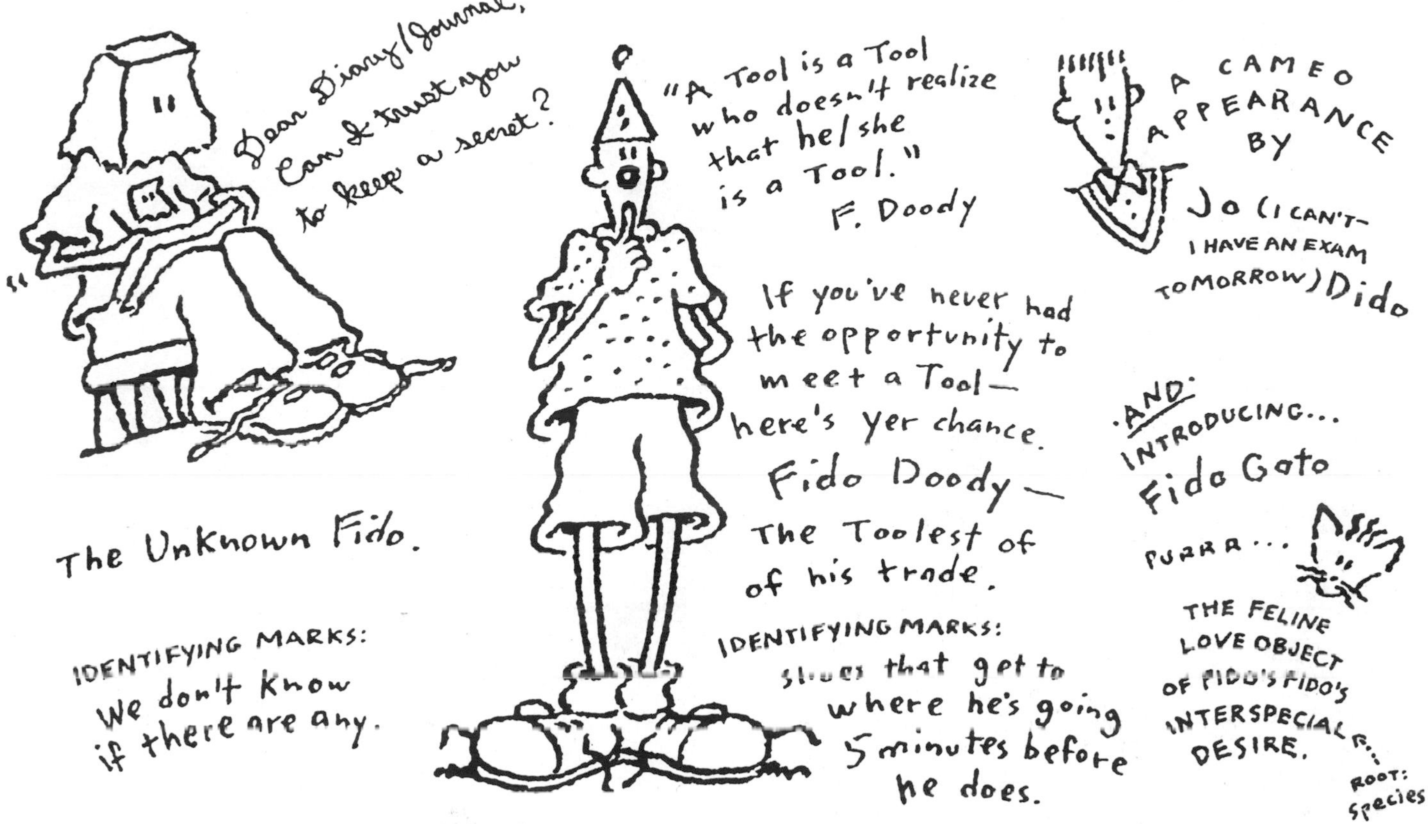

"Dear Diary/Journal, Can I trust you to keep a secret?"
The Unknown Fido.
IDENTIFYING MARKS:
We don't know if there are any.
"A Tool is a Tool who doesn't realize that he/she is a Tool."
F. Doody
If you've never had the opportunity to meet a Tool— here's yer chance.
Fido Doody—
The Toolest of of his trade.
IDENTIFYING MARKS:
shoes that get to where he's going 5 minutes before he does.
A CAMEO APPEARANCE BY
Jo (I CAN'T- I HAVE AN EXAM TOMORROW) Dido
AND
INTRODUCING...
Fido Gato
PURRR...
THE FELINE LOVE OBJECT OF FIDO'S FIDO'S INTERSPECIAL R... DESIRE.
ROOT: Species

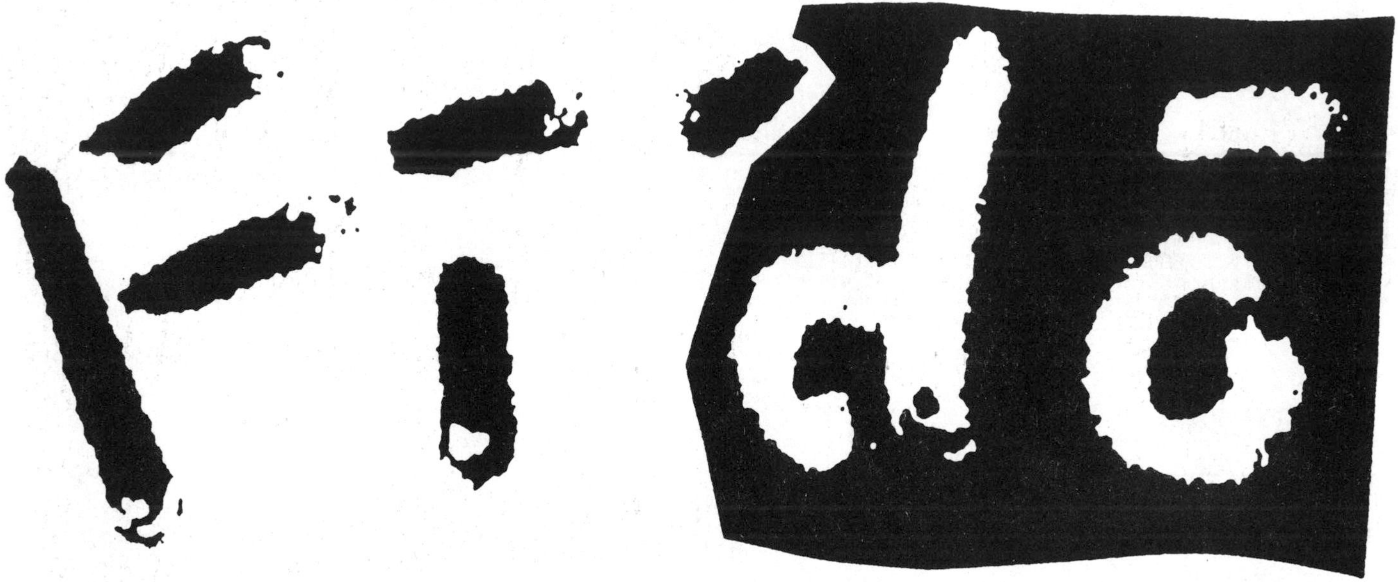
Fido

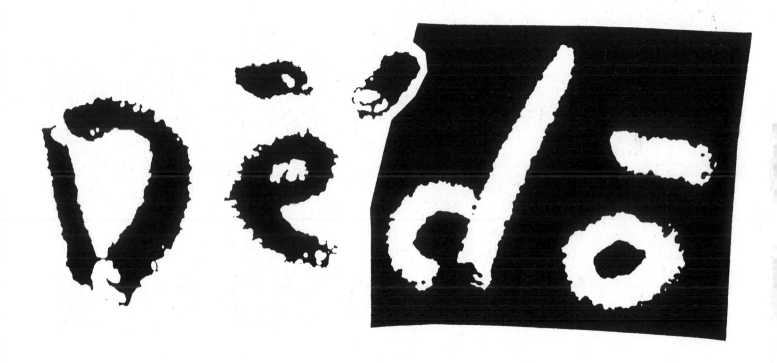

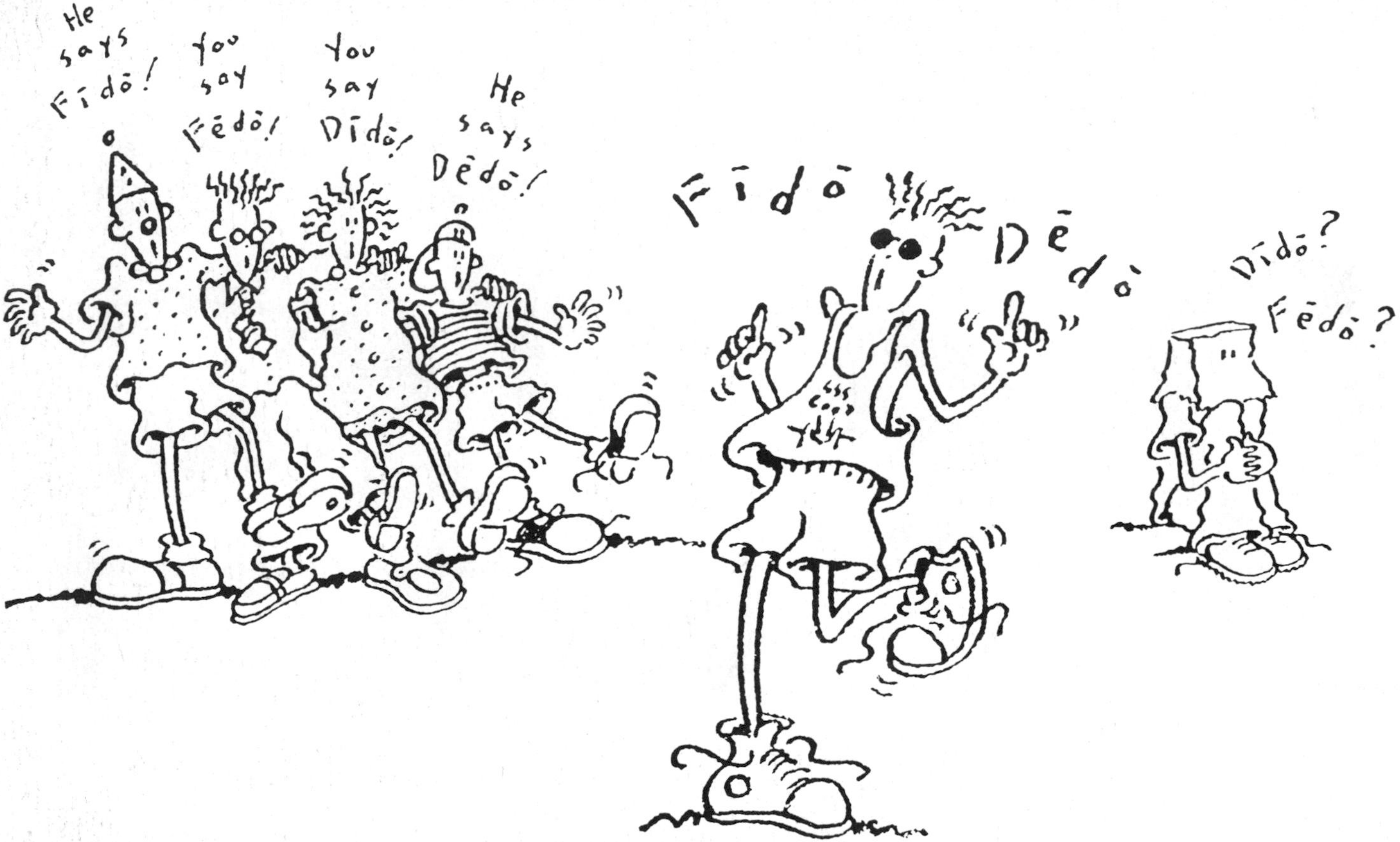
He says Fīdō!
You say Fēdō!
You say Dīdō!
He says Dēdō!
Fīdō
Dēdō
Dīdō?
Fēdō?

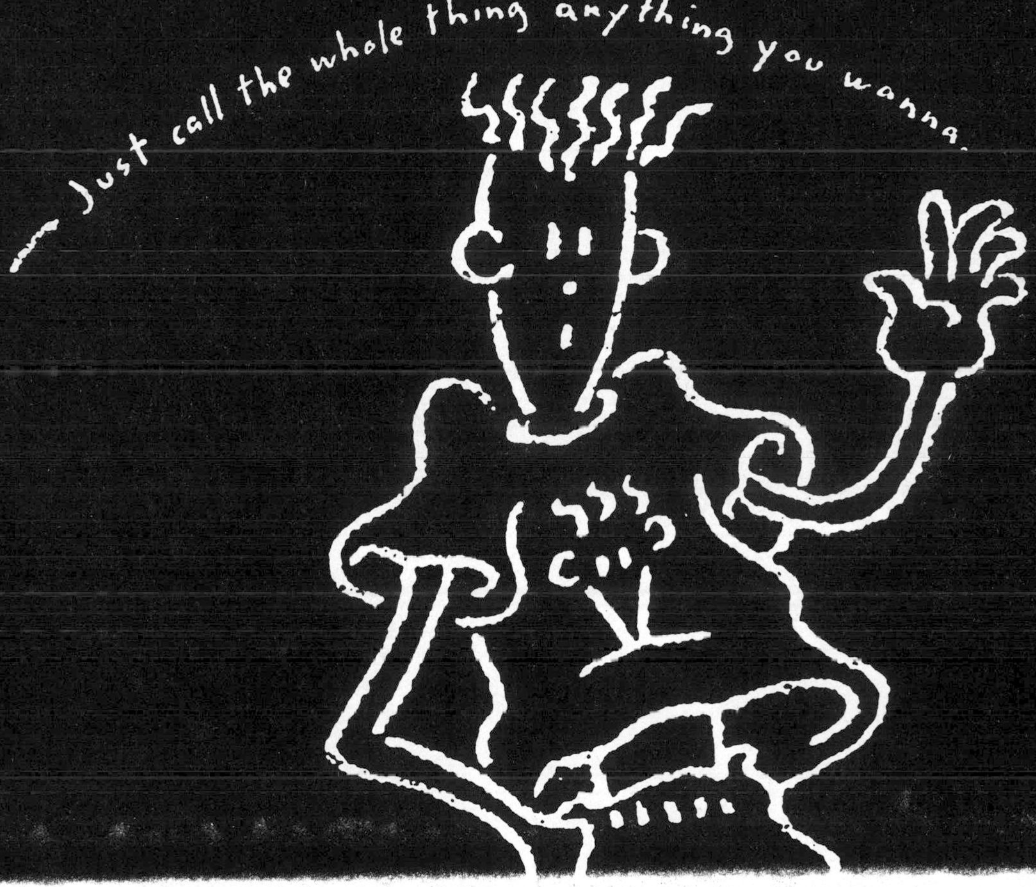
— Just call the whole thing anything you wanna.

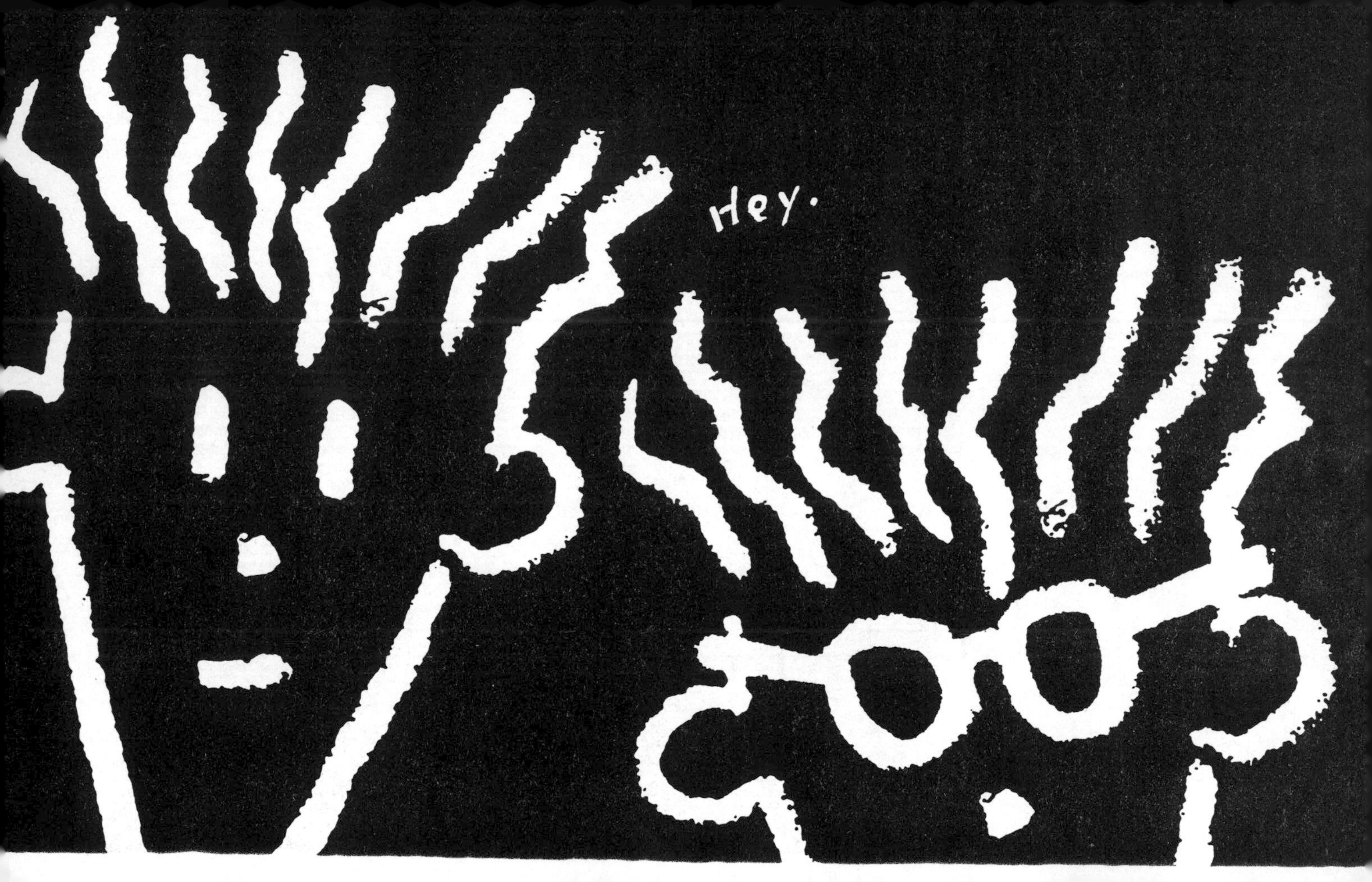
Hey.

they met.
they had a conversation.
it wasn't deep.

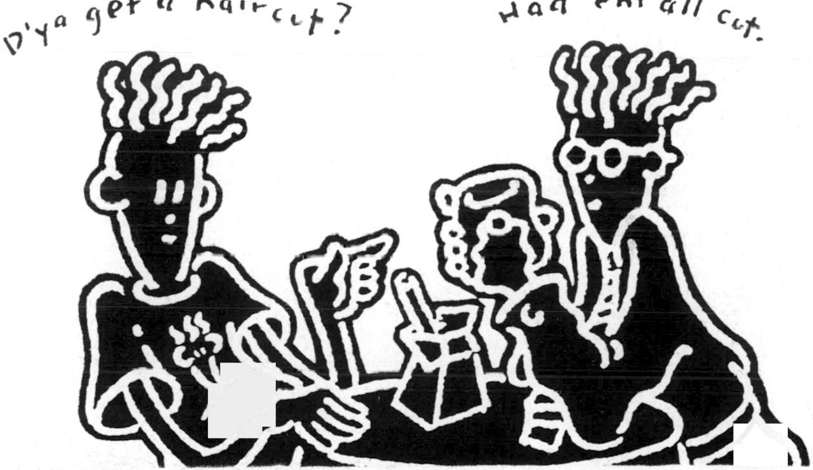
D'ya get a haircut?
Had 'em all cut.

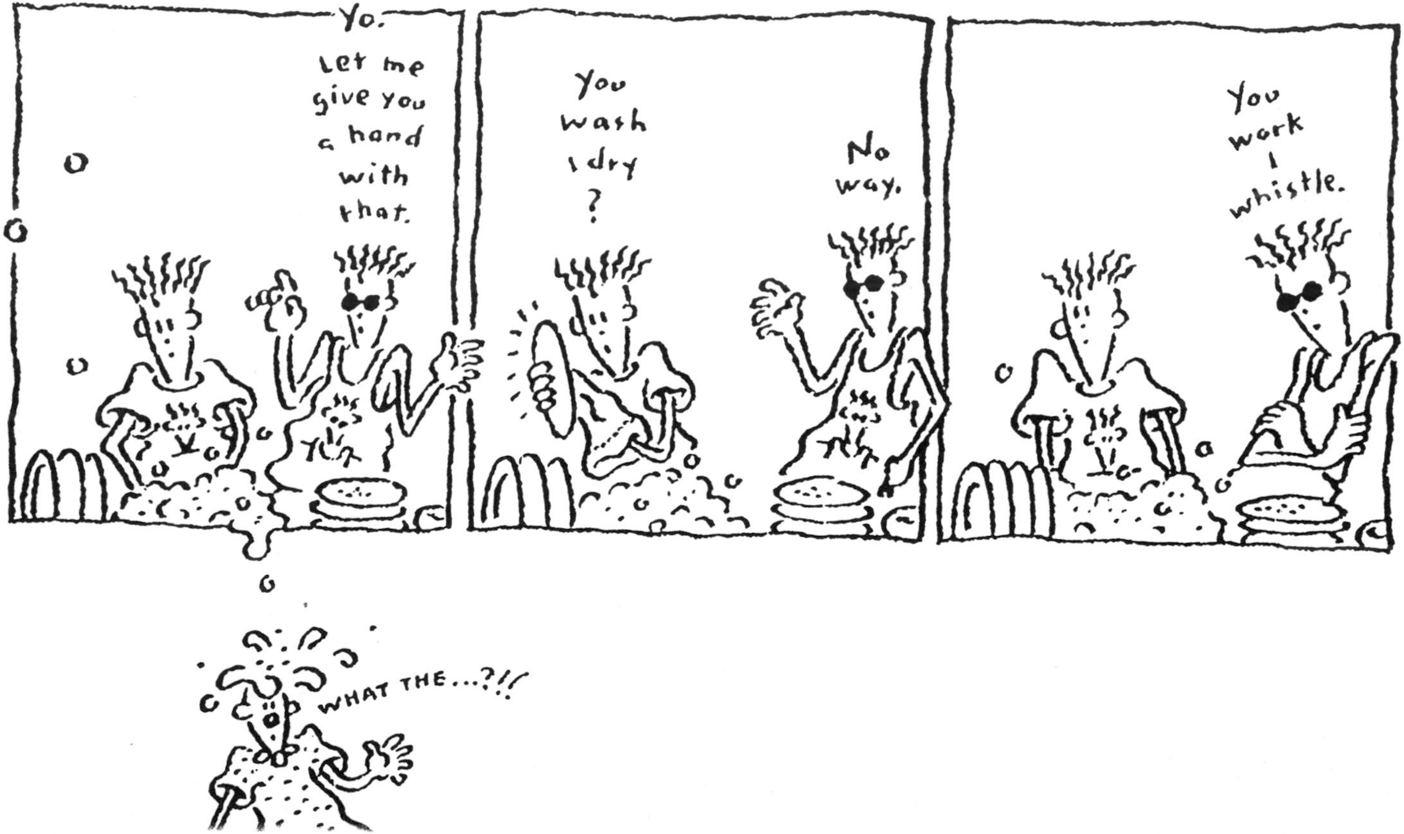
Yo.
Let me give you a hand with that.
You wash I dry ?
No way.
You work I whistle.
WHAT THE...?!!

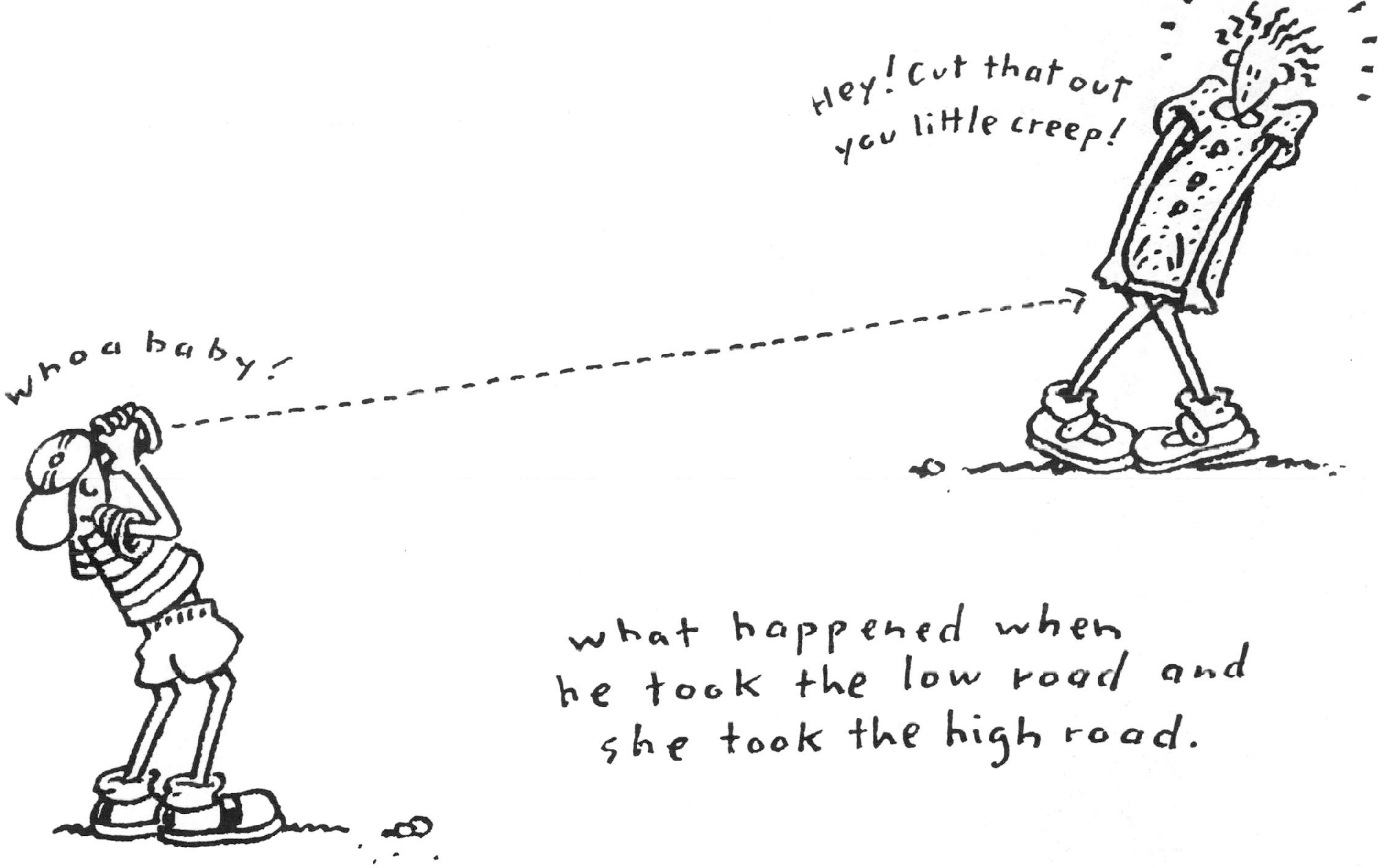
Hey! Cut that out you little creep!
whoa baby!

what happened when he took the low road and she took the high road.

Dear Sir :

We would be
delighted
to have you
work for our
company .

But not in
this life .

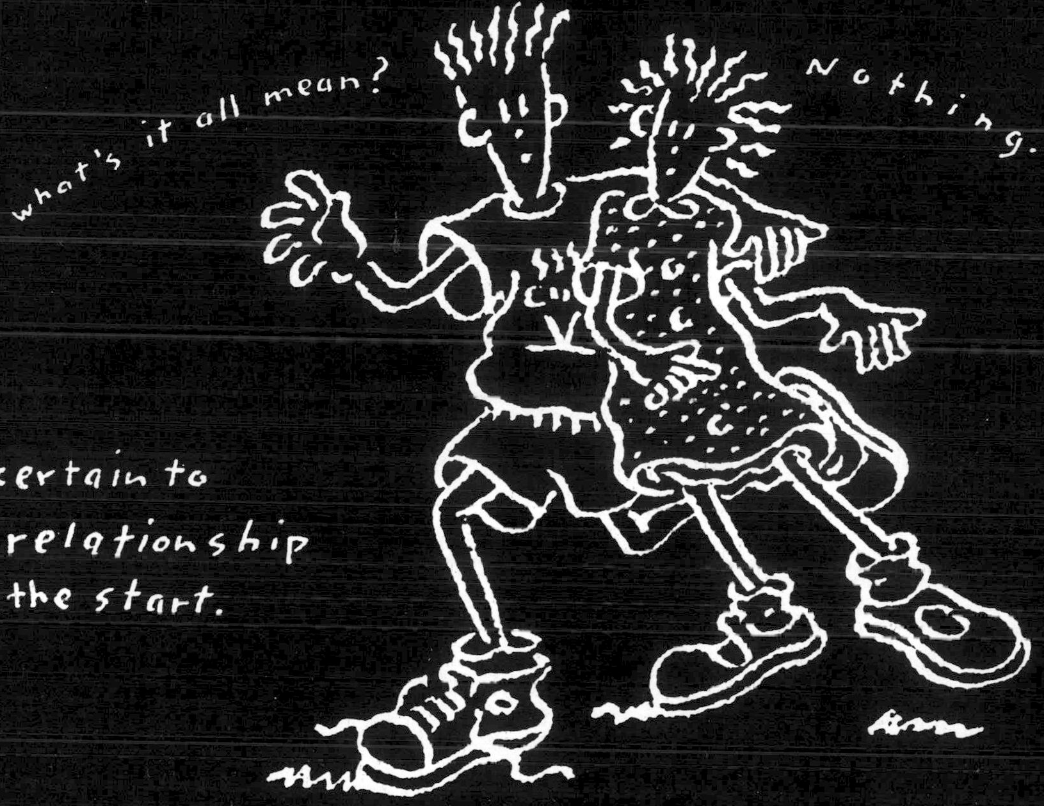
what's it all mean?
Nothing.

They made certain to define their relationship right from the start.

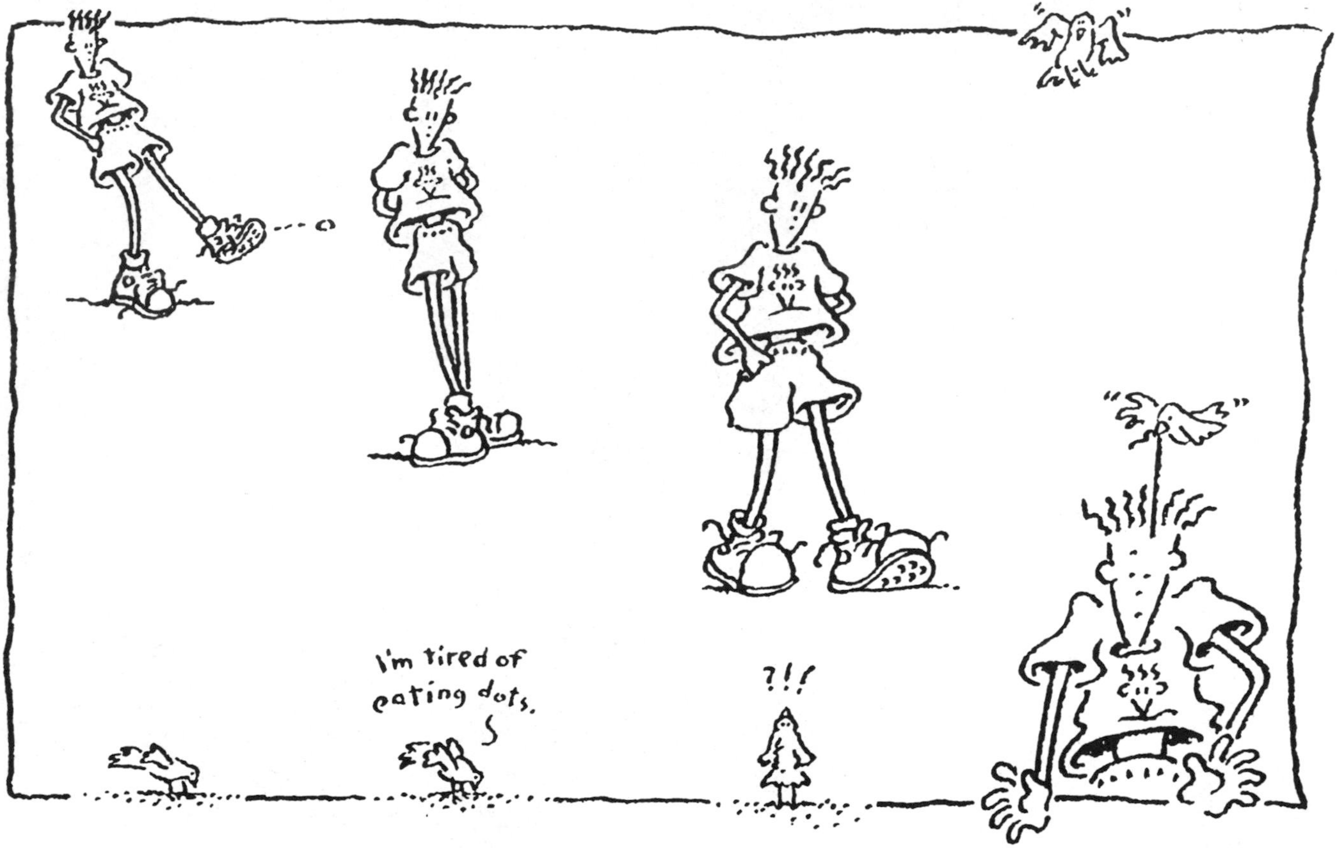
I'm tired of eating dots.
?!!

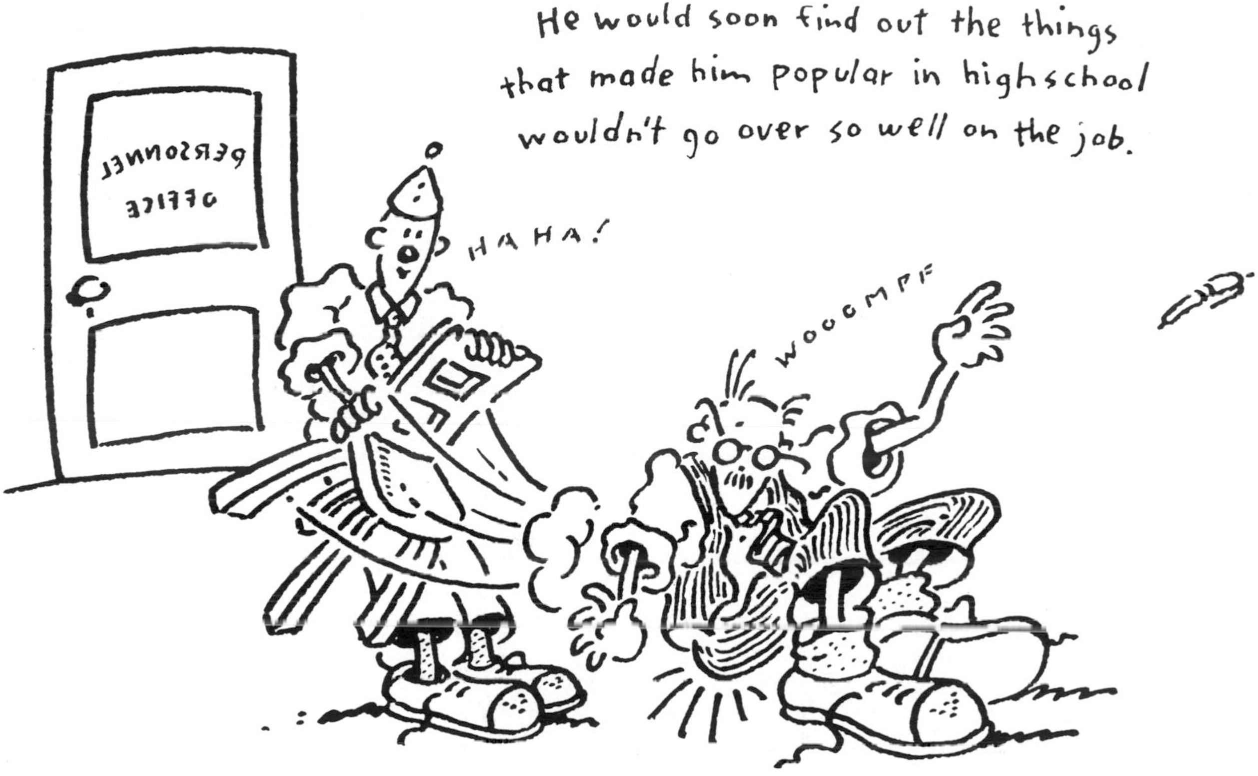
He would soon find out the things that made him popular in highschool wouldn't go over so well on the job.
PERSONNEL OFFICE
HAHA!
WOOOMPF

A "sniff" ROMANTIC

They had so much in common. They both loved dogs.

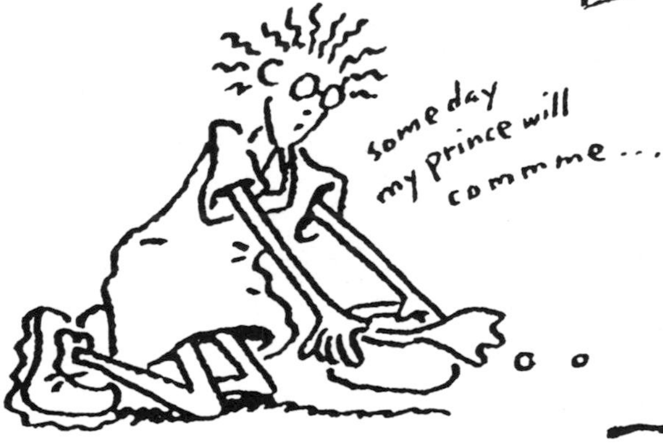

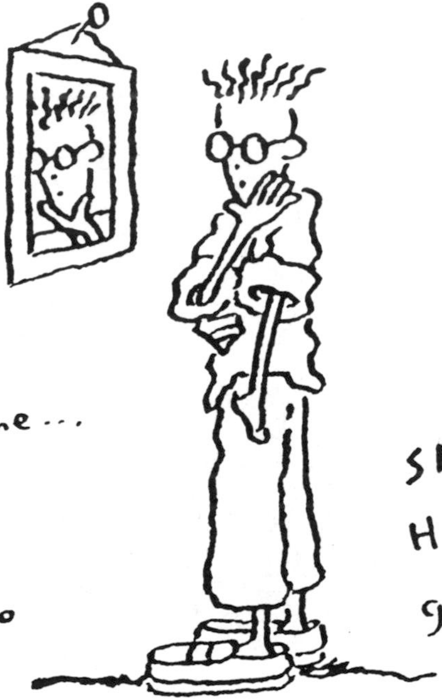

She loved beards. He was trying to grow one.

TRAGEDY.

"BOO HOO"

Alas, he lived in Peoria and she lived in Korea.

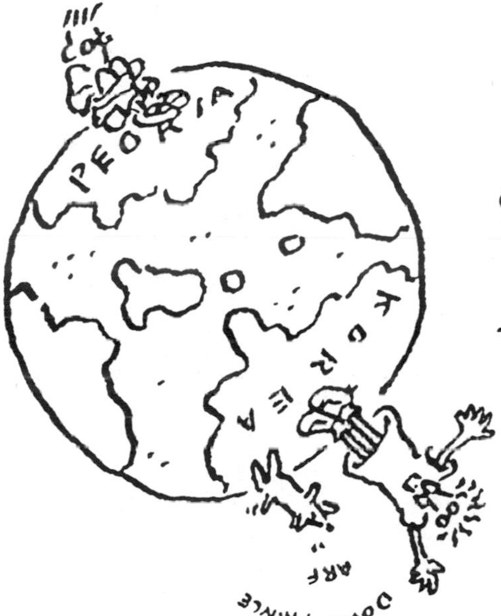
PEORIA
KOREA
"ARF"

Close, but no cigar. They never met.

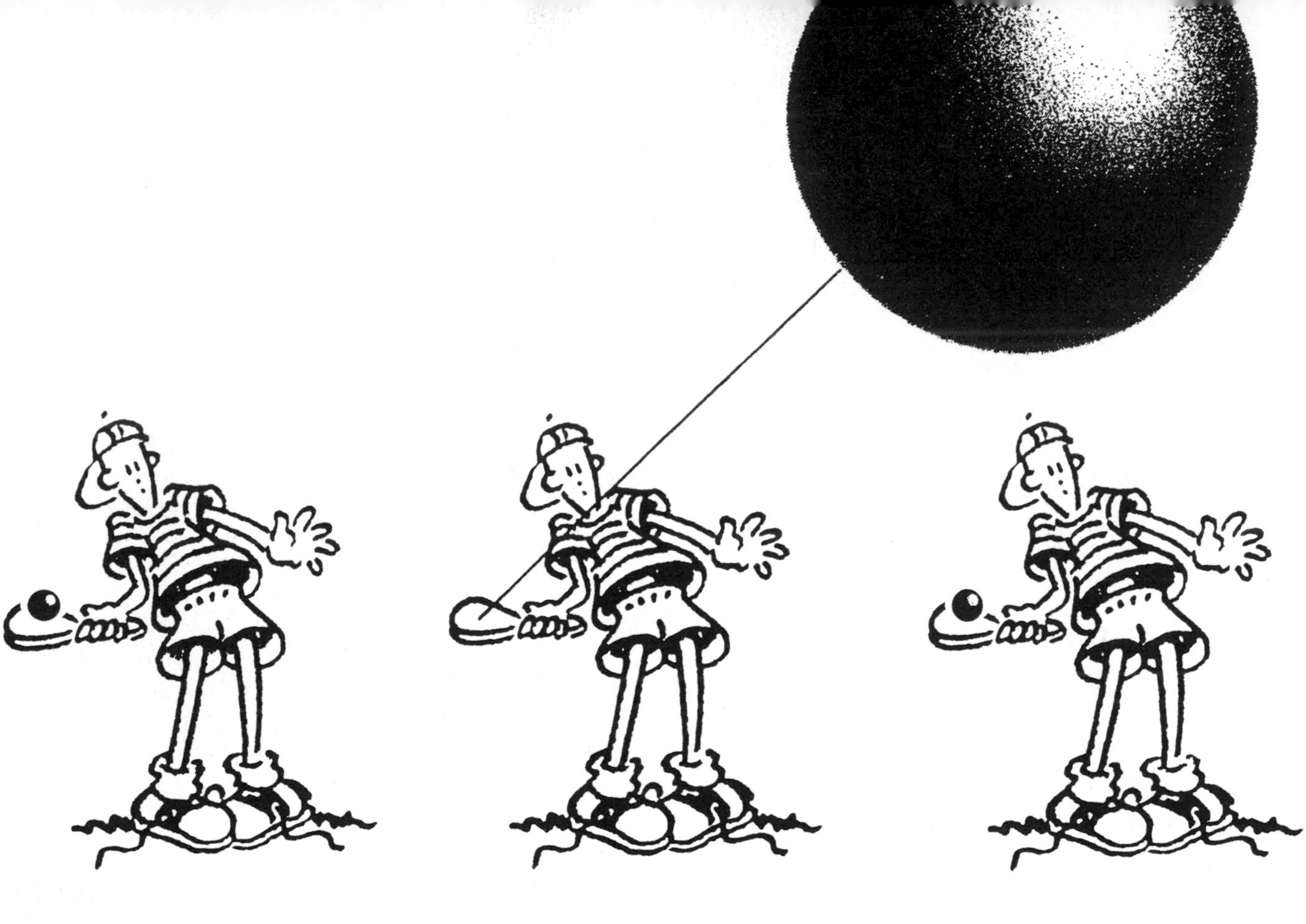

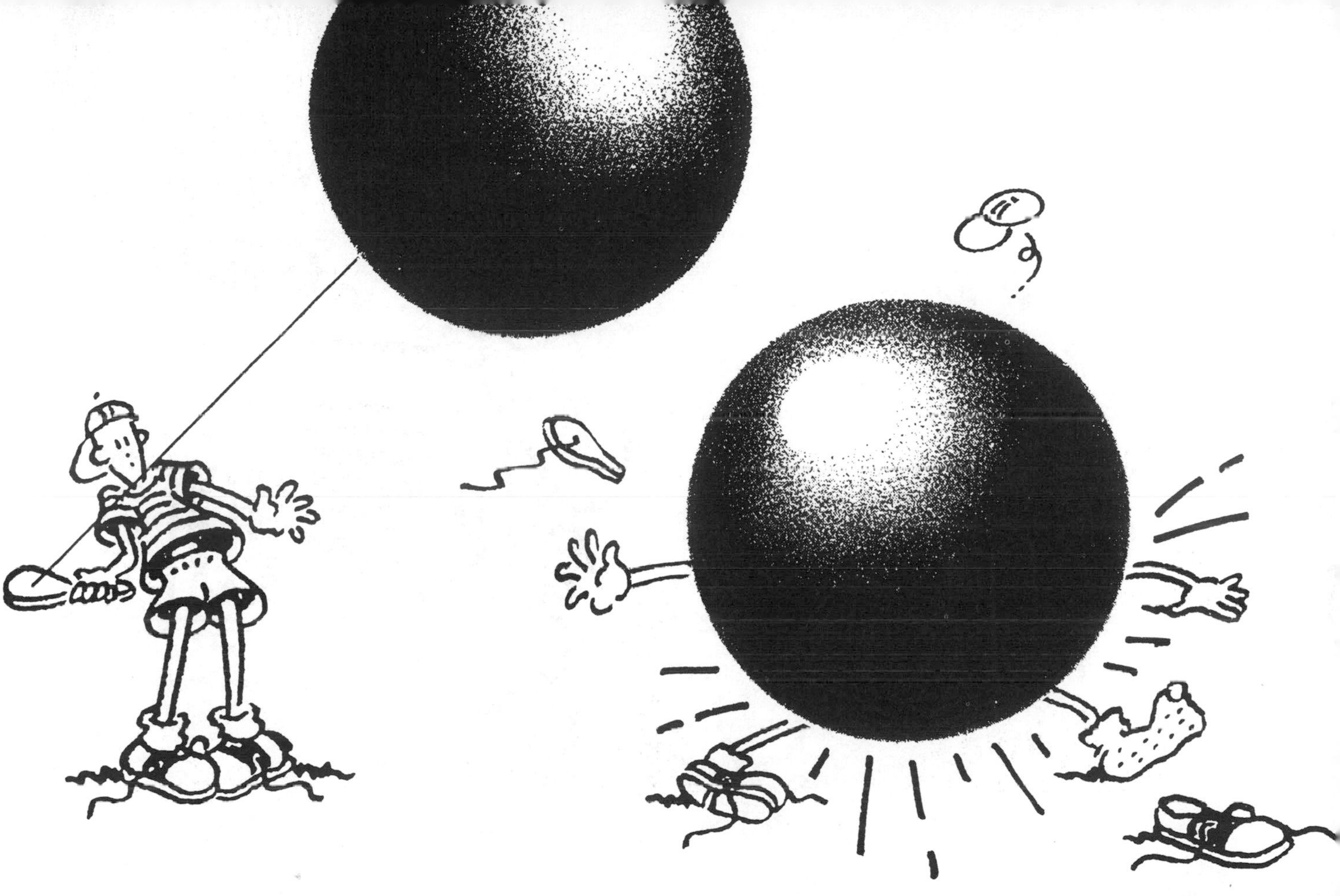

The most exciting thing to do at our house is watch the food in our new microwave oven go round and round.

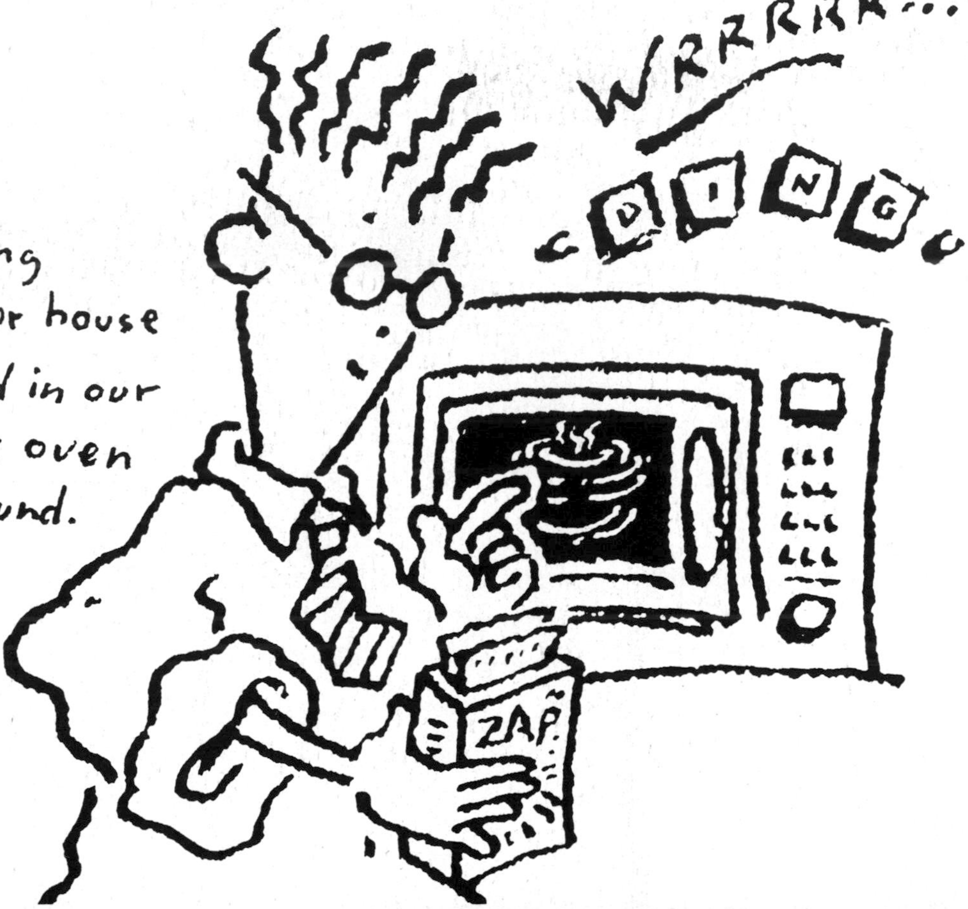

WRRRRRR...
DING
ZAP

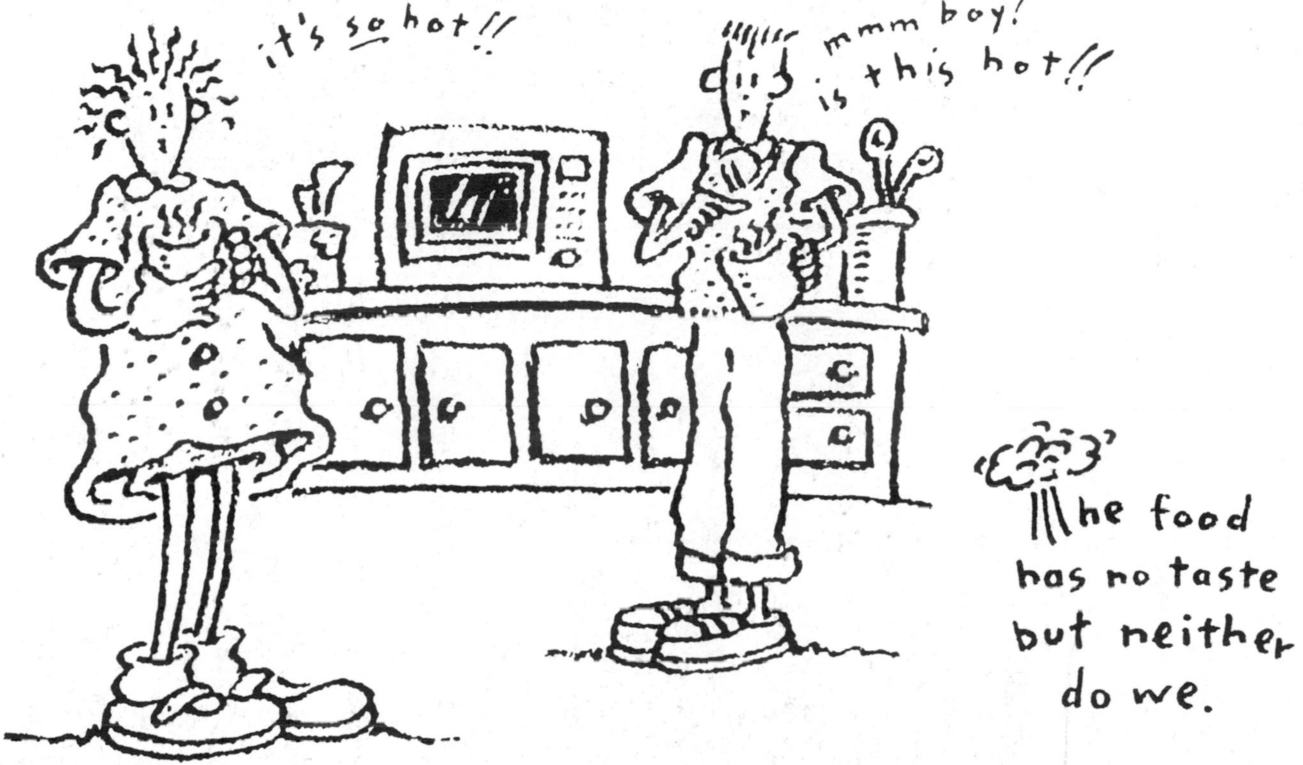
it's so hot!!
mmm boy! is this hot!!
The food has no taste but neither do we.

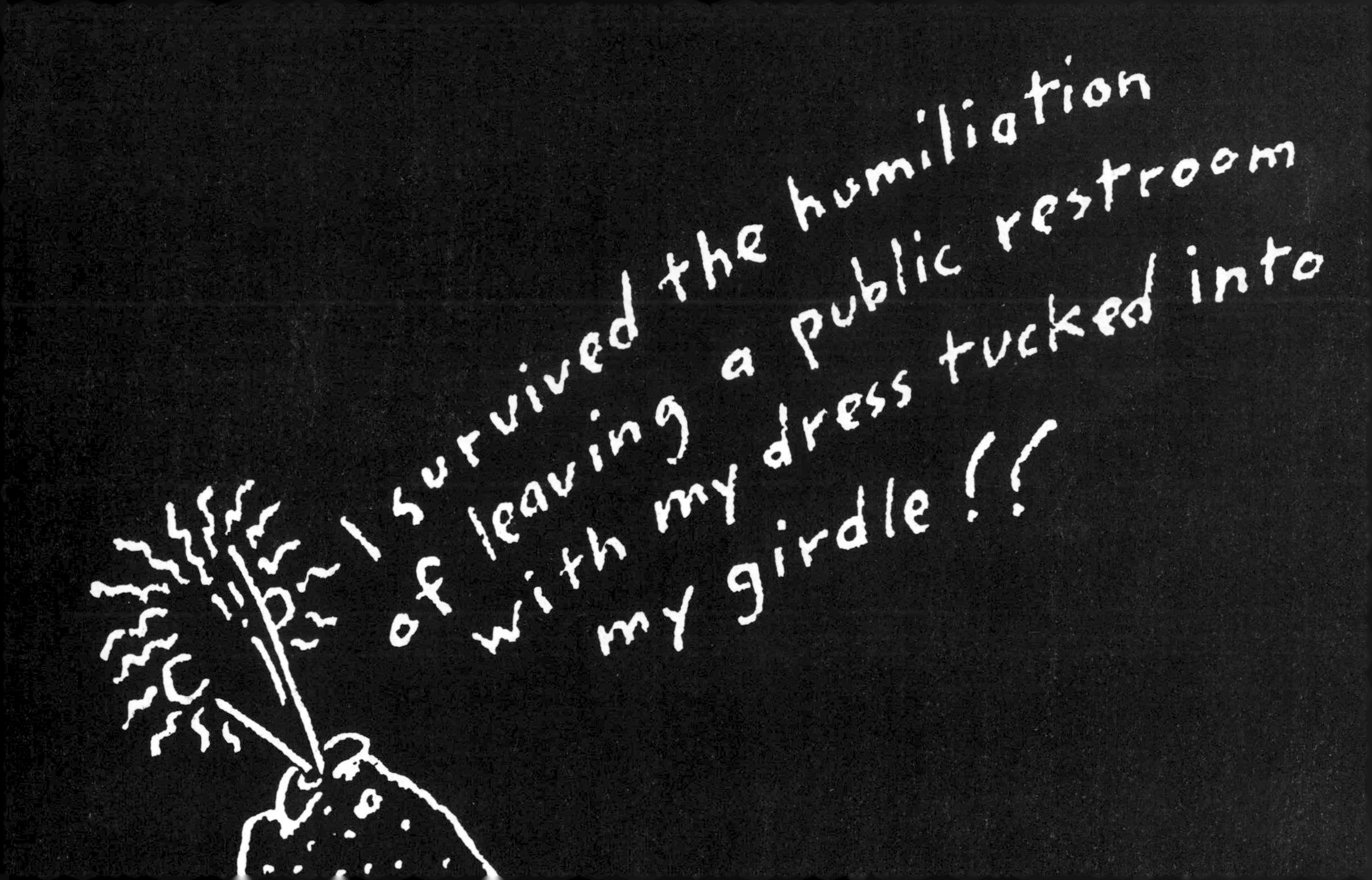
I survived the humiliation
of leaving a public restroom
with my dress tucked into
my girdle!!

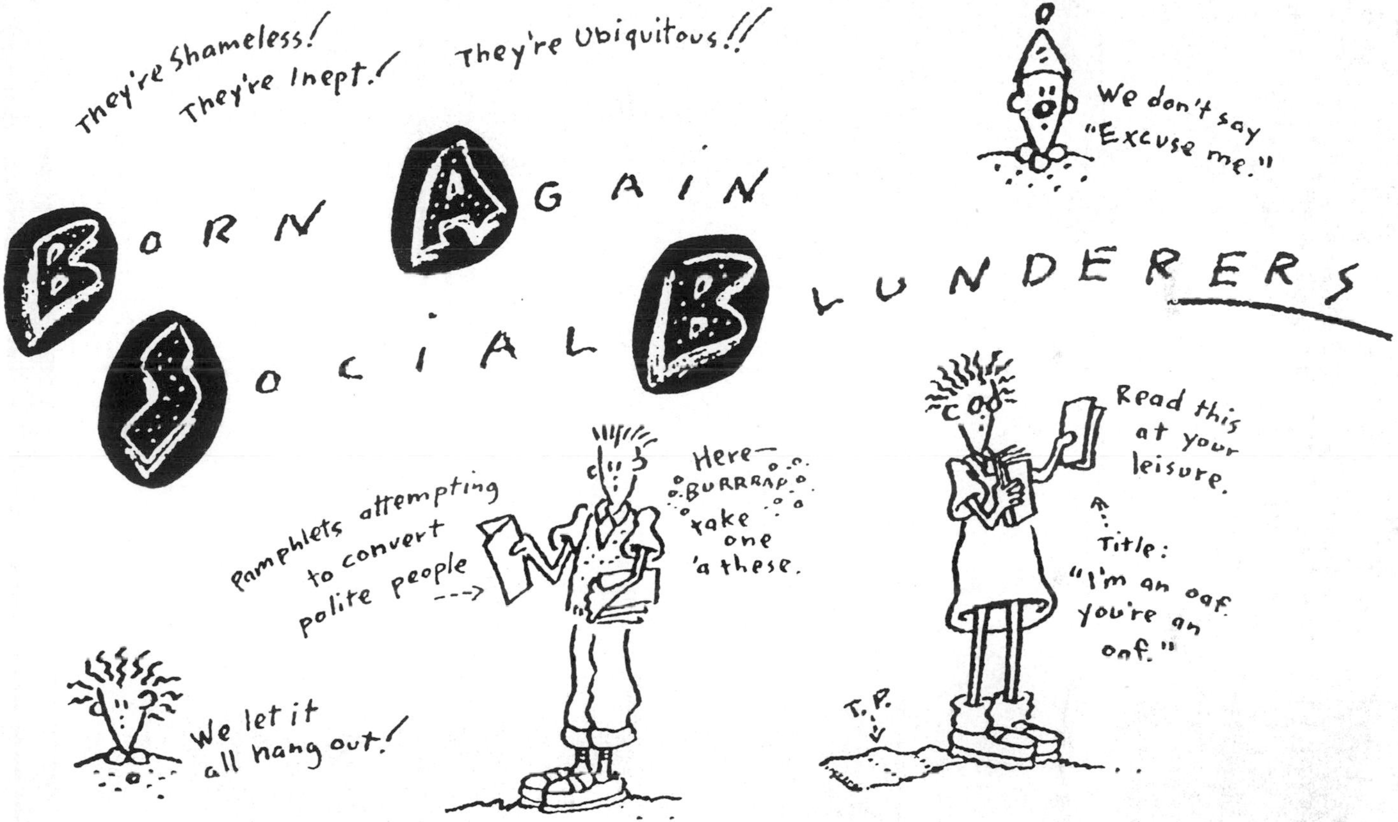
They're Shameless!
They're Inept.!
They're Ubiquitous!!
BORN AGAIN SOCIAL BLUNDERERS
We don't say "Excuse me."
Pamphlets attempting to convert polite people
Here— BURRRAP take one 'a these.
Read this at your leisure.
Title: "I'm an oaf. you're an oaf."
T.P.
We let it all hang out!

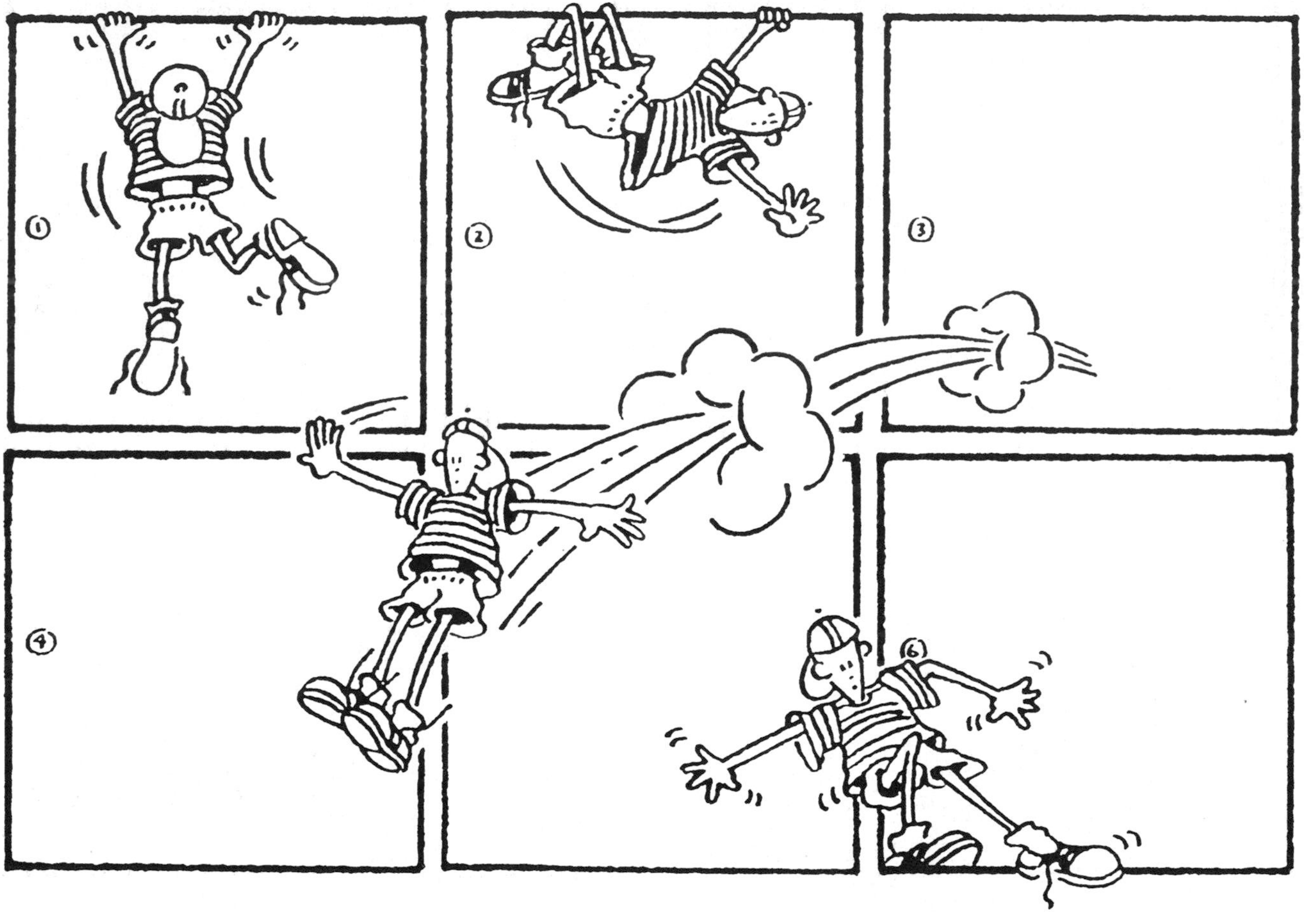
1
2
3
4
6

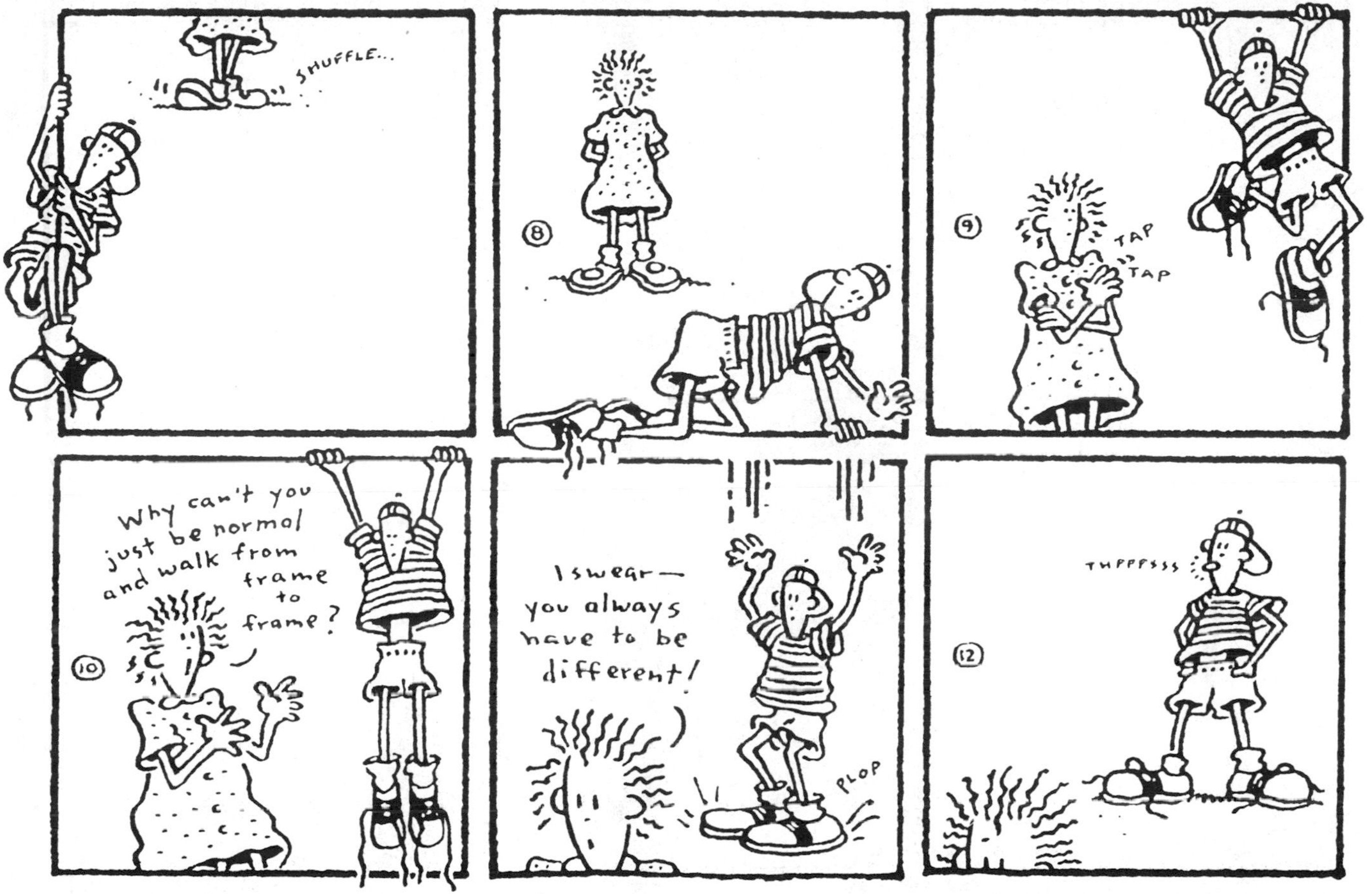
SHUFFLE...
8
9
TAP
TAP
10
Why can't you just be normal and walk from frame to frame?
I swear— you always have to be different!
PLOP
12
THPPPSSS

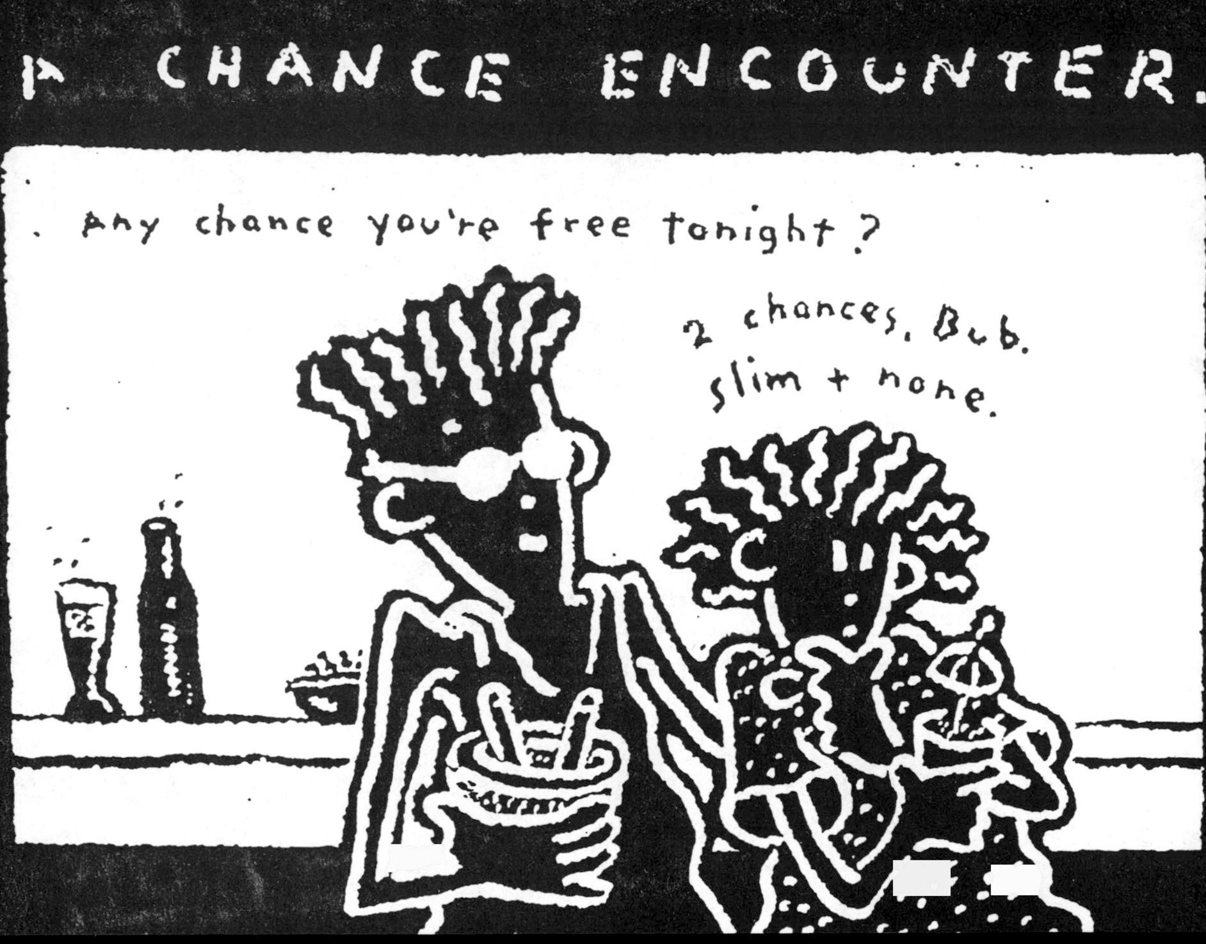
A CHANCE ENCOUNTER.
Any chance you're free tonight?
2 chances, Bub.
slim + none.

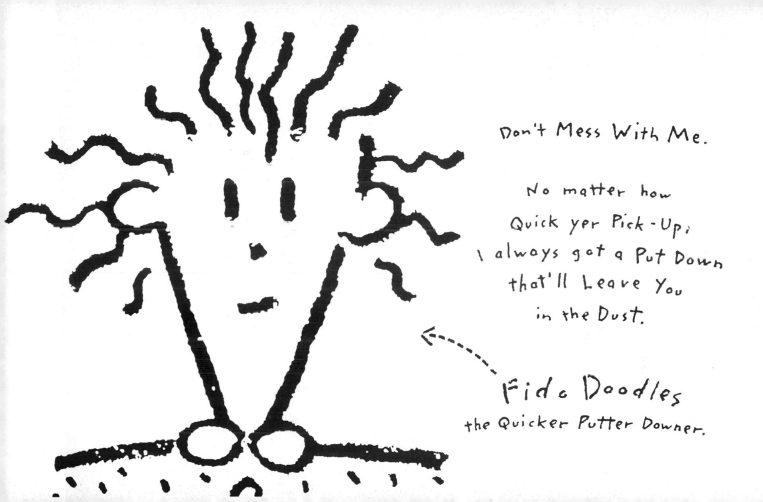

Don't Mess With Me.

No matter how
Quick yer Pick-Up,
I always got a Put Down
that'll Leave You
in the Dust.

Fido Doodles
the Quicker Putter Downer.

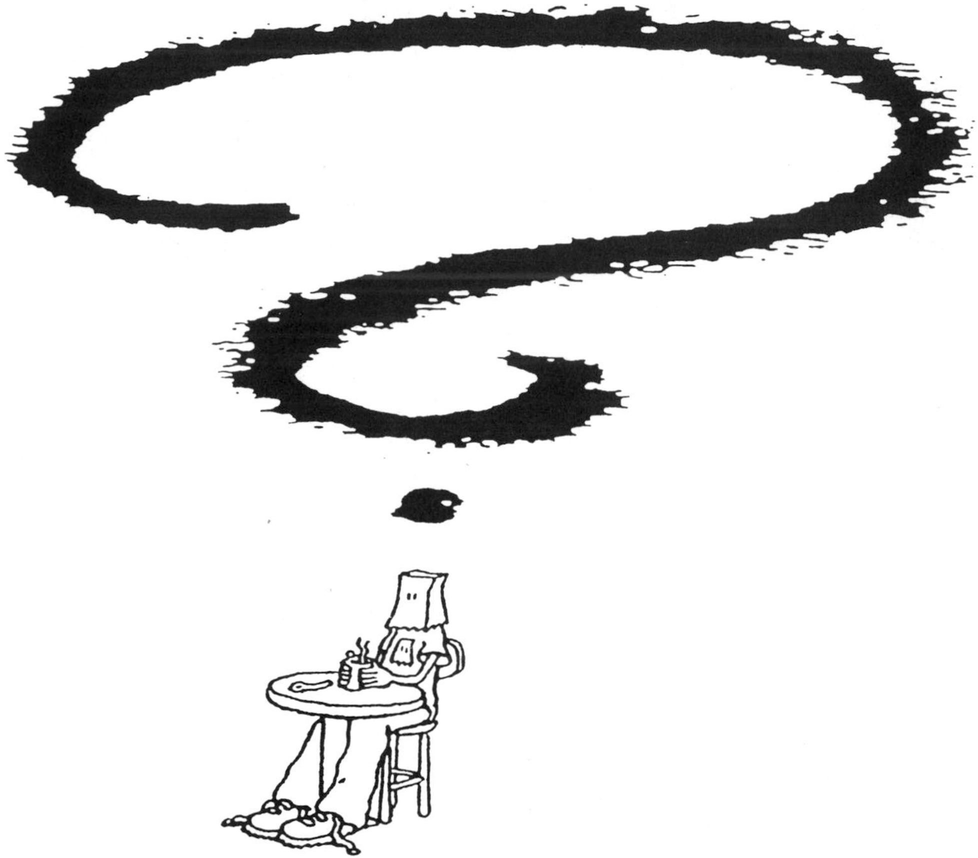

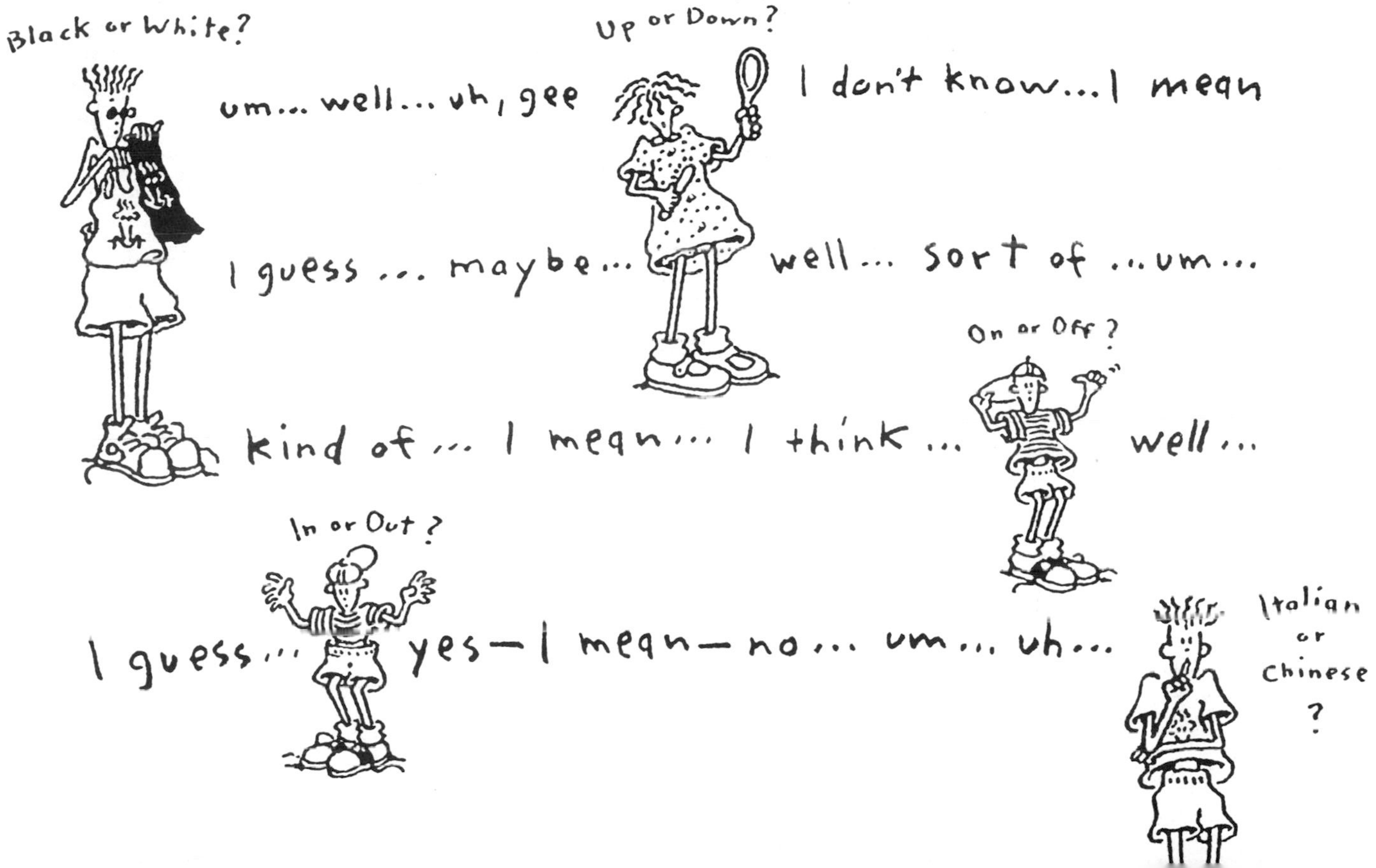
Black or White?
um... well... uh, gee
Up or Down?
I don't know... I mean
I guess ... maybe...
well... sort of ...um...
On or Off?
kind of ... I mean... I think ...
well...
In or Out?
I guess...
yes—I mean—no... um... uh...
Italian or Chinese ?

so... you think I'm wishy-washy?... Hmmm?
You think I can't make up my mind?!... Hmm?
you think I'm..uh, indecisive and
have trouble making choices...
is that it? Huh?!! is that
what you think ?!!?..?
...
oh yea? well let me tell

You something, Bub...
I am absolutely, po-
sitively, undeniably,
undoubtedly,
unquestionably

unequivocally
either — who
way
is O.K. with

certain that fever—

me.

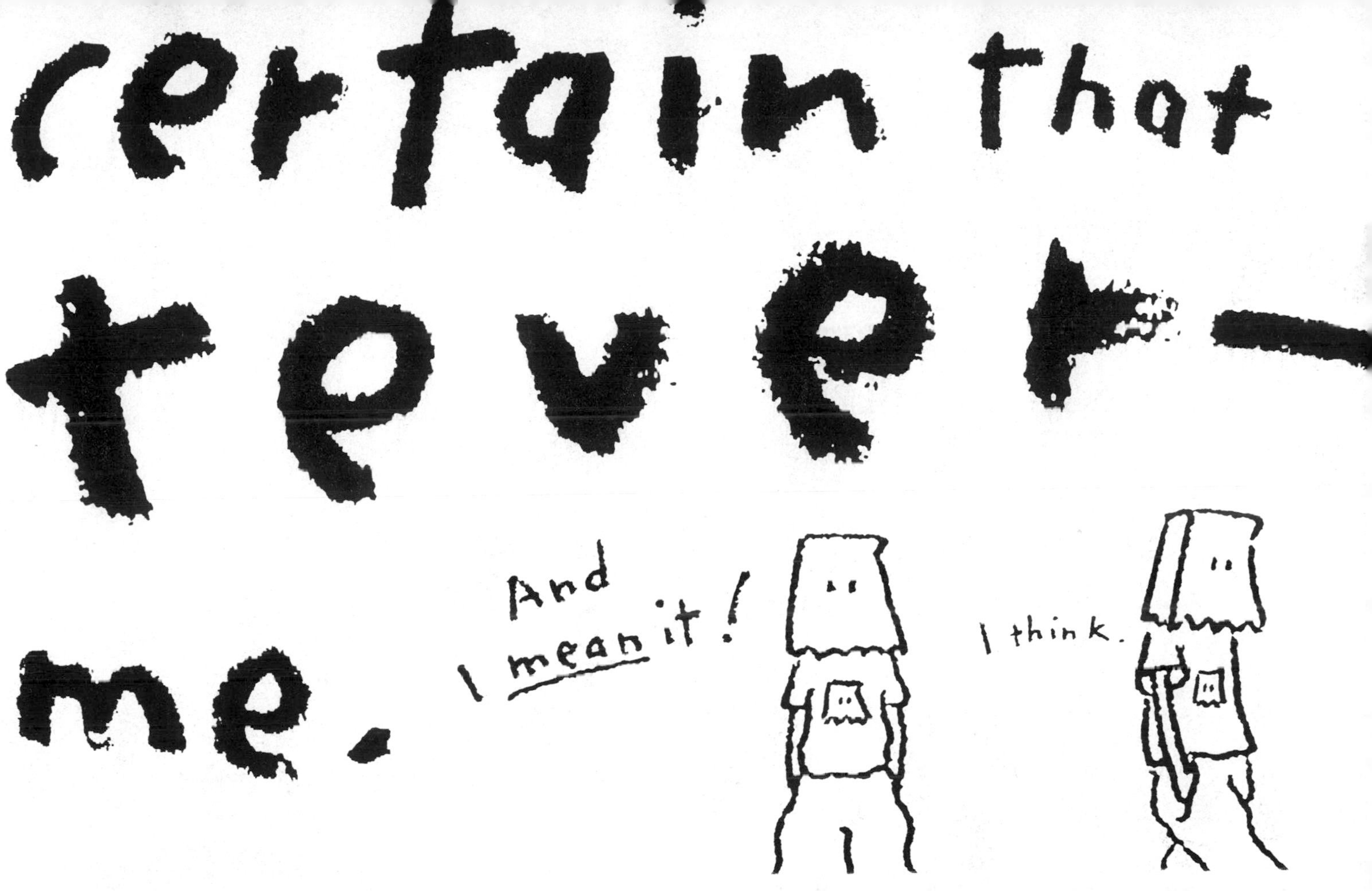

And I mean it!
I think.

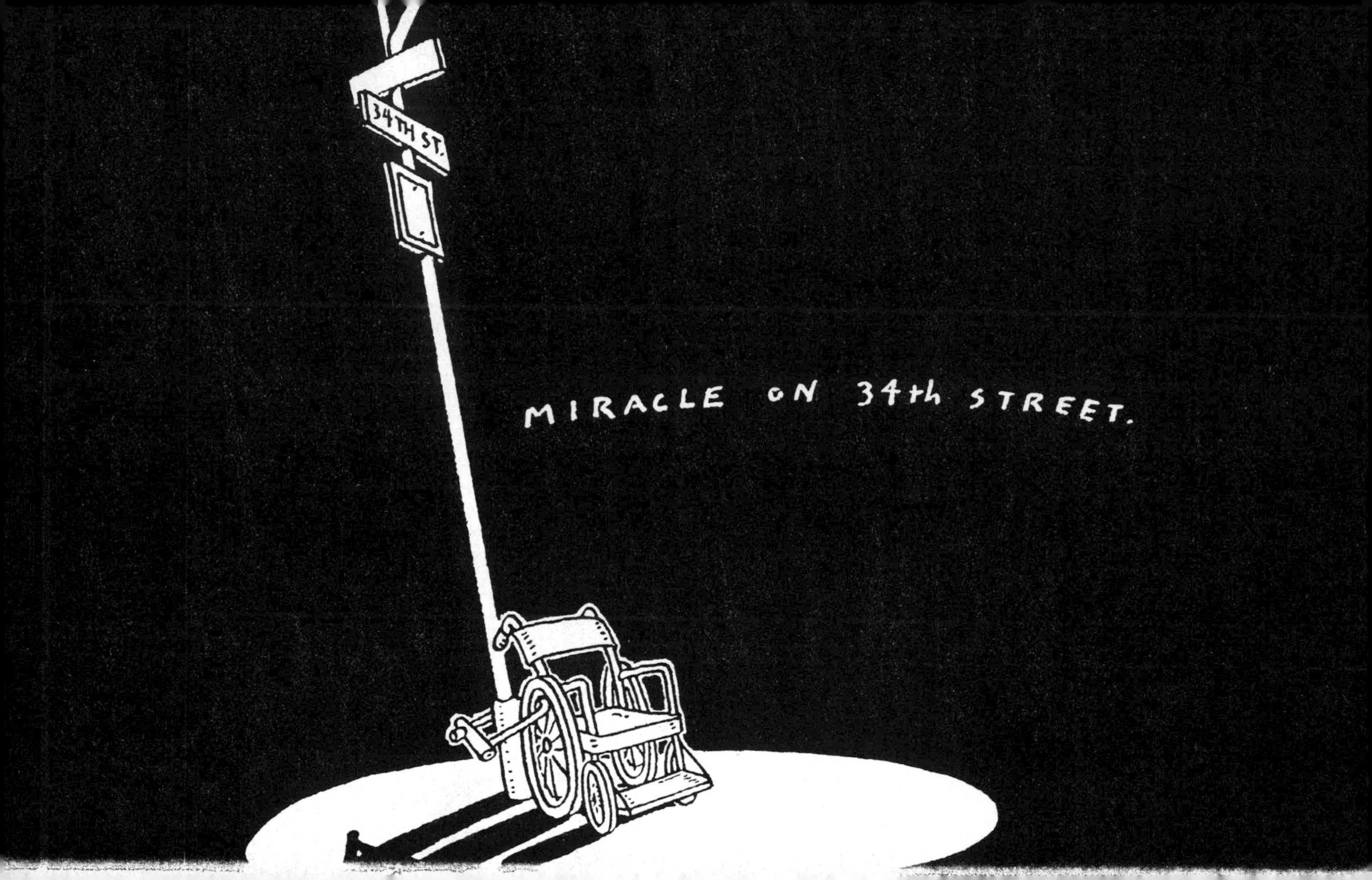
34TH ST.
MIRACLE ON 34th STREET.

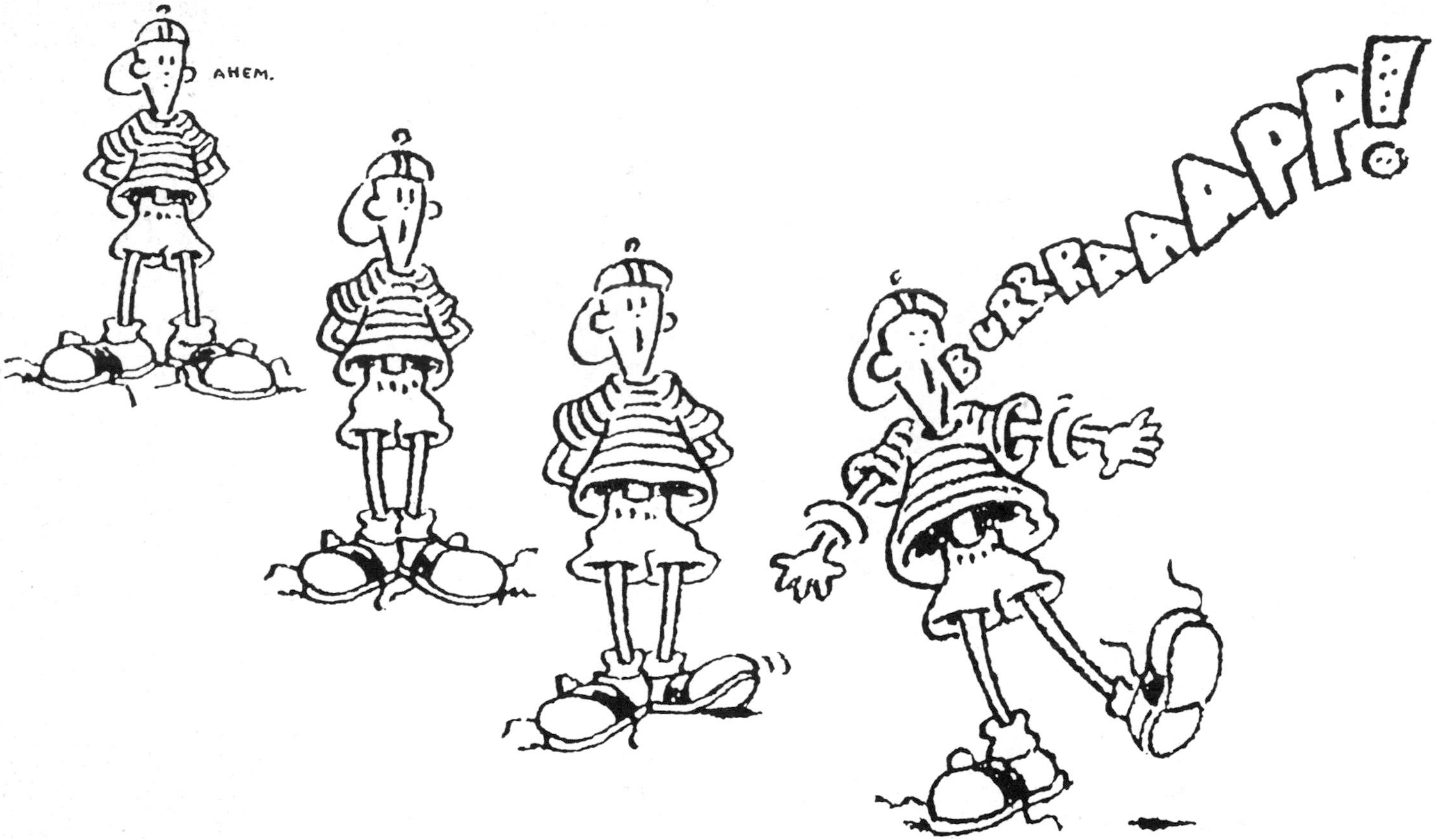

AHEM.
BURRRAAAAPP!

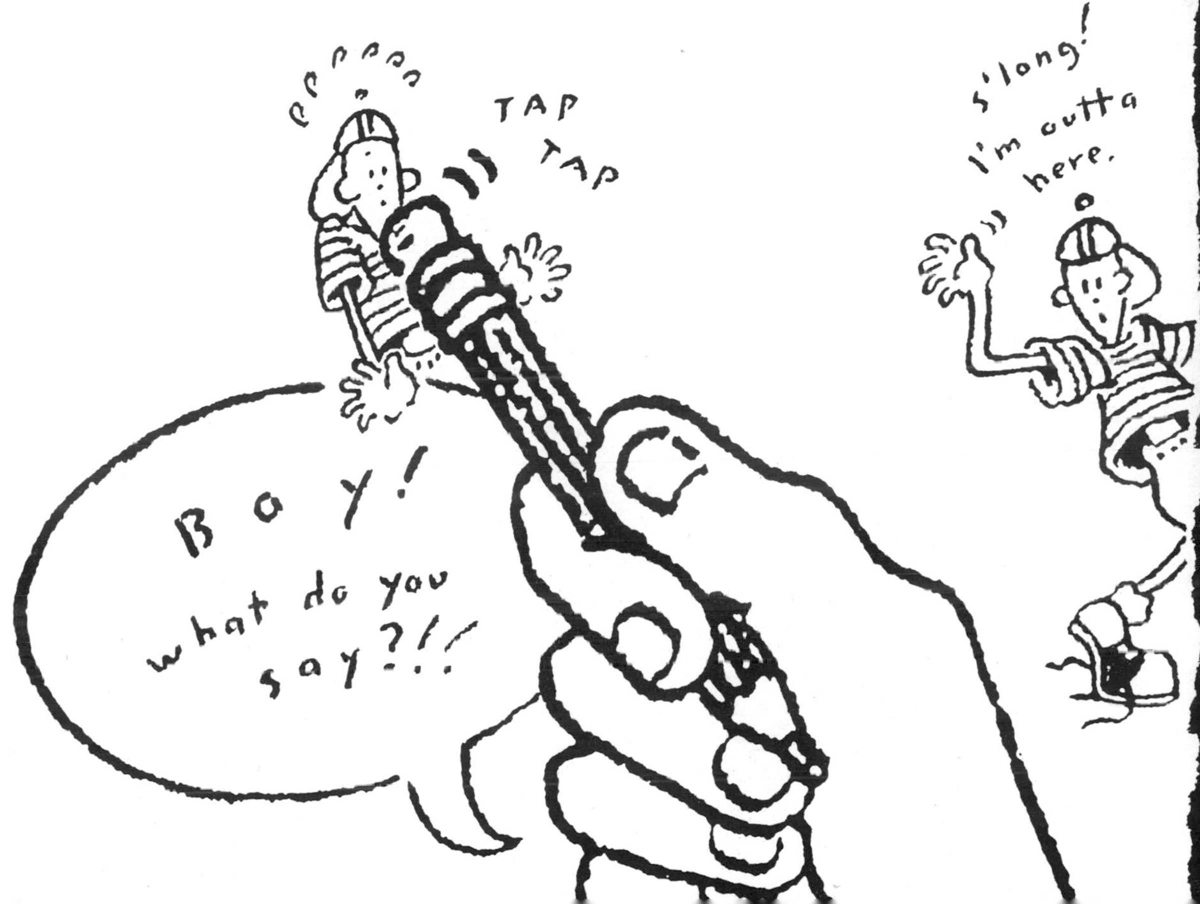
TAP TAP
Boy! what do you say?!!
s'long! I'm outta here.

Dear Reader:
Please overlook this unconscionable intrusion upon the high ethical and moral standards that we hold so dear. We beg you to understand that while we are doing everything in our power to attempt to control the uncontrollable, Boy will be Boy —and— characters will be characters.

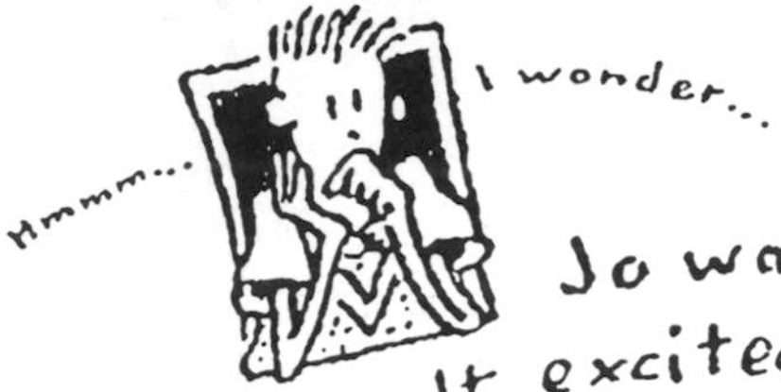
Hmmm...
I wonder...

Jo was unaccustomed to all the attention. It excited him, for sure, but he was puzzled, too. Was it due to his new tie 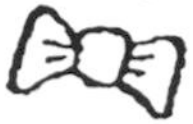 or the wallet, containing 850 dollars and numerous credit cards, that he found 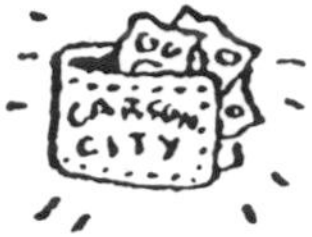
CARSON CITY
on the floor of the cab last night.

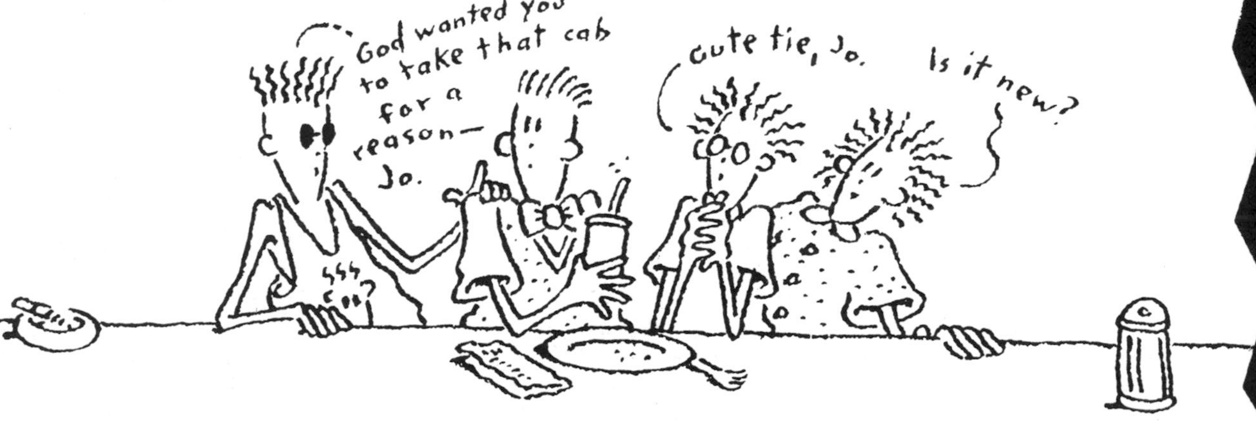
God wanted you to take that cab for a reason— Jo.
Cute tie, Jo.
Is it new?

It was just as well that Jo had a policy of not going to the café twice in one day.

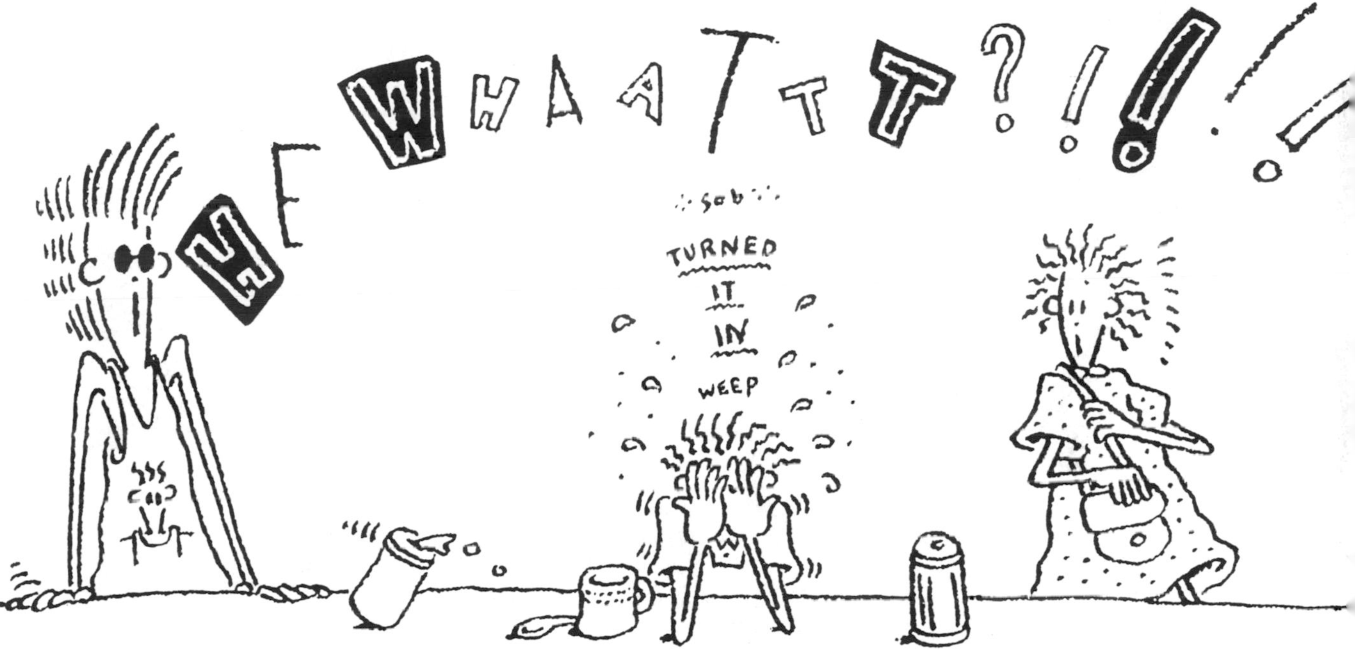

EEWHAATTT?!!!!
sob
TURNED
IT
IN
WEEP

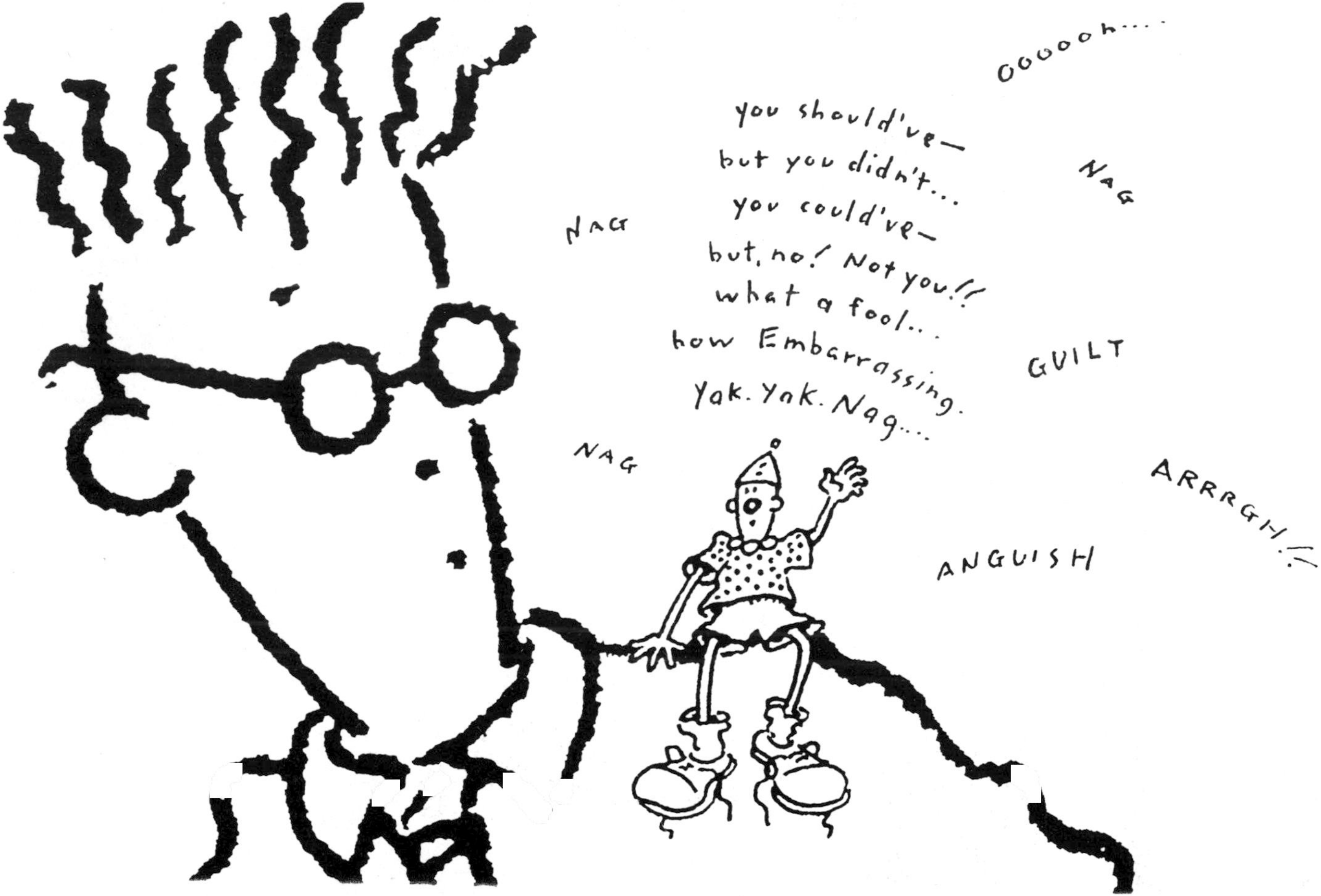
Oooooh....
you should've—
but you didn't...
you could've—
but, no! Not you!!
what a fool...
how Embarrassing.
Yak. Yak. Nag....
NAG
NAG
NAG
GUILT
ARRRGH!!
ANGUISH

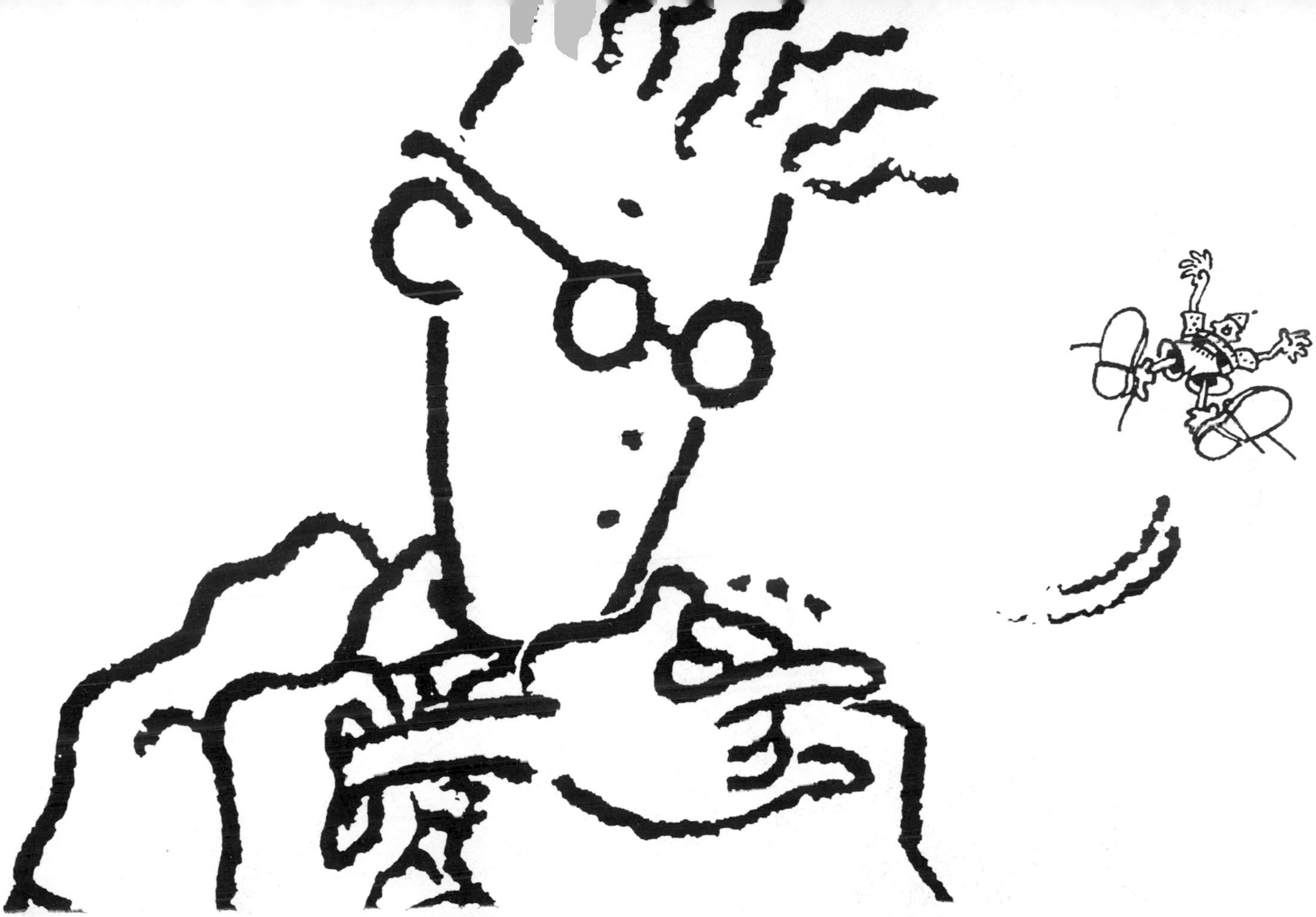

Fido's Fido tries ethnic food.

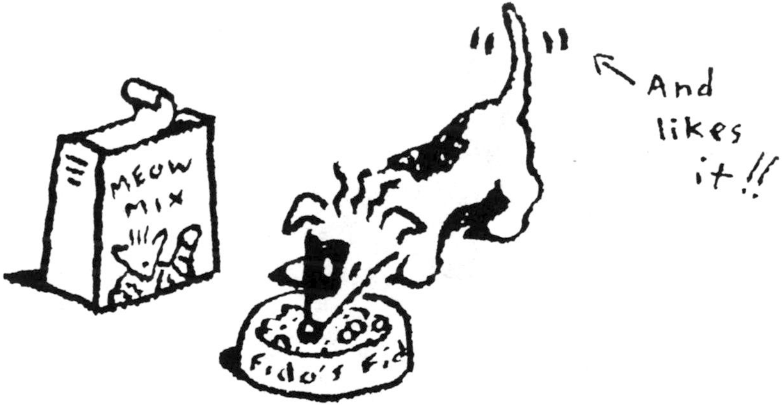
MEOW MIX
Fido's Fid
" "
And likes it!!

Fido's Fido crosses the Collar Line.

the Dog's Dish →

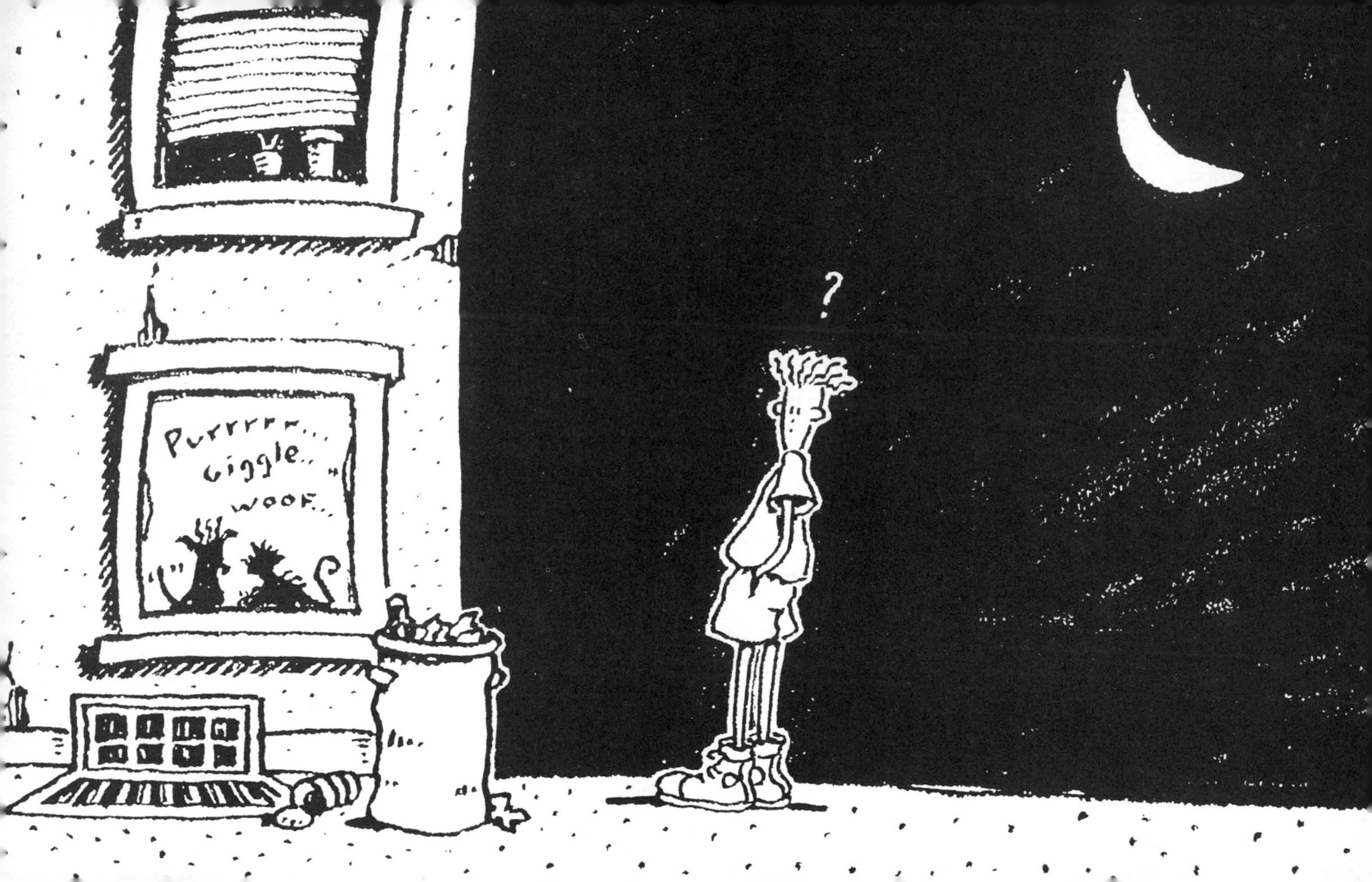
Purrrrr...
Giggle..
WOOF..
?

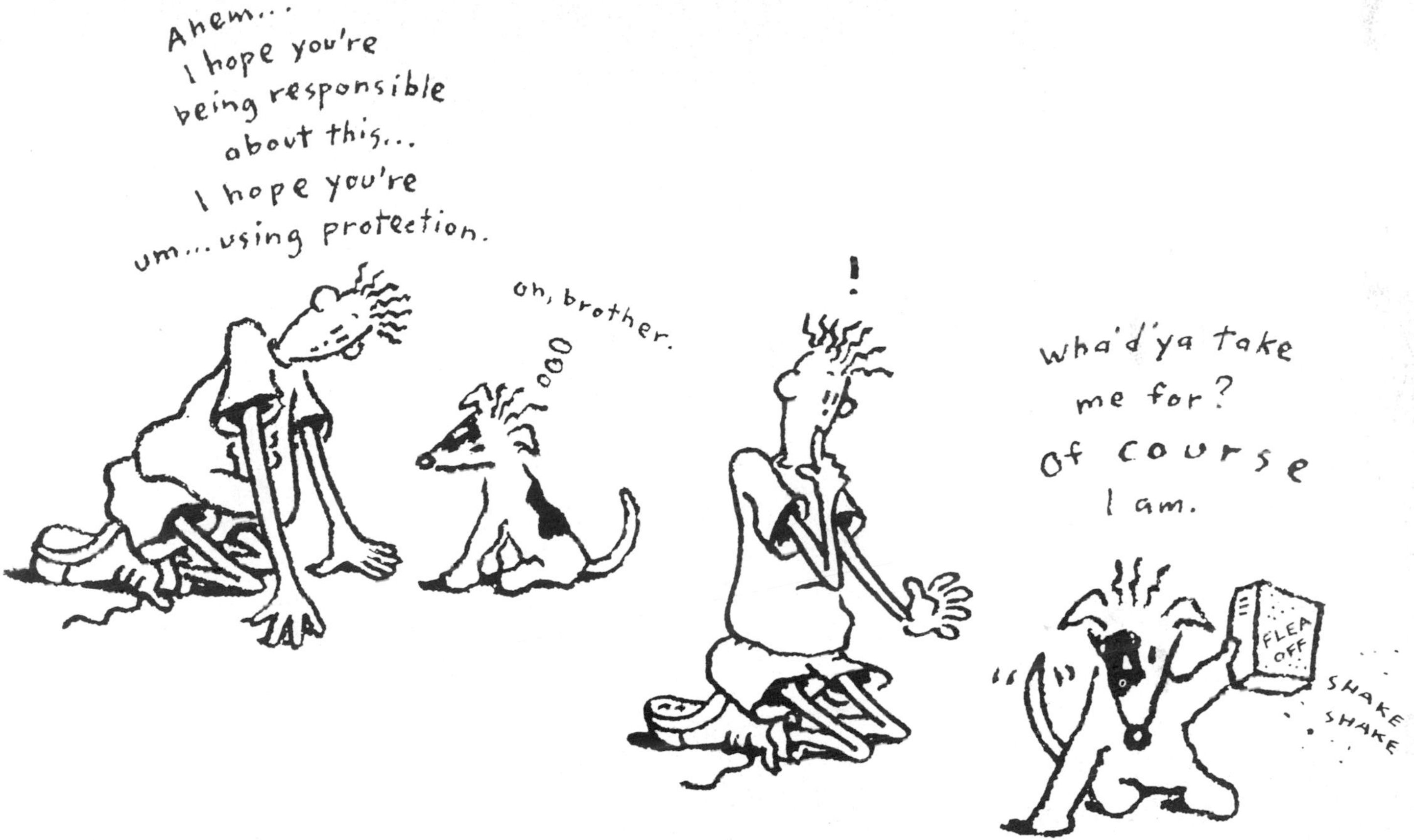

Ahem...
I hope you're
being responsible
about this...
I hope you're
um... using protection.
ooo
oh, brother.
!
Wha'd'ya take
me for?
Of course
I am.
FLEA OFF
SHAKE
SHAKE

Enter our fuzzy Romeo + Juliet — as they paw their way toward the quaint East Village digs that our hero Mutt fondly calls "HOME"...

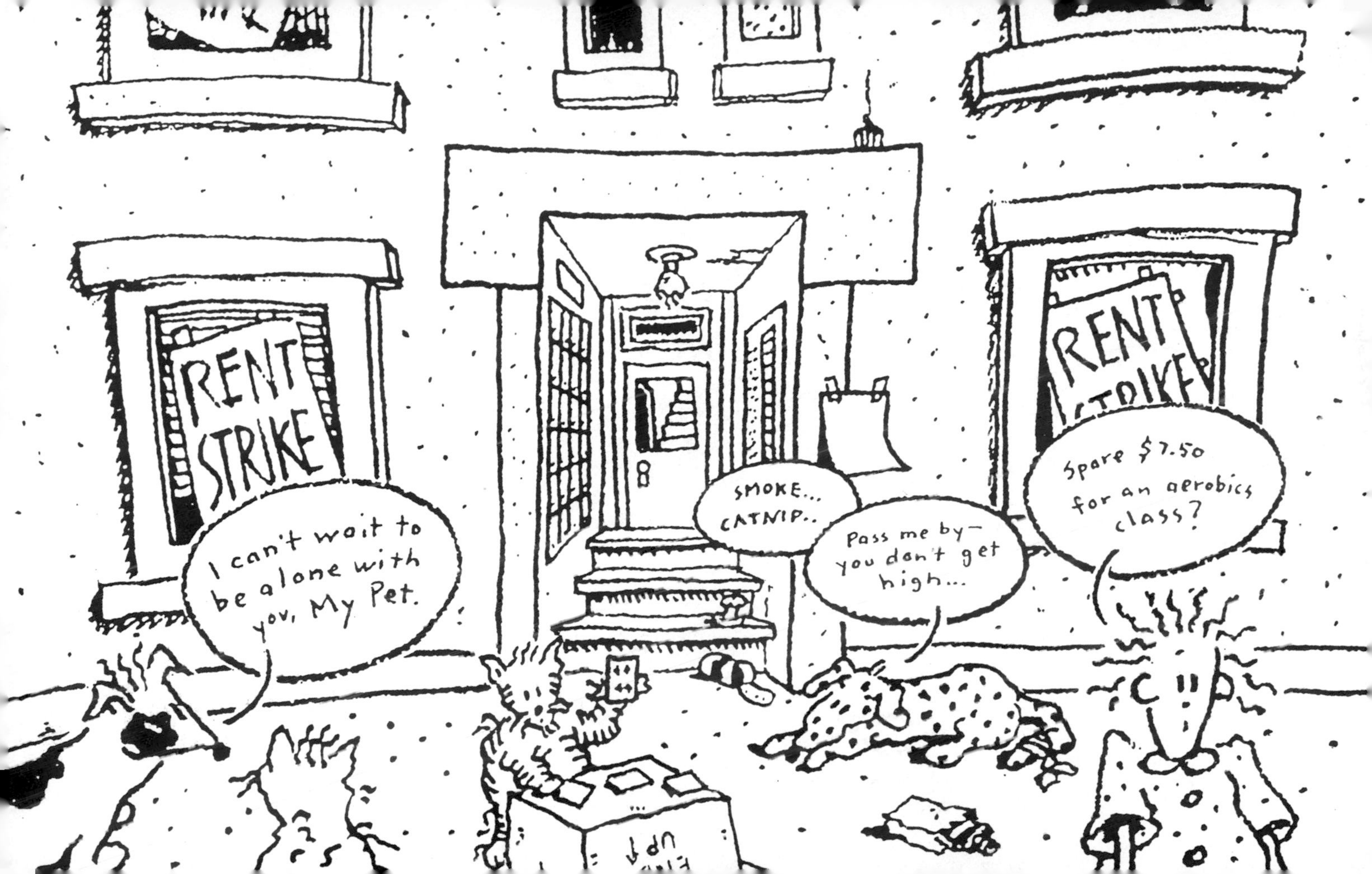
RENT STRIKE
RENT STRIKE
I can't wait to be alone with you, My Pet.
SMOKE... CATNIP..
Pass me by— you don't get high...
Spare $7.50 for an aerobics class?
UP

MOMENTS LATER THEY ARRIVE, UNHARMED. ONLY TO FIND...

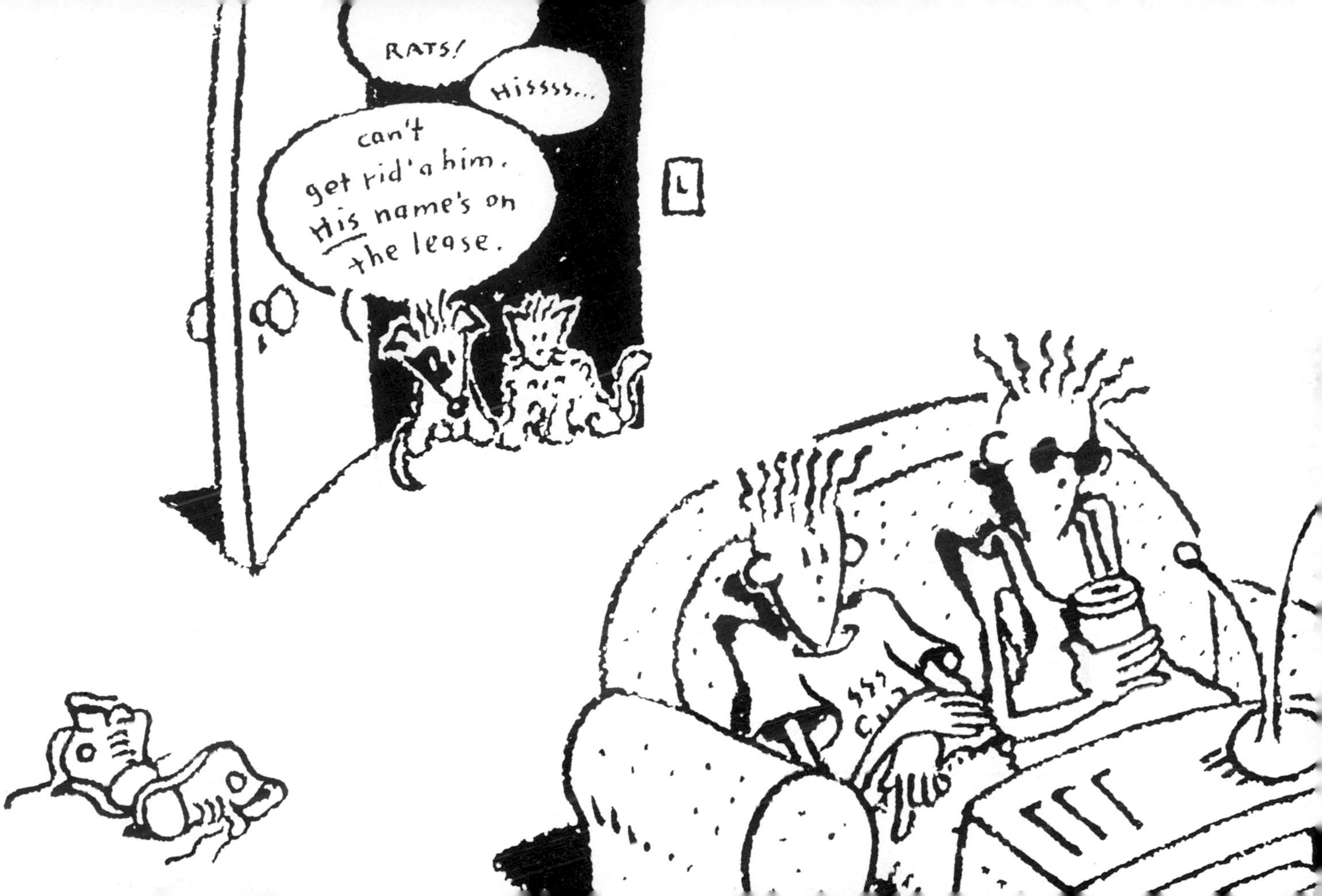
RATS!
HISSSS...
can't get rid'a him. His name's on the lease.

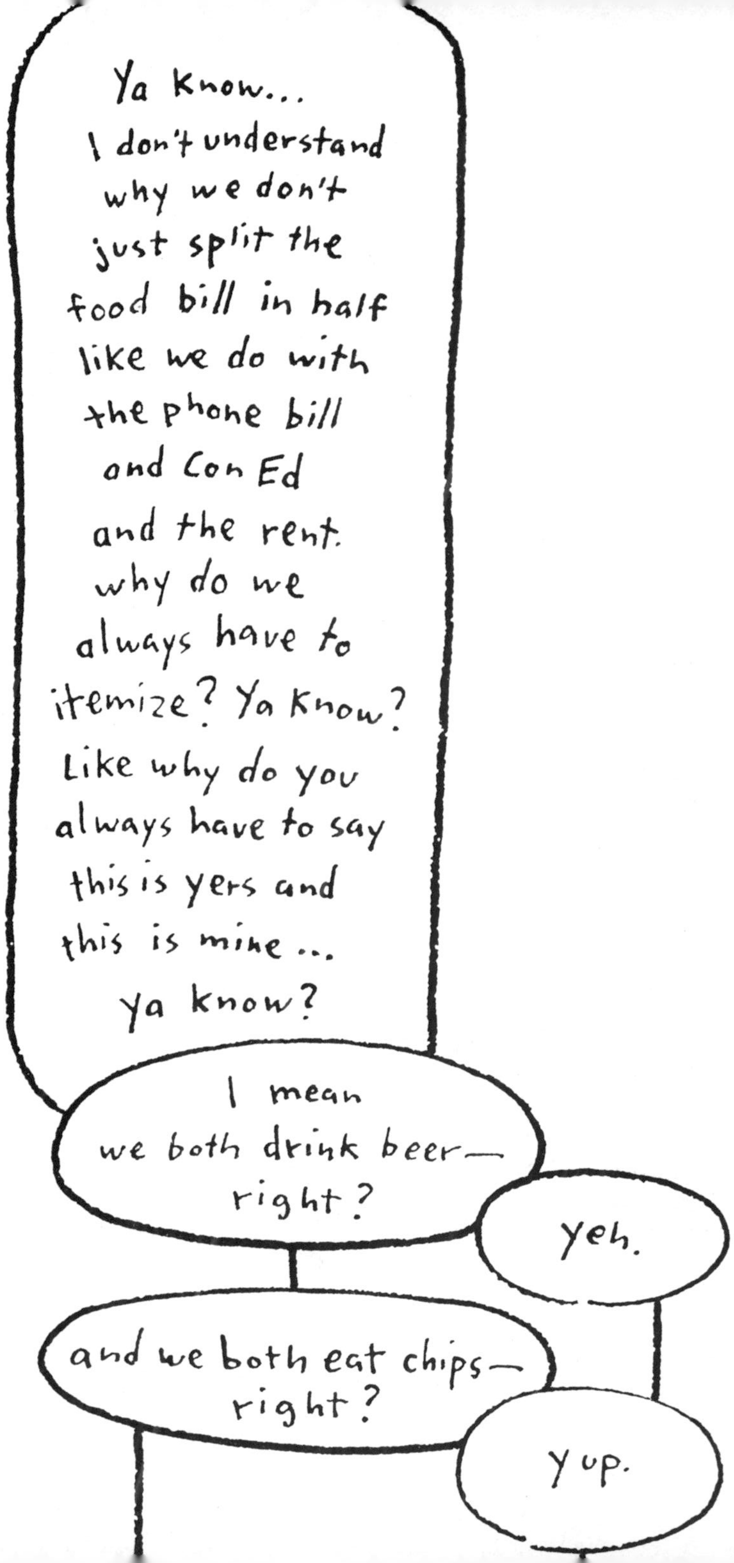
Ya know... I don't understand why we don't just split the food bill in half like we do with the phone bill and Con Ed and the rent. why do we always have to itemize? Ya know? Like why do you always have to say this is yers and this is mine... ya know?
I mean we both drink beer— right?
yeh.
and we both eat chips— right?
yup.

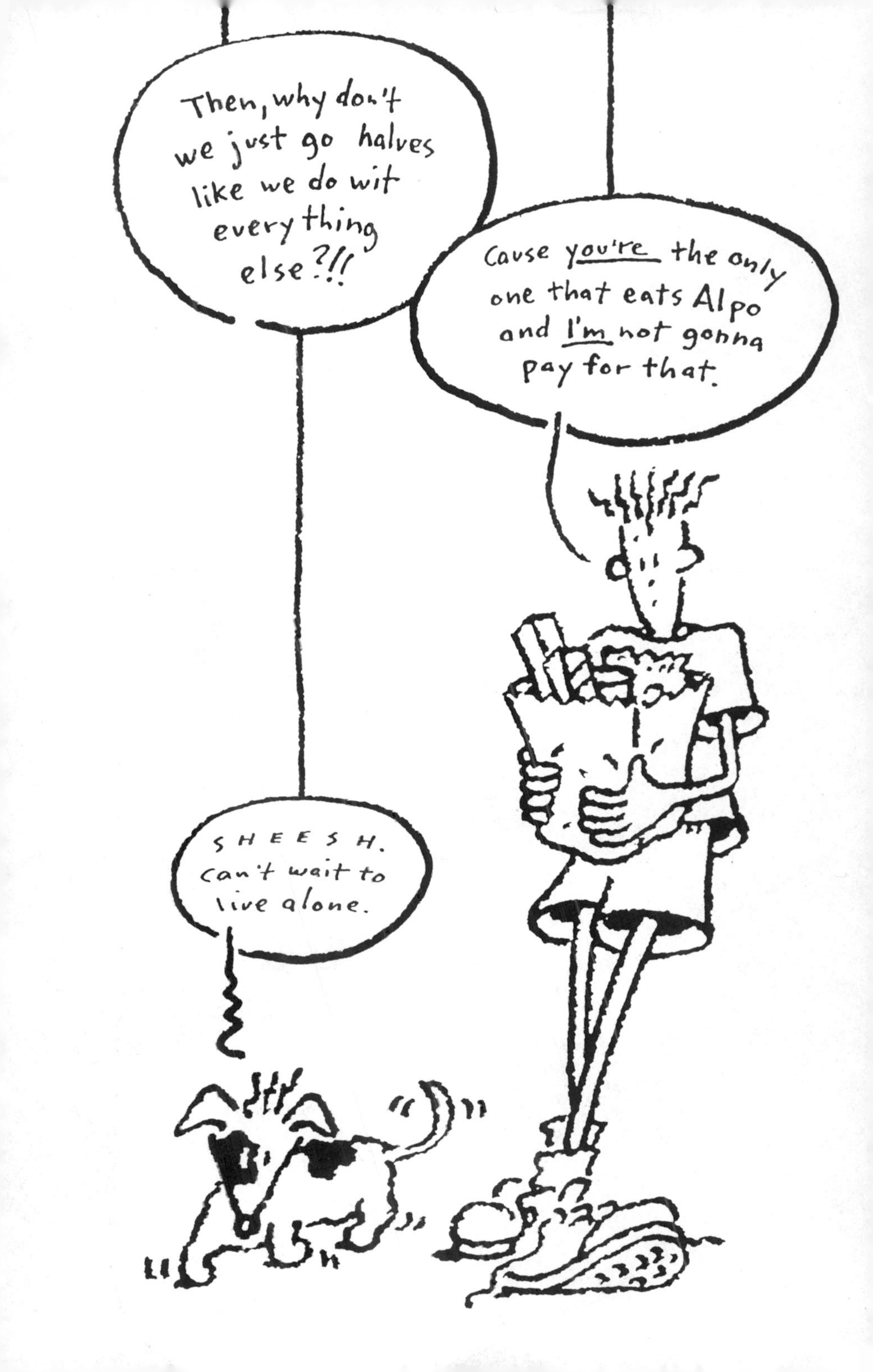
Then, why don't we just go halves like we do wit everything else?!!
Cause you're the only one that eats Alpo and I'm not gonna pay for that.
SHEESH. Can't wait to live alone.

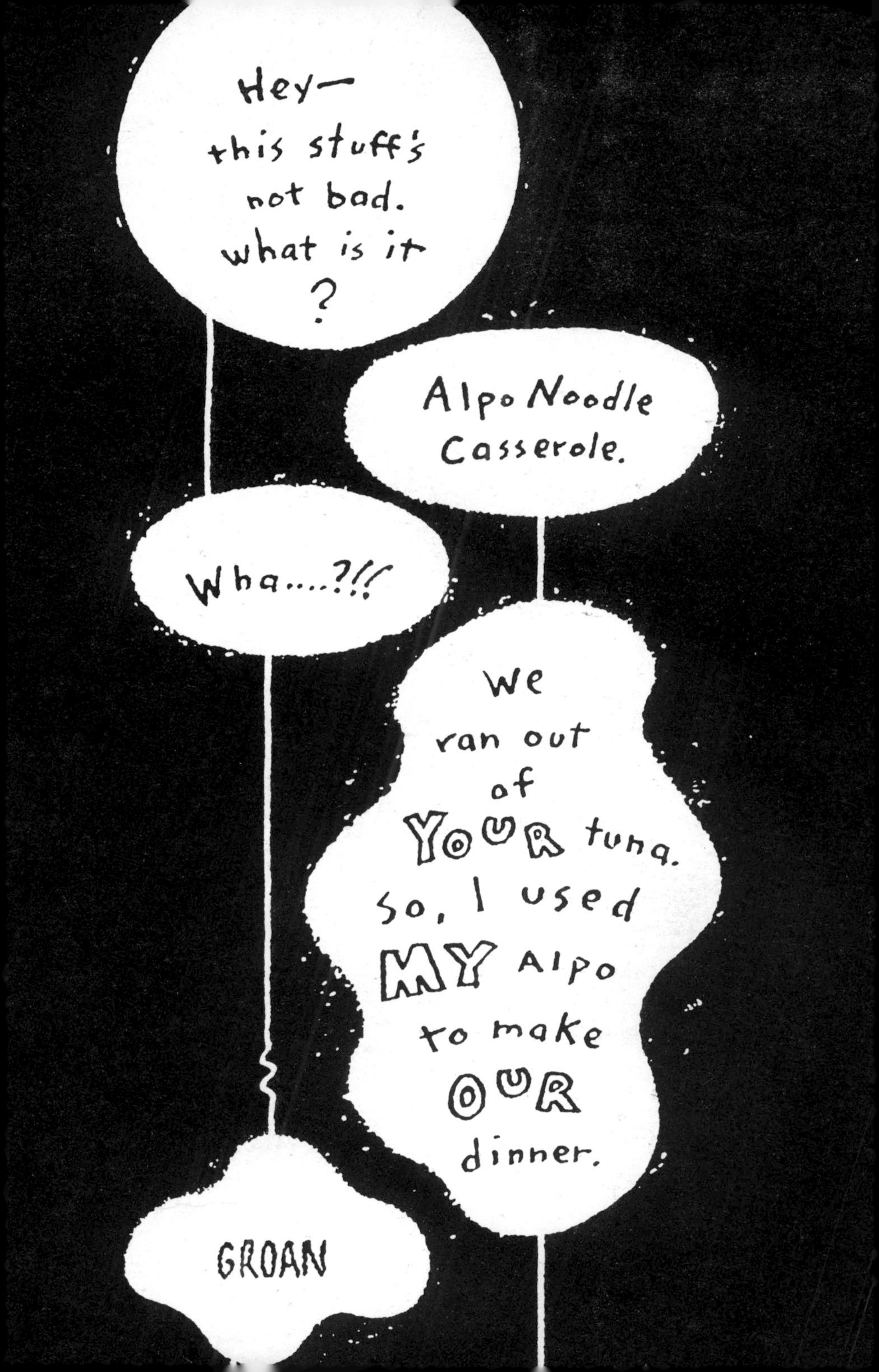
Hey— this stuff's not bad. what is it ?
Alpo Noodle Casserole.
Wha....?!!
We ran out of YOUR tuna. So, I used MY Alpo to make OUR dinner.
GROAN

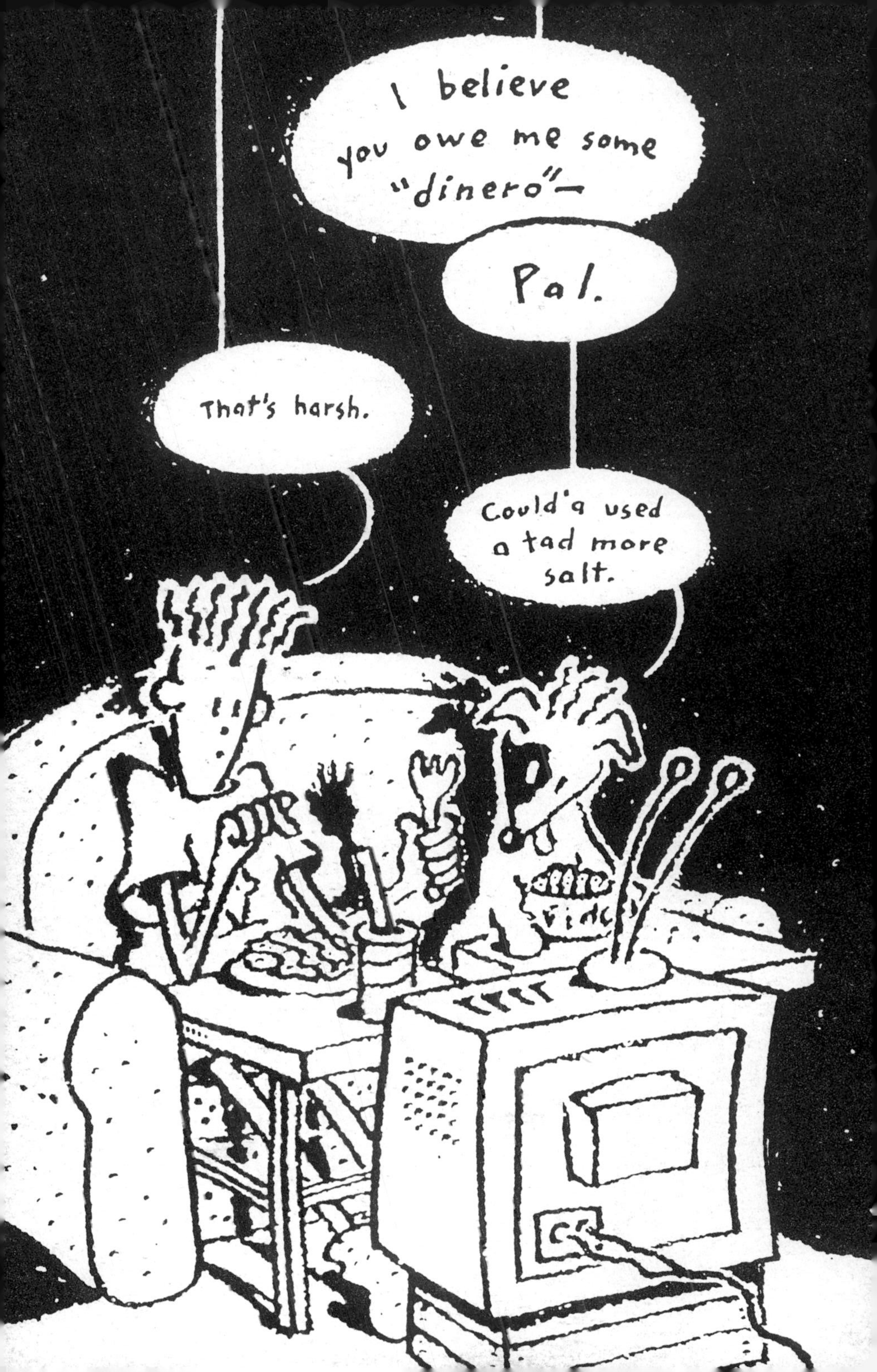
I believe you owe me some "dinero"—
Pal.
That's harsh.
Could'a used a tad more salt.

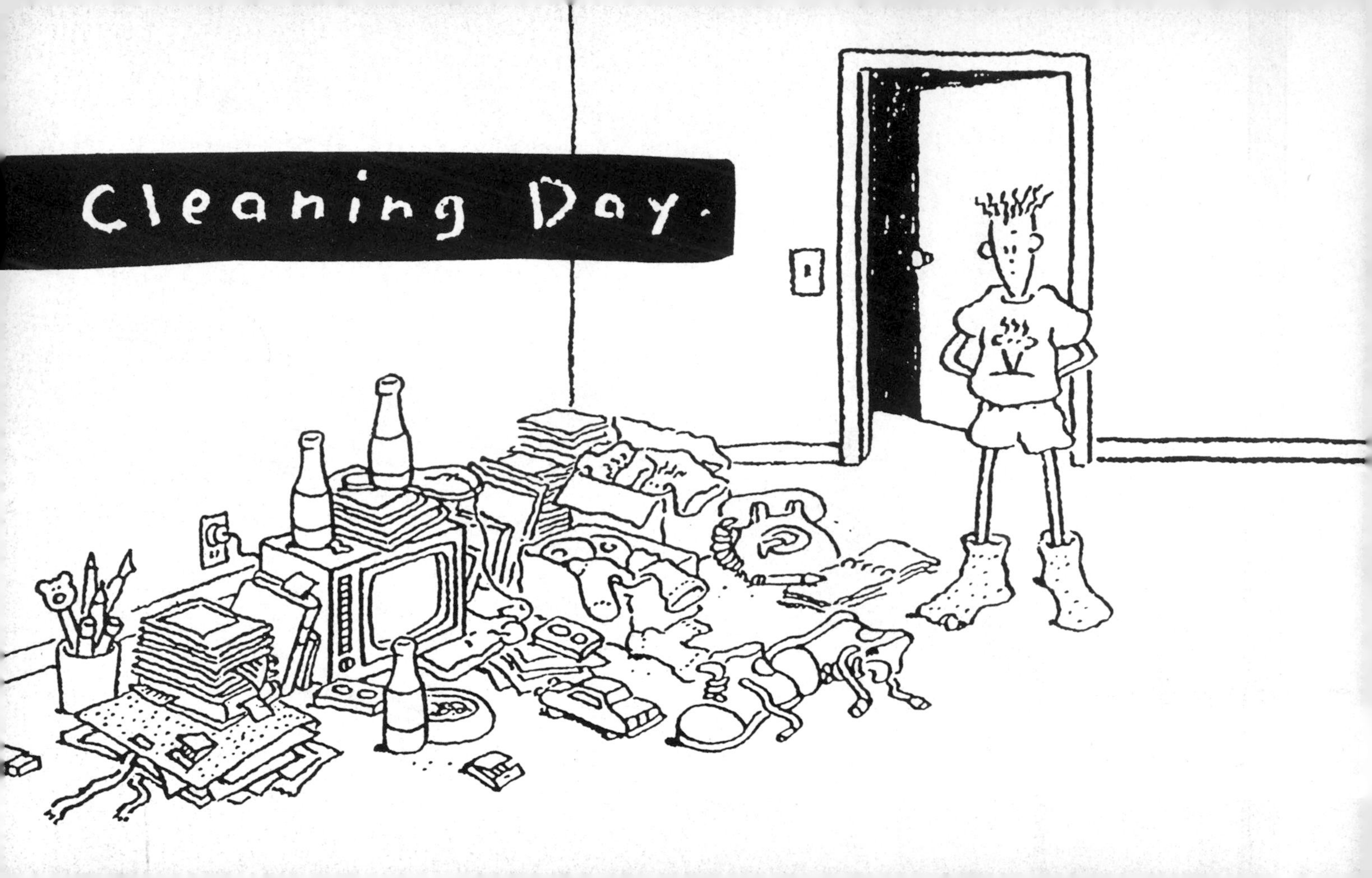
Cleaning Day.

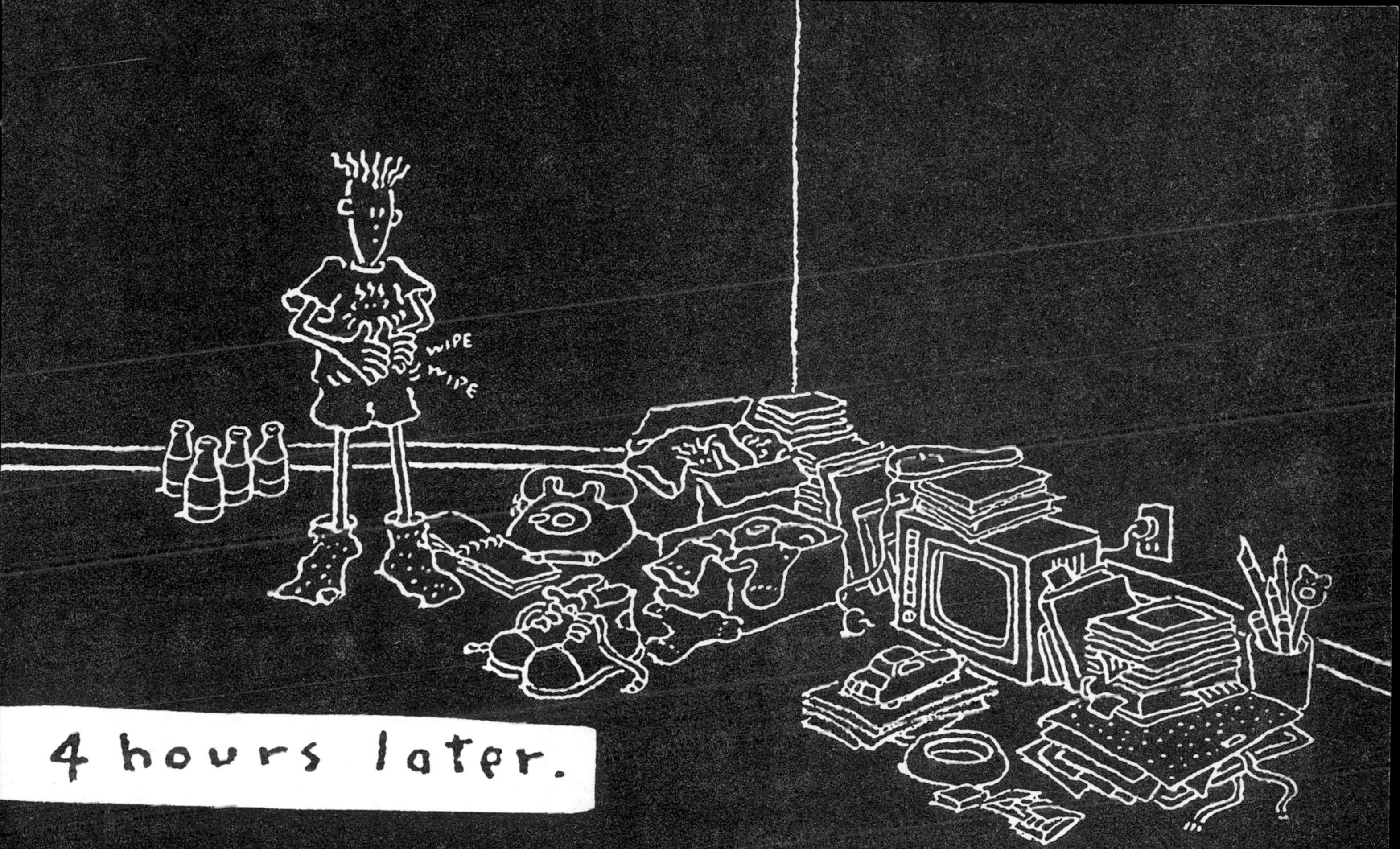
WIPE
WIPE
4 hours later.

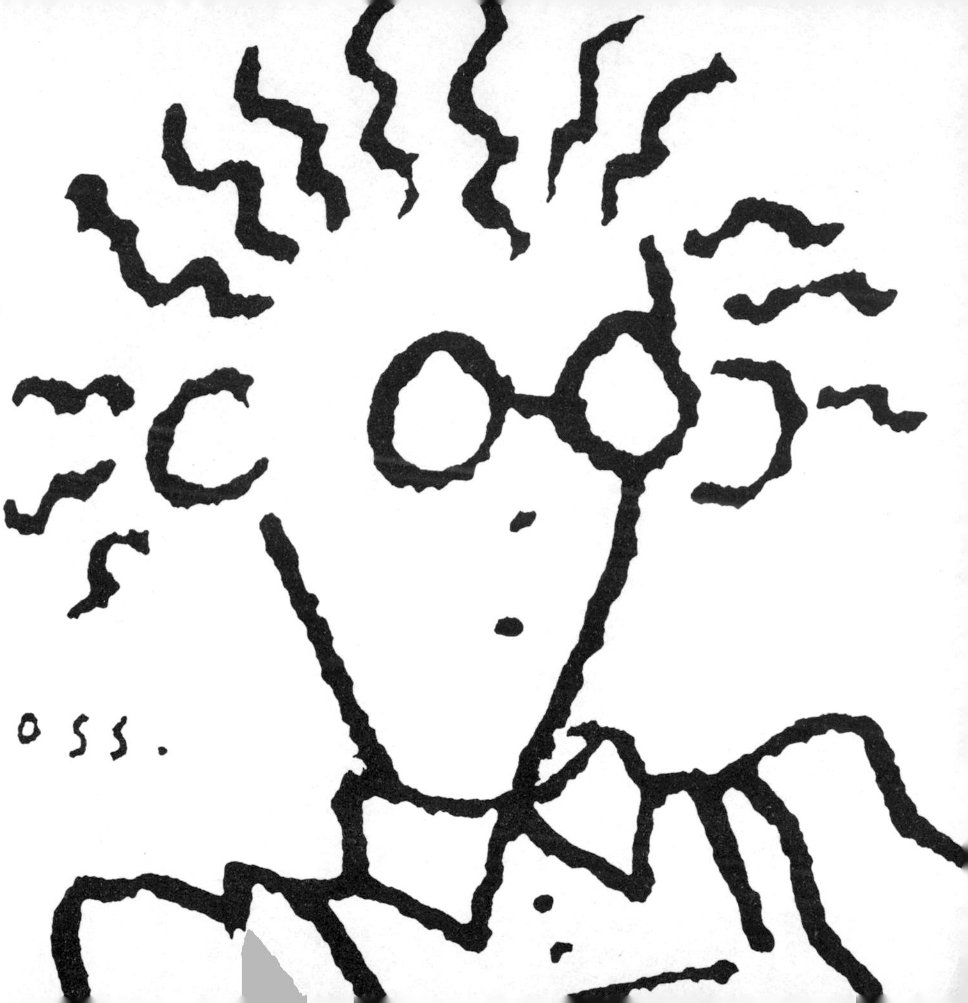
Dribble Dido

HER·OWN BOSS.

A desperate attempt to control *some* aspect of her daily existence.

DROOP
STAY
KNEESOCKS—
STAY!!!

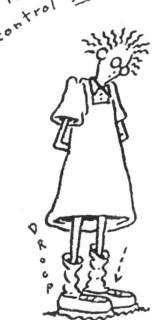

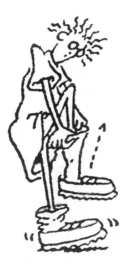

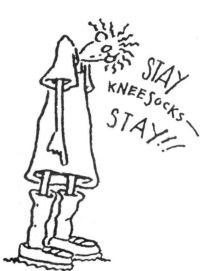

HER OWN BOSS.

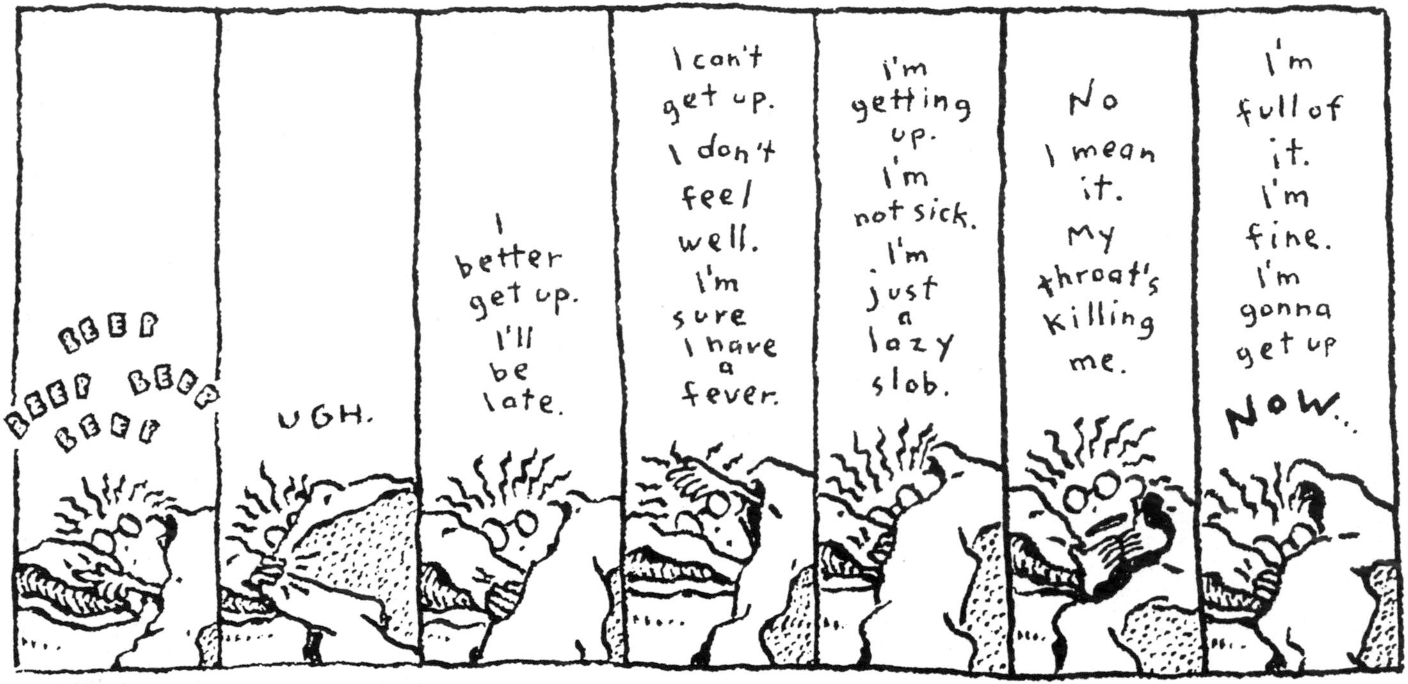
BEEP
BEEP BEEP BEEP
BEEP
UGH.
I better get up. I'll be late.
I can't get up. I don't feel well. I'm sure I have a fever.
I'm getting up. I'm not sick. I'm just a lazy slob.
No I mean it. My throat's killing me.
I'm full of it. I'm fine. I'm gonna get up
NOW...

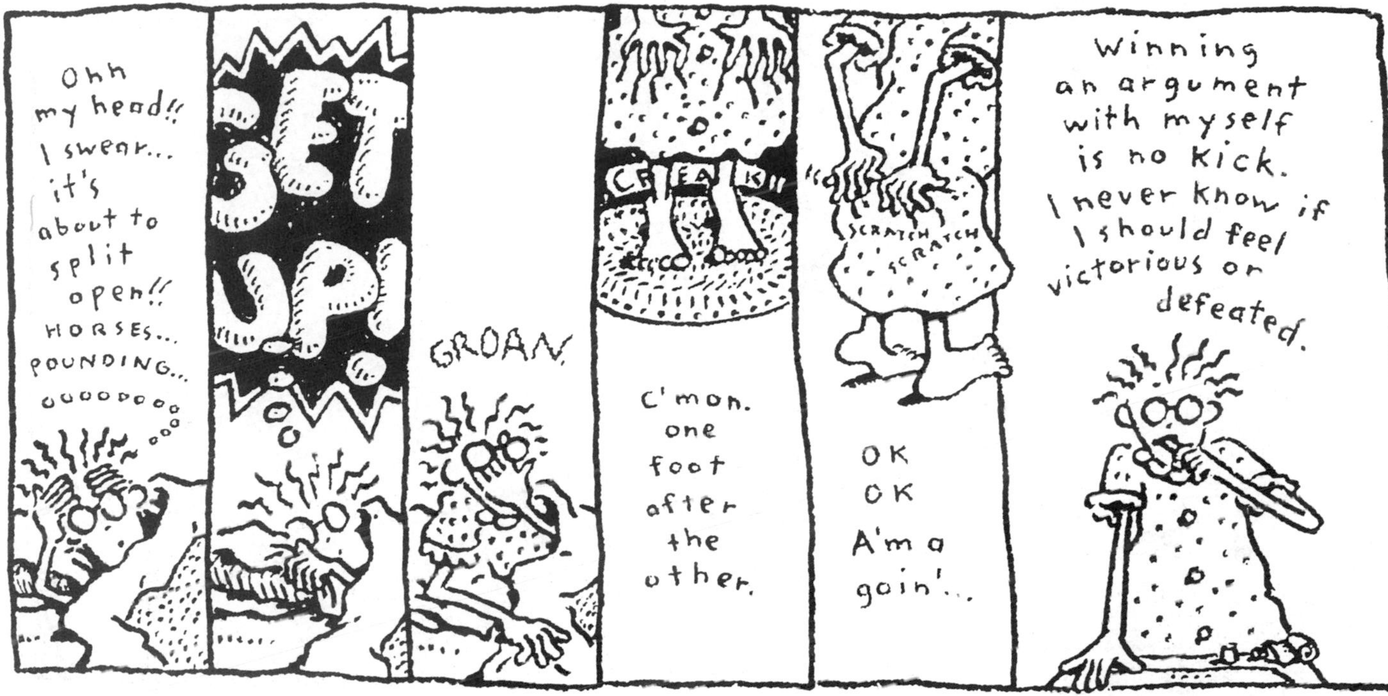
Ohh my head!! I swear... it's about to split open!! HORSES... POUNDING... oooooooooooo
SET UP!
GROAN.
CREAK
C'mon. one foot after the other.
SCRATCH SCRATCH
OK OK A'm a goin'...
Winning an argument with myself is no kick. I never know if I should feel victorious or defeated.

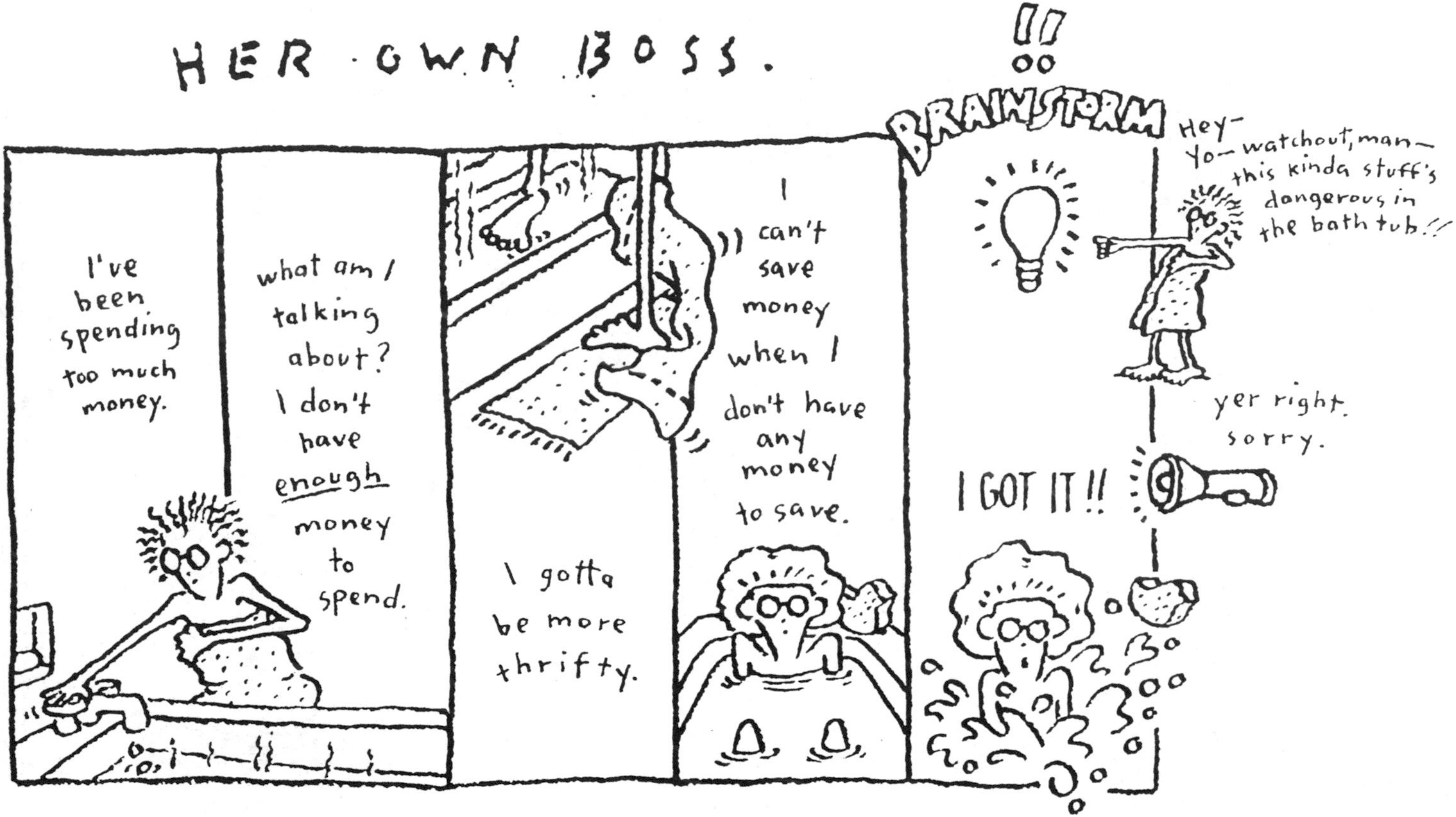
HER OWN BOSS.
I've been spending too much money.
what am I talking about? I don't have enough money to spend.
I gotta be more thrifty.
I can't save money when I don't have any money to save.
BRAINSTORM
!!
I GOT IT!!
Hey- Yo- watchout, man- this kinda stuff's dangerous in the bath tub!!
yer right. sorry.

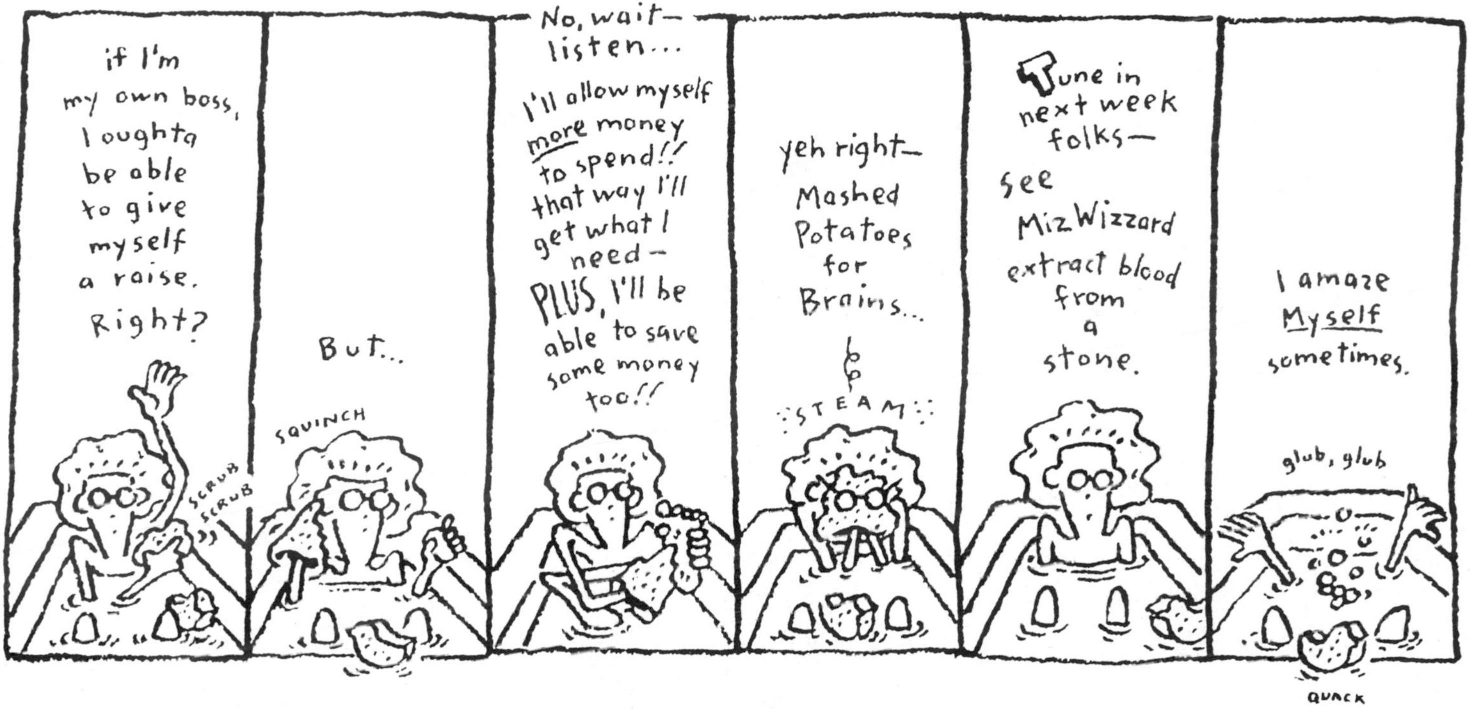
if I'm my own boss, I oughta be able to give myself a raise. Right?
SCRUB SCRUB
But...
SQUINCH
No, wait— listen...
I'll allow myself more money to spend!! that way I'll get what I need— PLUS, I'll be able to save some money too!!
yeh right— Mashed Potatoes for Brains...
STEAM
Tune in next week folks— see MizWizzard extract blood from a stone.
I amaze Myself sometimes.
glub, glub
QUACK

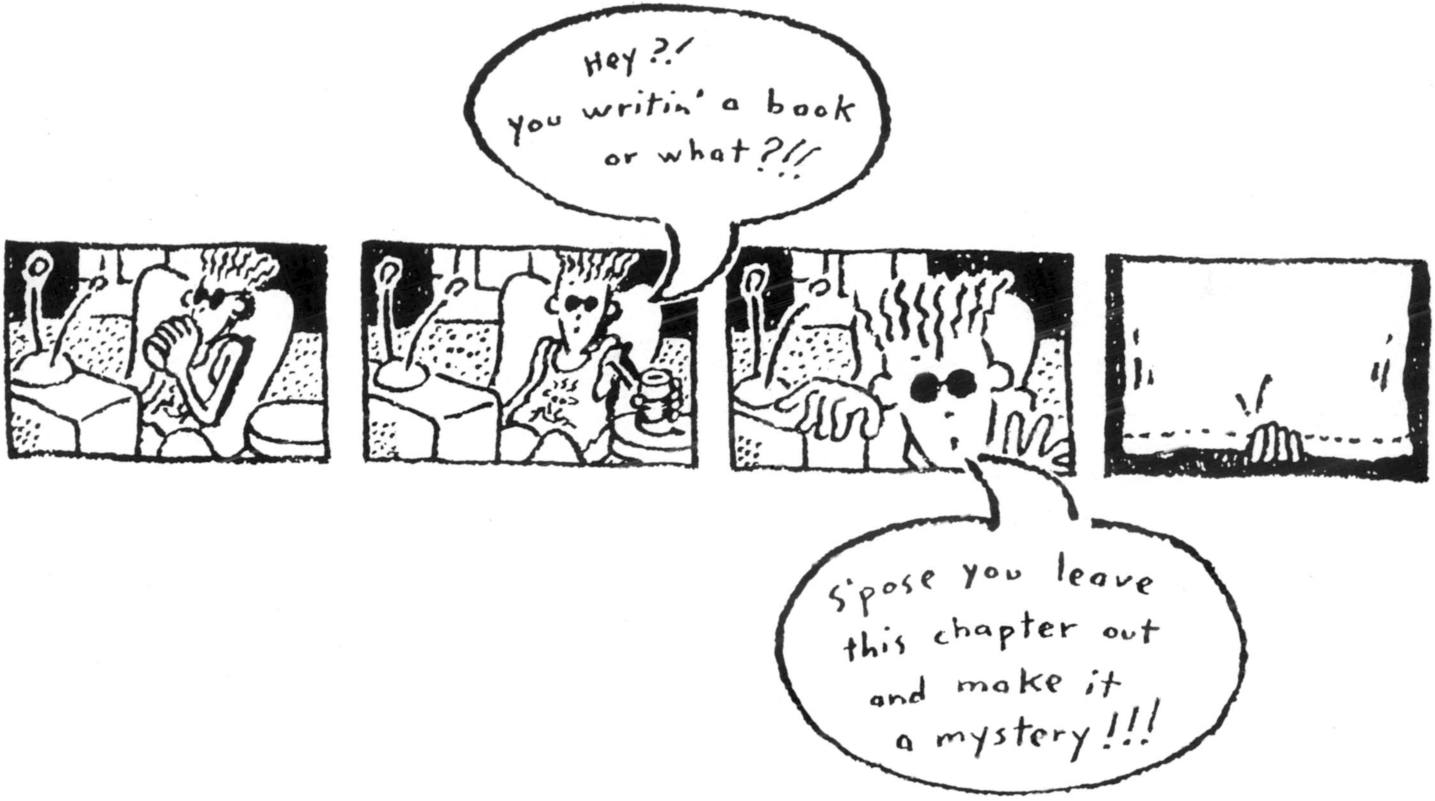
Hey?! you writin' a book or what?!!
S'pose you leave this chapter out and make it a mystery!!!

Mr. Cool is humbled.

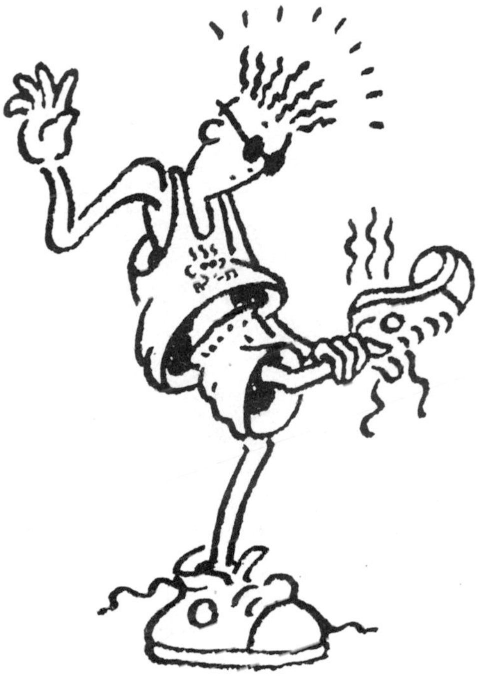

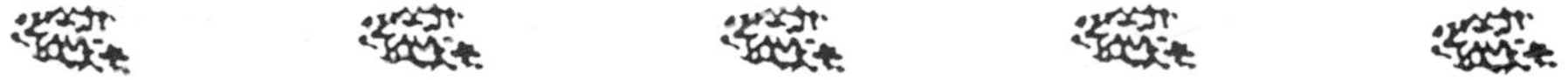

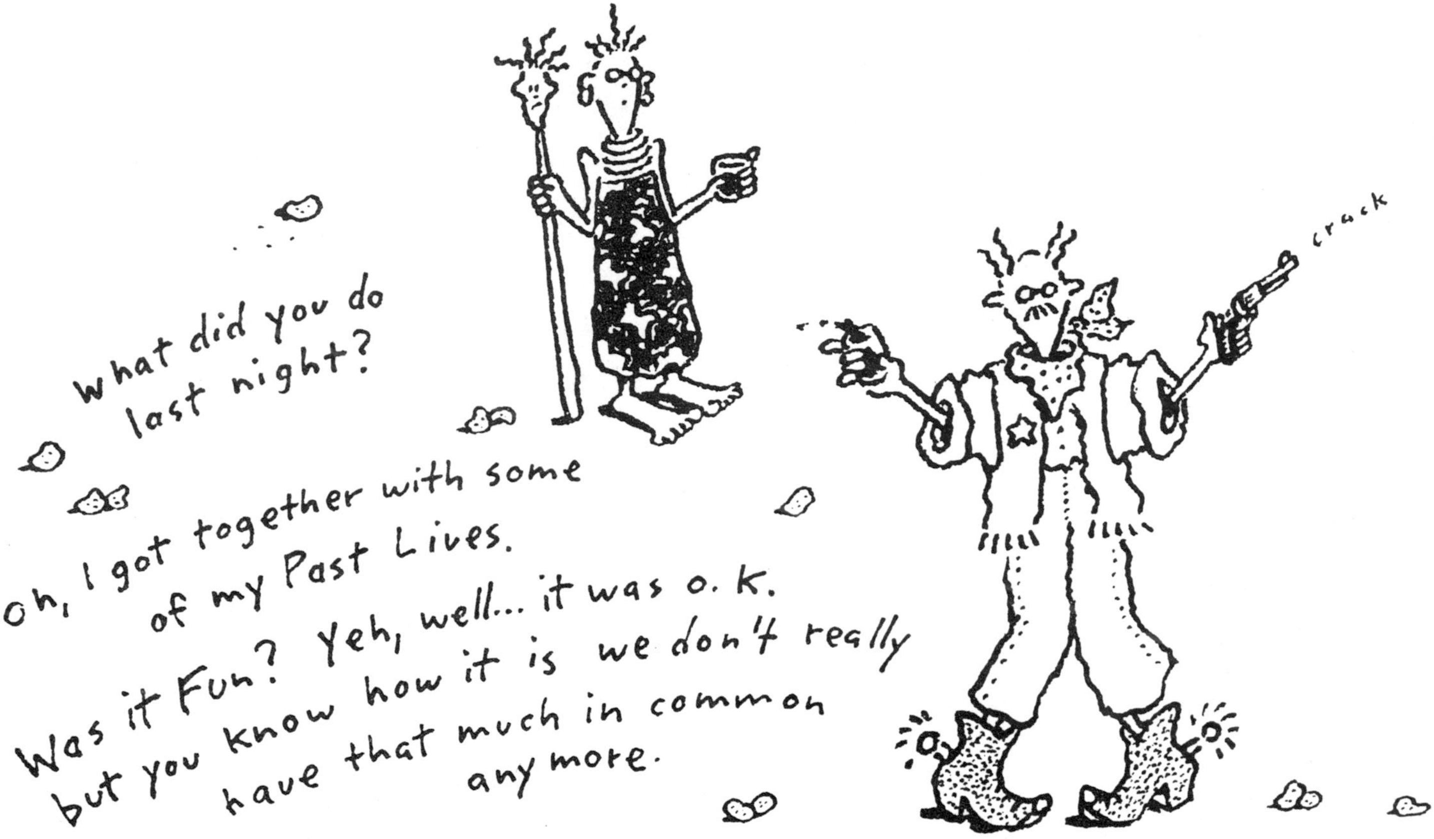
What did you do last night?
Oh, I got together with some of my Past Lives.
Was it Fun? Yeh, well... it was o. k. but you know how it is we don't really have that much in common anymore.
crack

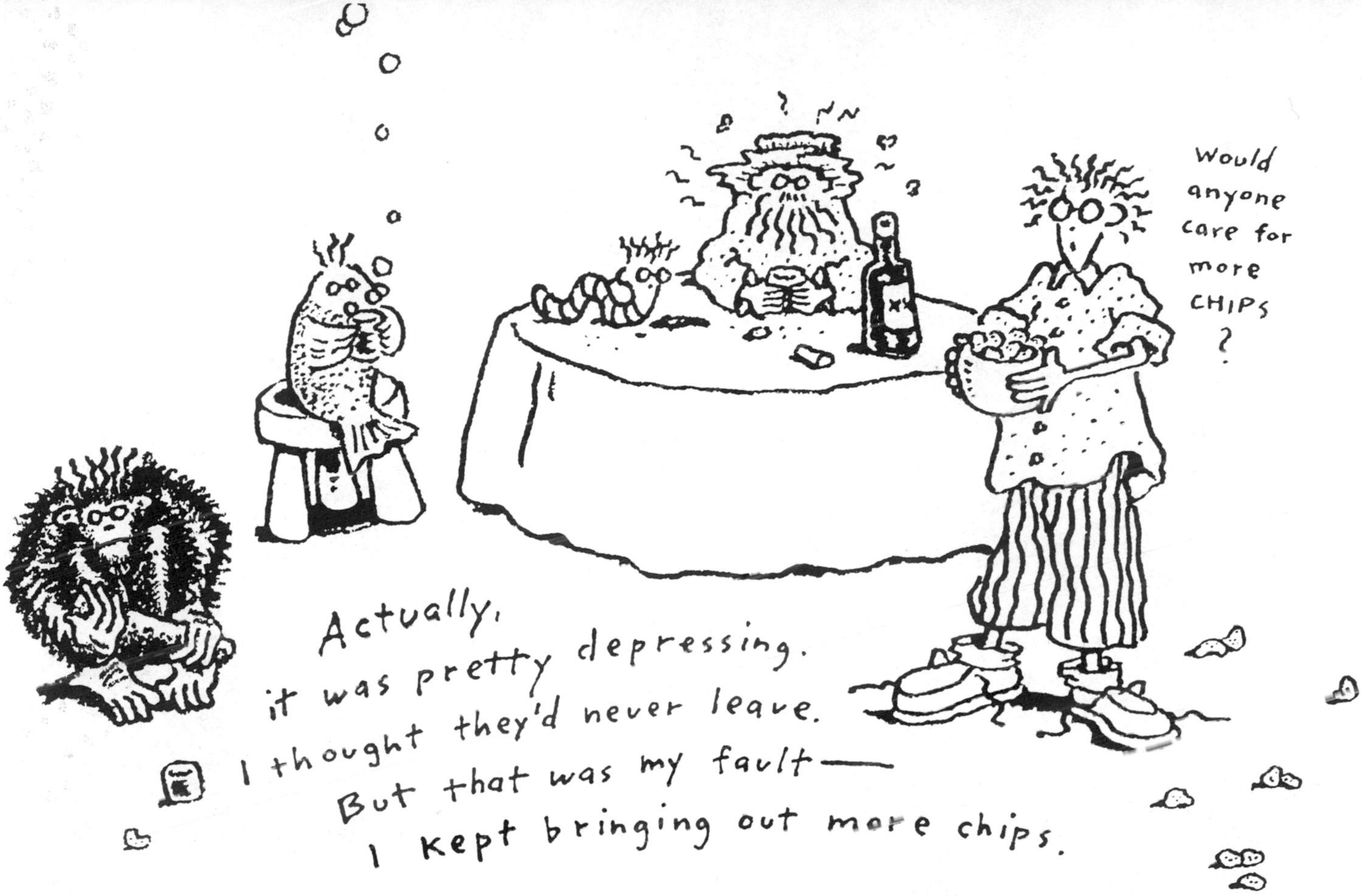
Would anyone care for more CHIPS ?
Actually, it was pretty depressing.
I thought they'd never leave.
But that was my fault—
I kept bringing out more chips.

sigh...

Finally, she resigned herself to the fact that she would never have thick and lustrous hair. Nor would she ever have a body like Gina Lollobrigida. At last, she was at peace in her own skin.

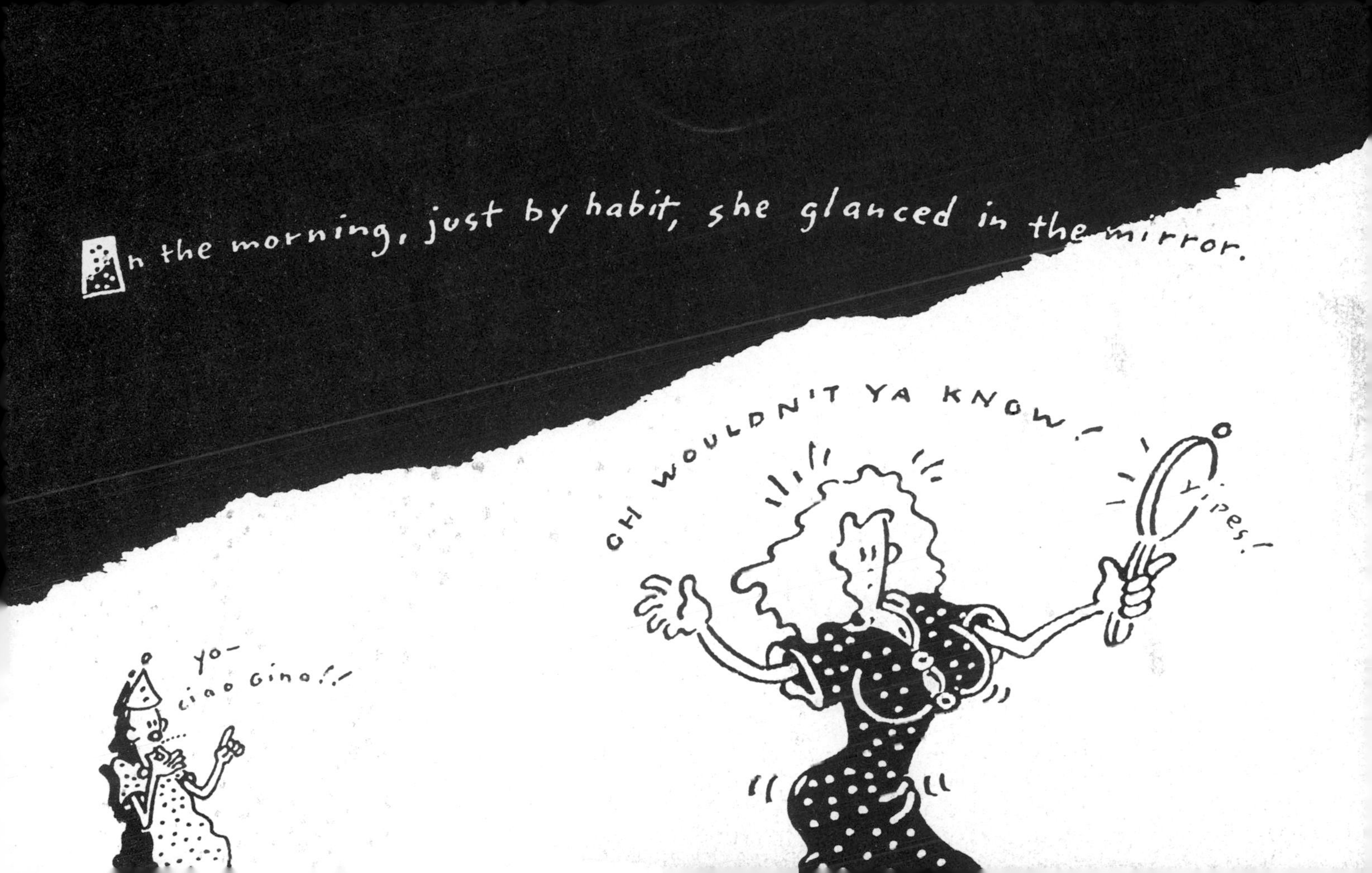
In the morning, just by habit, she glanced in the mirror.
OH WOULDN'T YA KNOW!
YIPES!
yo-
ciao Gino!!

Hmmm...

A Brief Affair.

It began with a glance from across a crowded room.

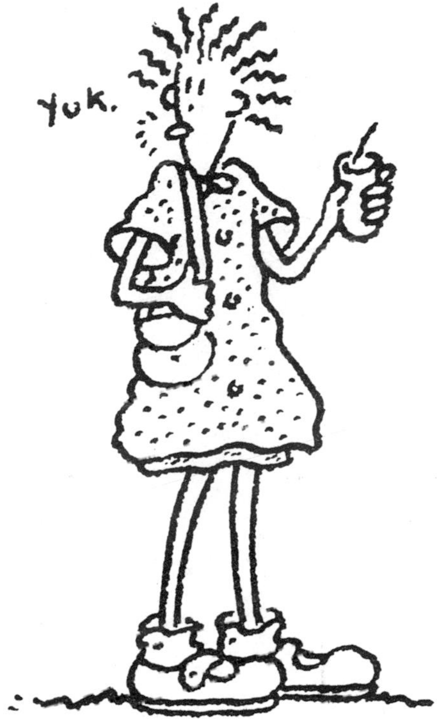
Yuk.

That's where it ended.

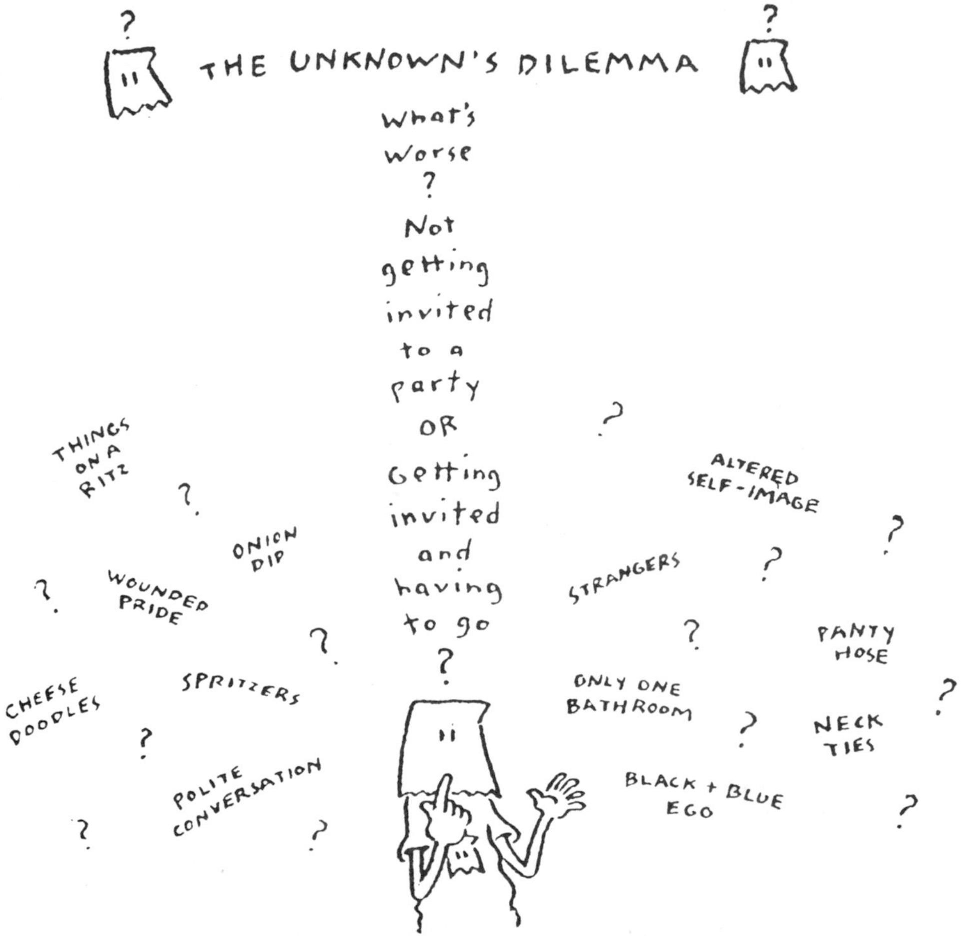
THE UNKNOWN'S DILEMMA
What's worse ? Not getting invited to a party OR Getting invited and having to go ?
THINGS ON A RITZ
ONION DIP
WOUNDED PRIDE
CHEESE DOODLES
SPRITZERS
POLITE CONVERSATION
ALTERED SELF-IMAGE
STRANGERS
PANTY HOSE
ONLY ONE BATHROOM
NECK TIES
BLACK + BLUE EGO

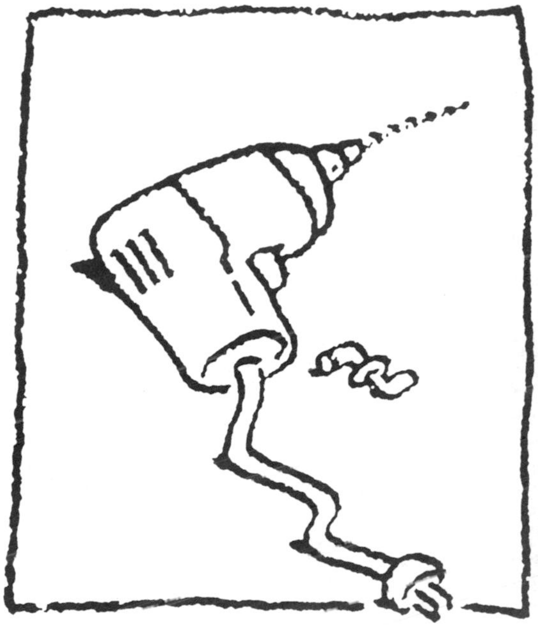

Power Tool.

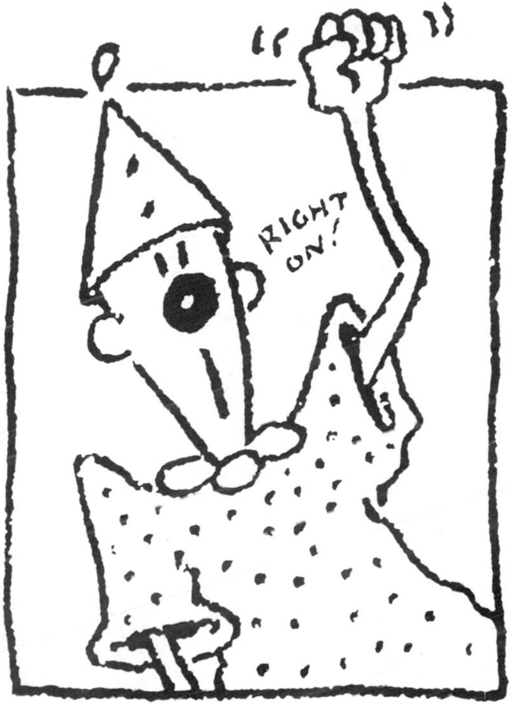
RIGHT ON!

Tool Power.

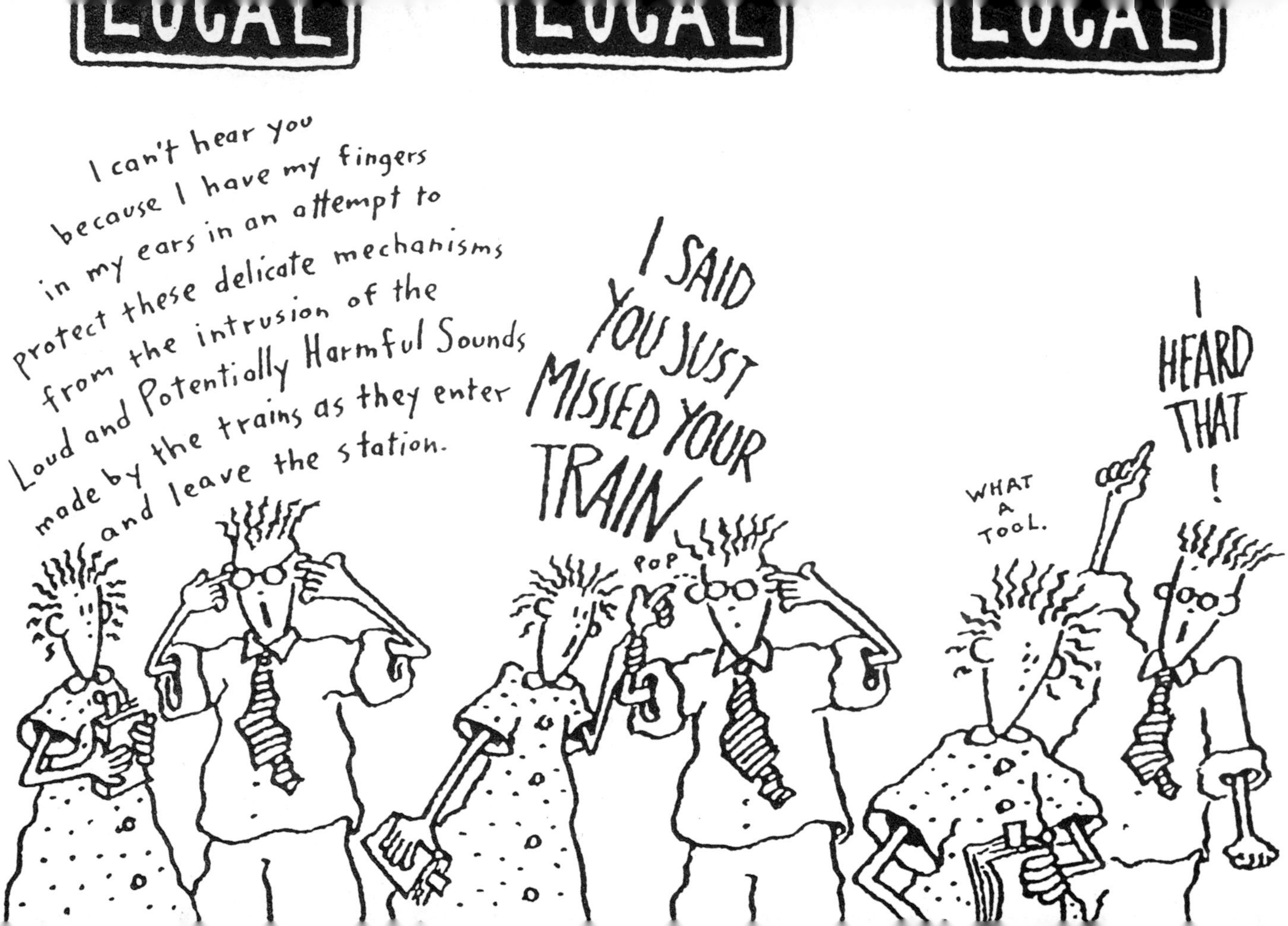
LOCAL
LOCAL
LOCAL
I can't hear you because I have my fingers in my ears in an attempt to protect these delicate mechanisms from the intrusion of the Loud and Potentiolly Harmful Sounds made by the trains as they enter and leave the station.
I SAID YOU JUST MISSED YOUR TRAIN
POP
WHAT A TOOL.
I HEARD THAT!

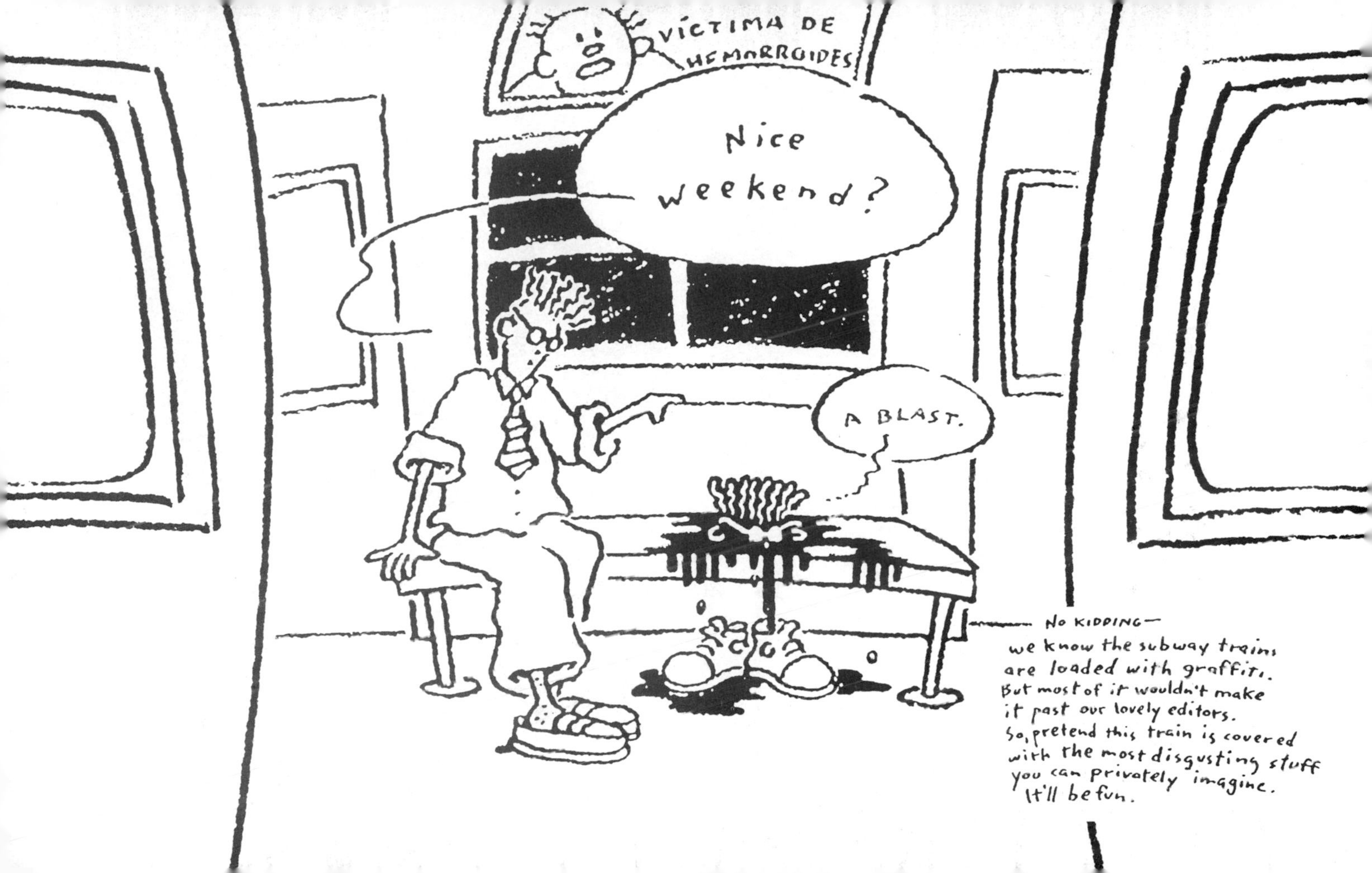
VÍCTIMA DE HEMORROIDES
Nice weekend?
A BLAST.
NO KIDDING—
we know the subway trains are loaded with graffiti. But most of it wouldn't make it past our lovely editors. So, pretend this train is covered with the most disgusting stuff you can privately imagine. It'll be fun.

THE REALLY BIG AND IMPORTANT MEETING.

I have a really big and important meeting coming up.
I have a really big and important meeting in a few days.

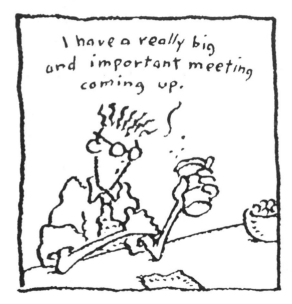

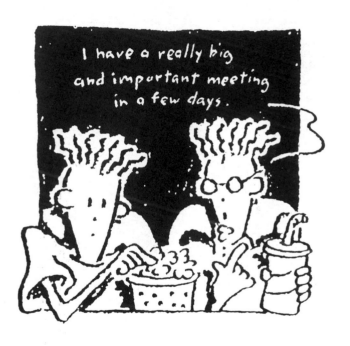

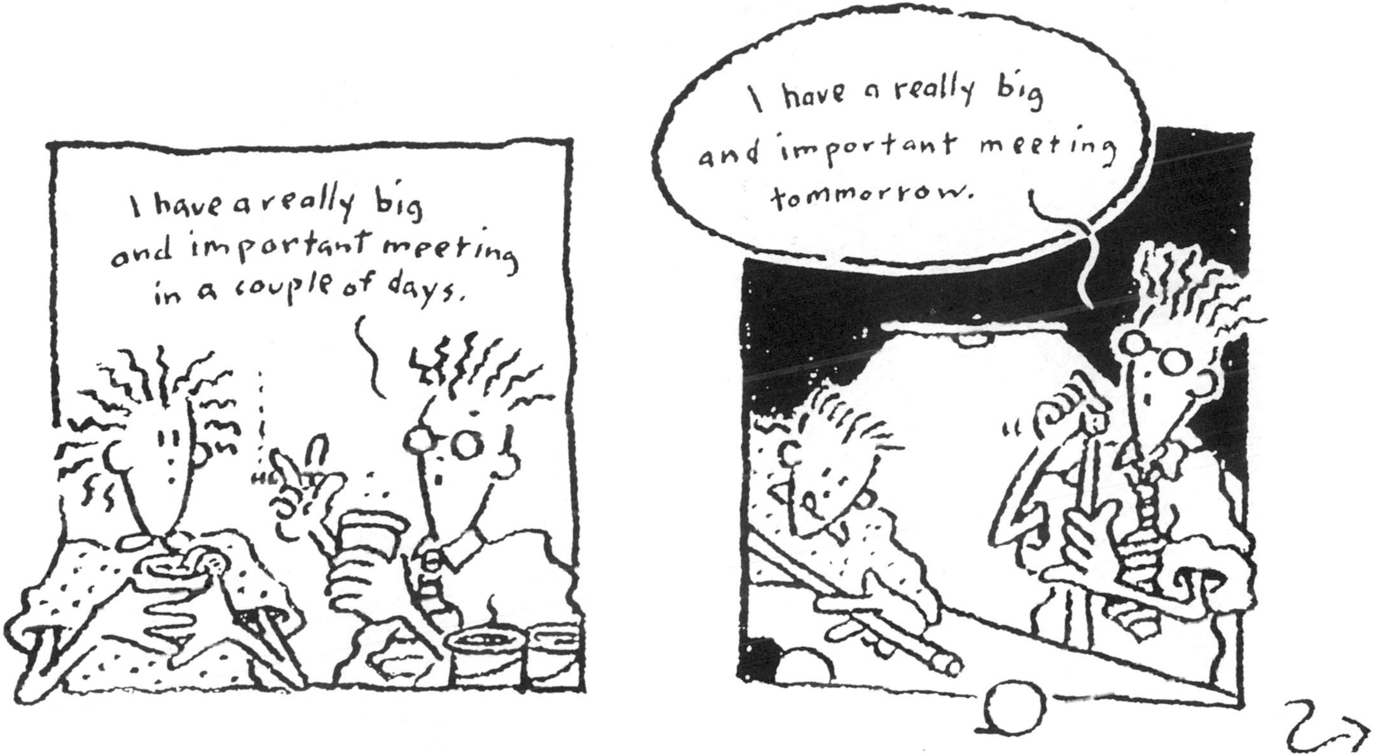
I have a really big and important meeting in a couple of days.
I have a really big and important meeting tommorrow.

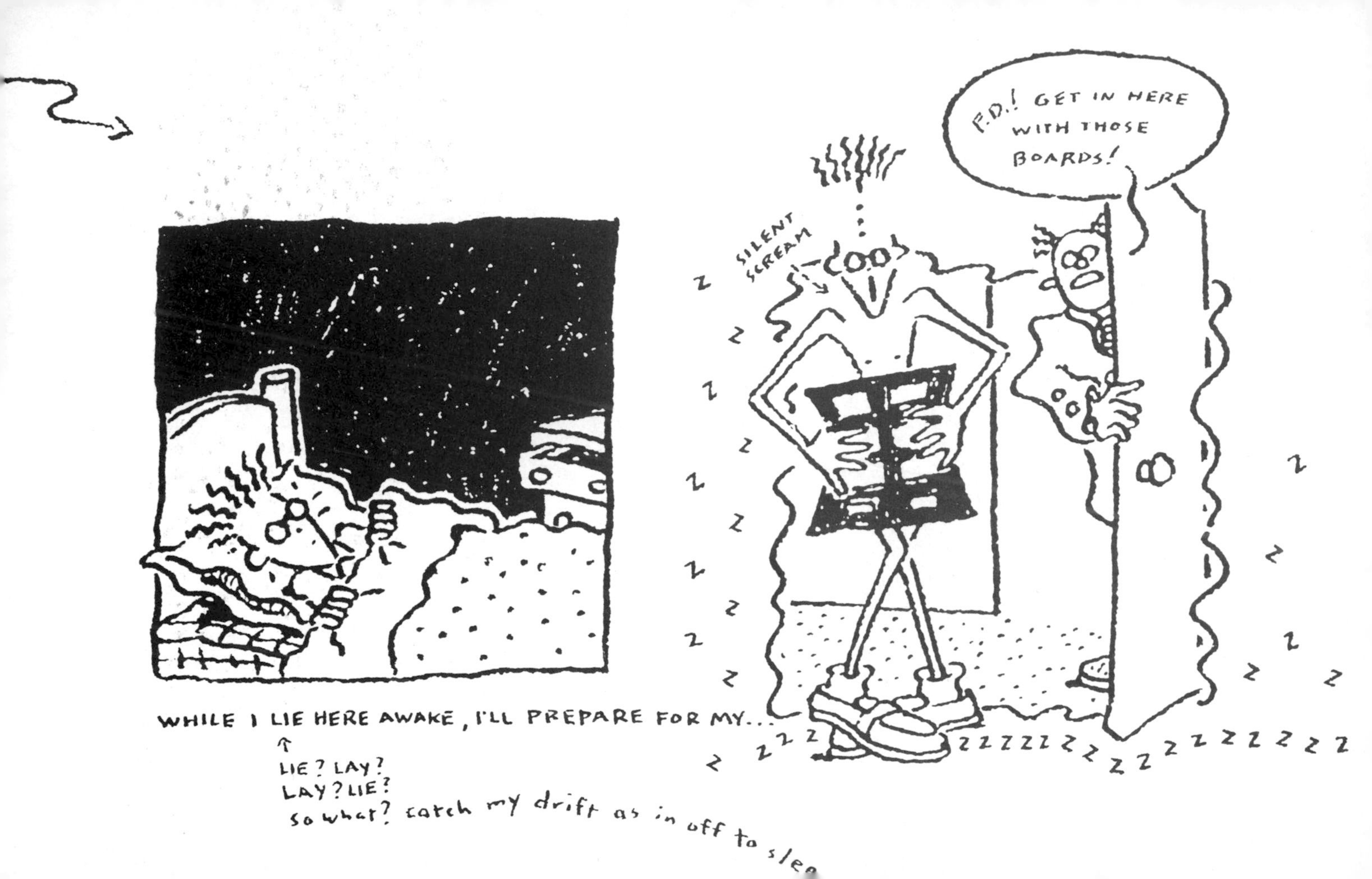
F.D.! GET IN HERE WITH THOSE BOARDS!
SILENT SCREAM
WHILE I LIE HERE AWAKE, I'LL PREPARE FOR MY...
LIE? LAY?
LAY? LIE?
so what? catch my drift as in off to slee
Z Z Z Z Z Z Z Z Z Z Z Z Z Z Z Z Z Z Z Z Z Z Z Z Z Z Z Z Z Z Z Z Z Z Z Z Z Z Z Z Z

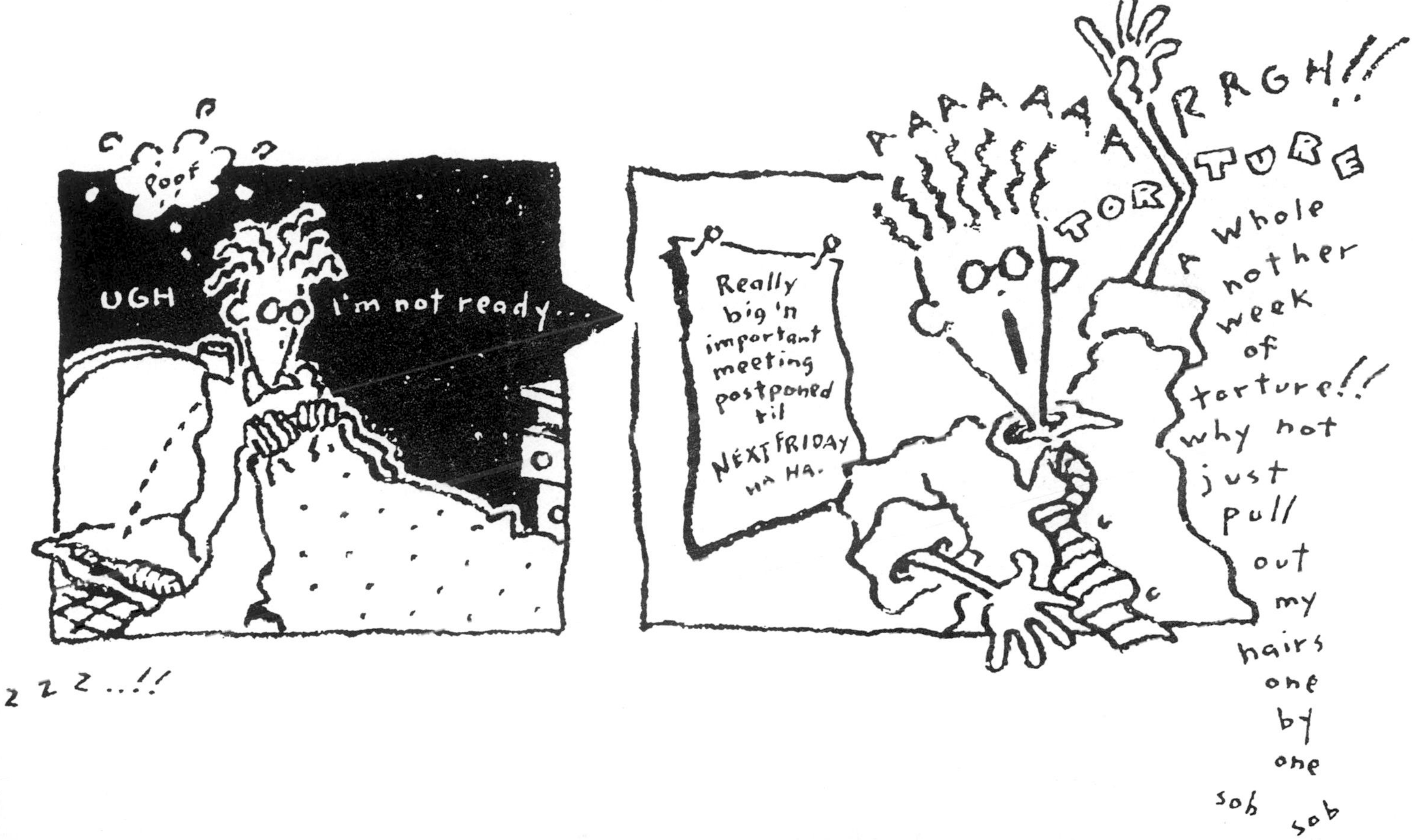

poof
UGH
I'm not ready...
z z z ..!!
Really big 'n important meeting postponed til NEXT FRIDAY HA HA.
AAAAAAAARRRGH!!
TORTURE
a whole nother week of torture!!! why not just pull out my hairs one by one
sob sob

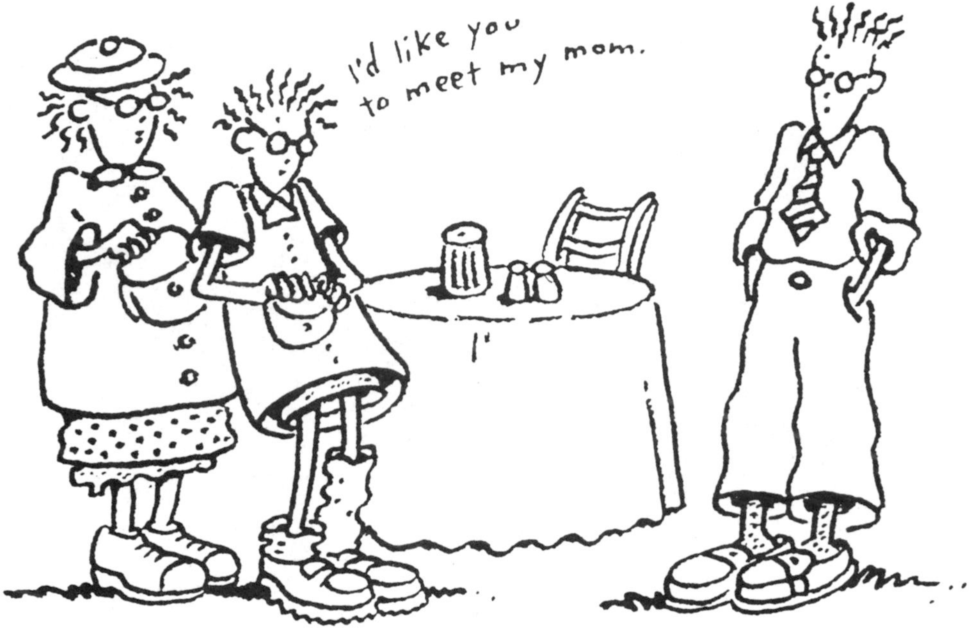
I'd like you
to meet my mom.

Not the kind of protection to bring on a date.

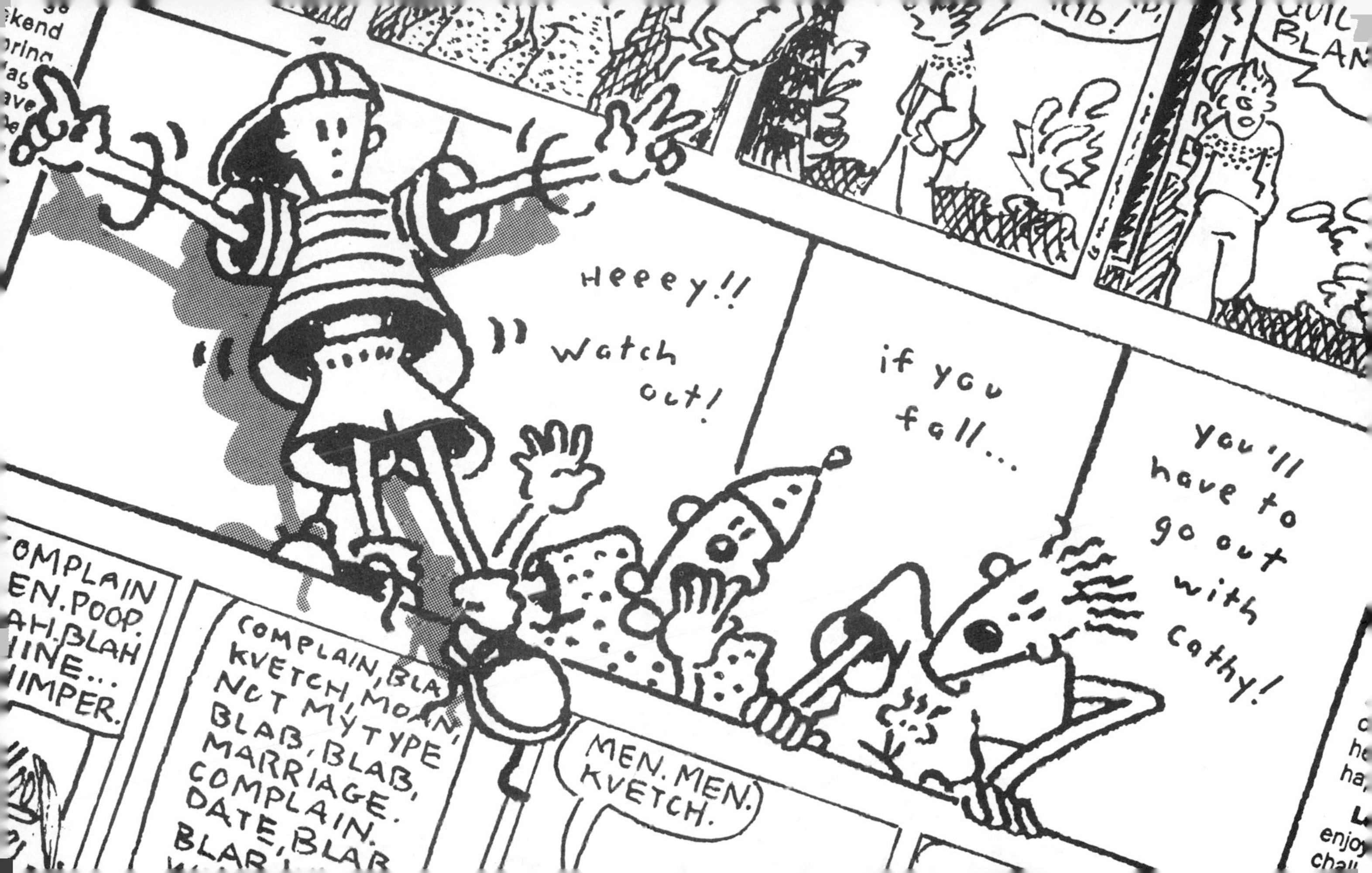
Heeey!!
watch out!
if you fall...
you'll have to go out with Cathy!
COMPLAIN, BLA KVETCH, MOAN, NOT MY TYPE BLAB, BLAB, MARRIAGE. COMPLAIN. DATE, BLAB
MEN. MEN. KVETCH.

An independent sort accustomed to making her own decisions, she decided to conduct a test at home. Half a load of laundry with her detergent, and half with The Current Leading Brand. The result? She felt both piles were white enough. Satisfied, she determined it would be months before she had to buy detergent again.

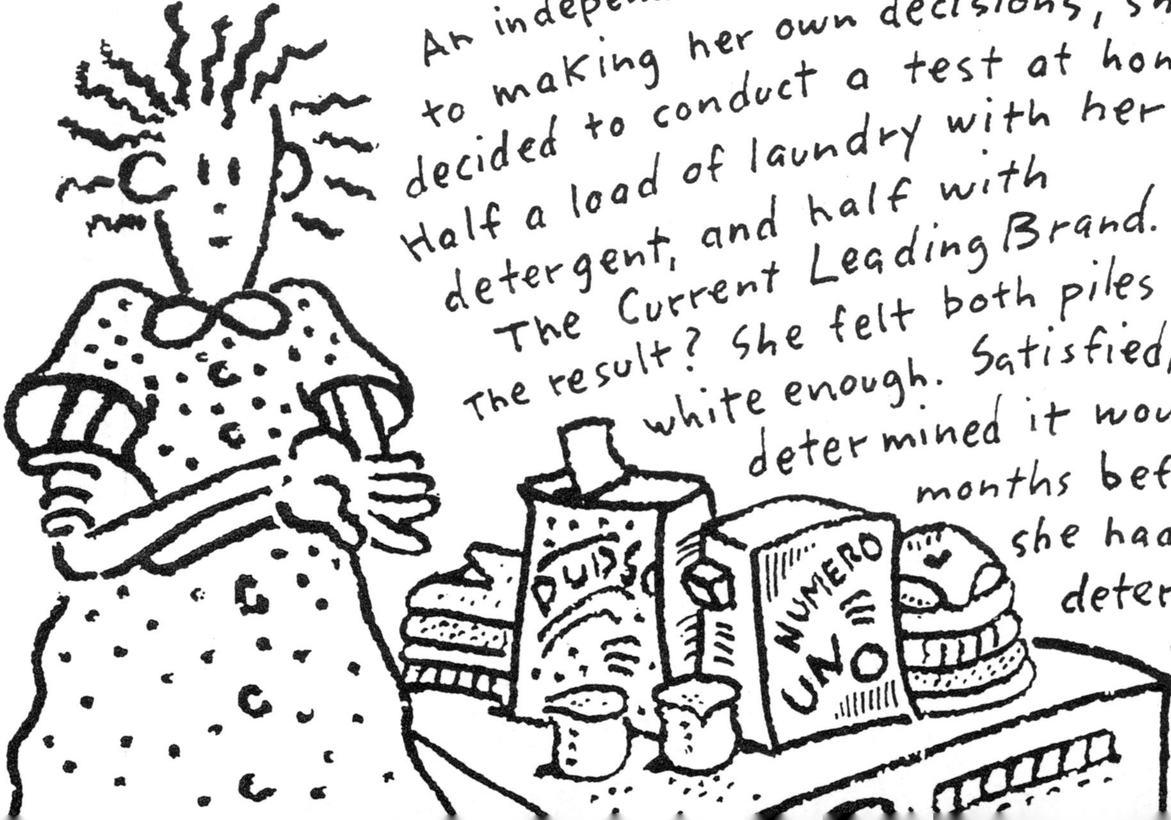
DUDS
NUMERO UNO

A peek at
Jackie O's
clothesline

UNAUTHORIZED ILLUSTRATION

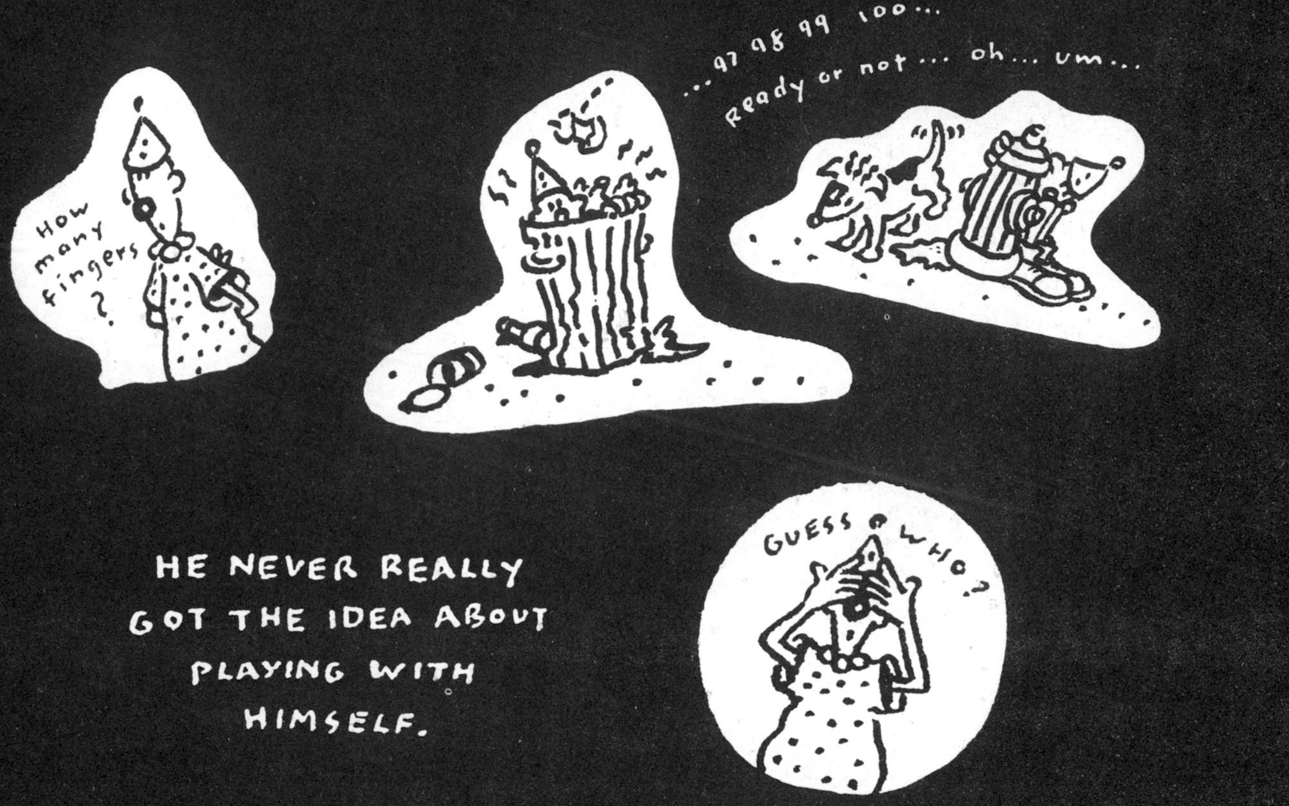
How many fingers ?
...97 98 99 100...
Ready or not... oh... um...
GUESS WHO?
HE NEVER REALLY GOT THE IDEA ABOUT PLAYING WITH HIMSELF.

tools are people too.

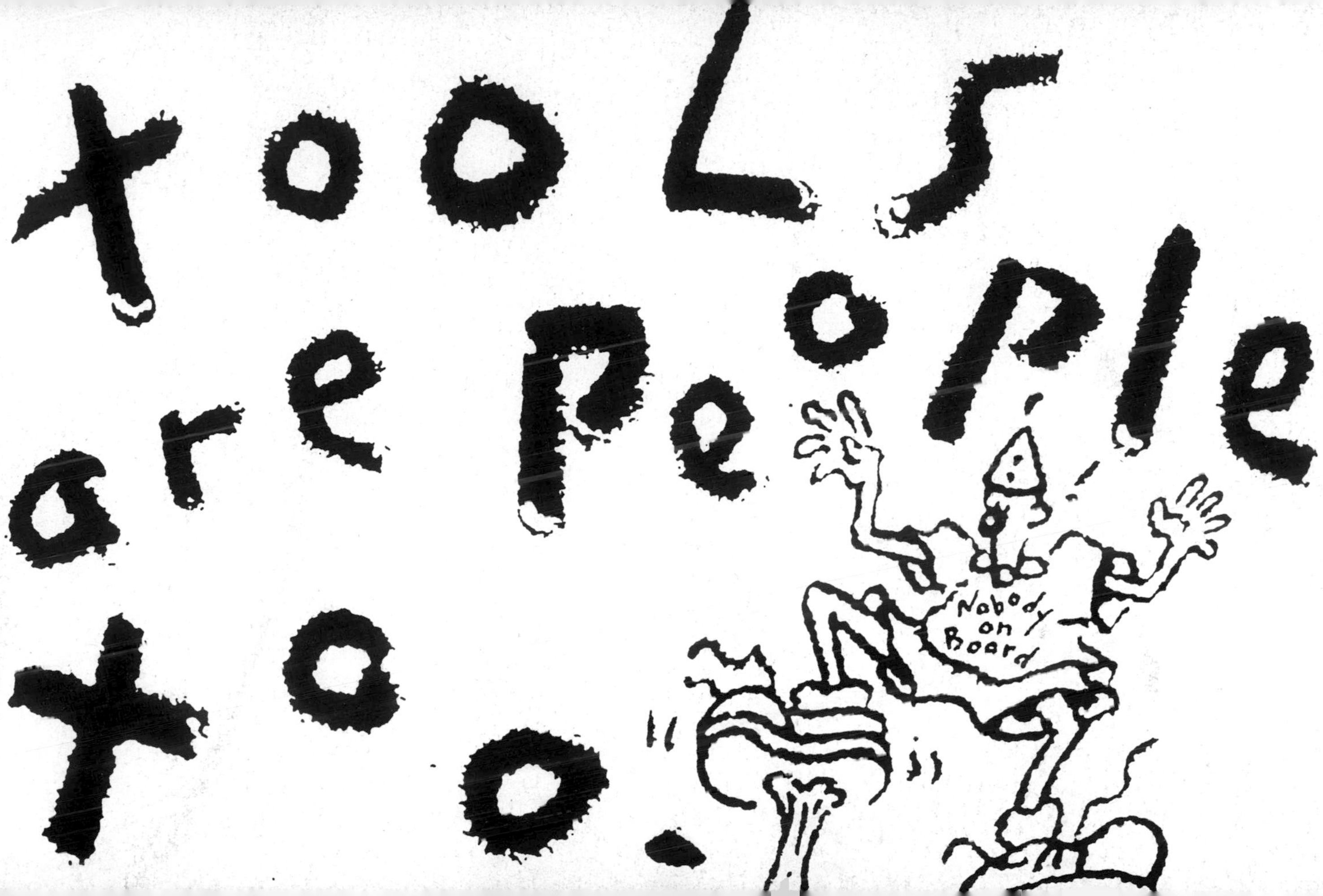
Nobody on Board

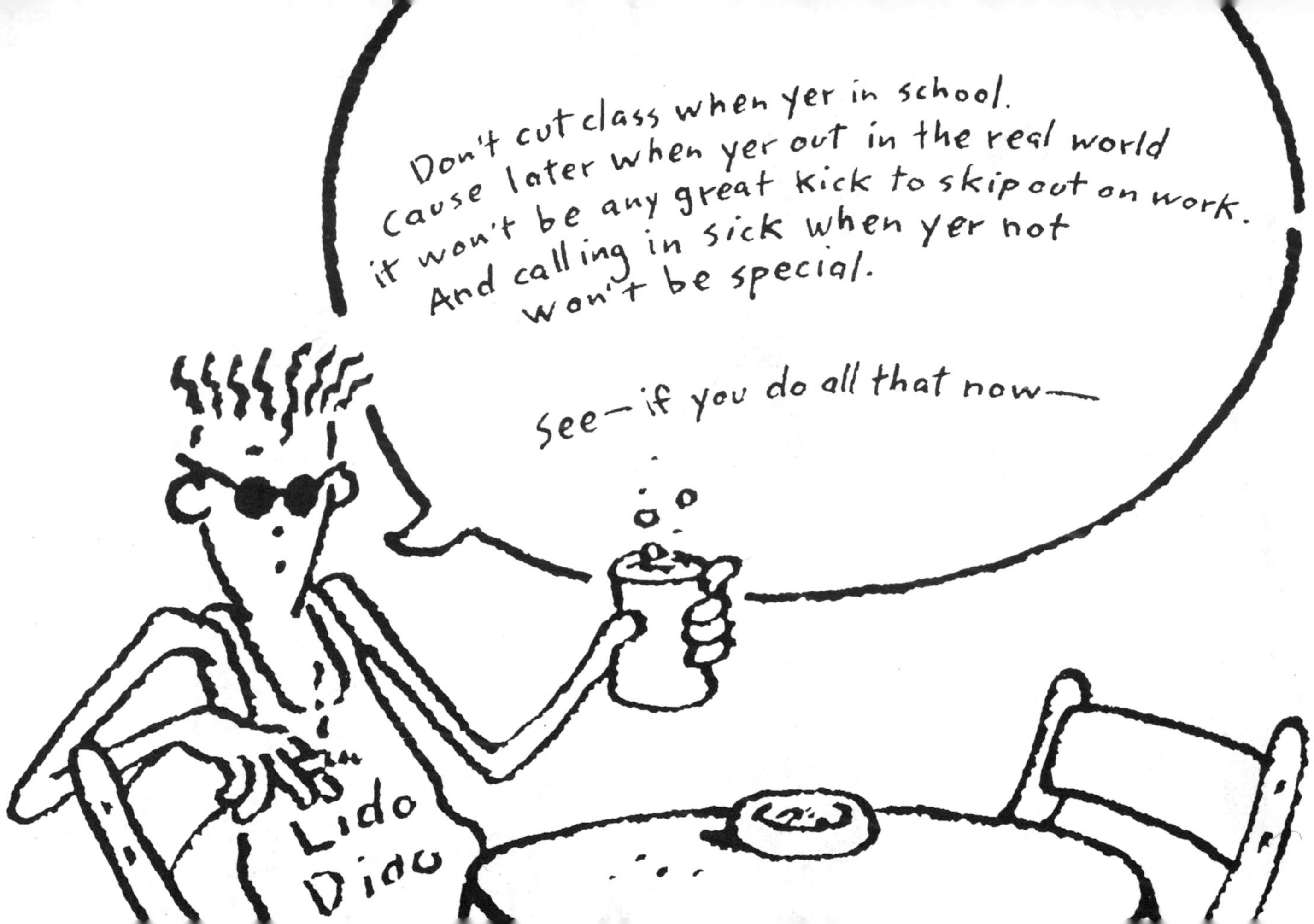
Don't cut class when yer in school.
Cause later when yer out in the real world
it won't be any great kick to skip out on work.
And calling in sick when yer not
won't be special.
See—if you do all that now—
Lido
Dido

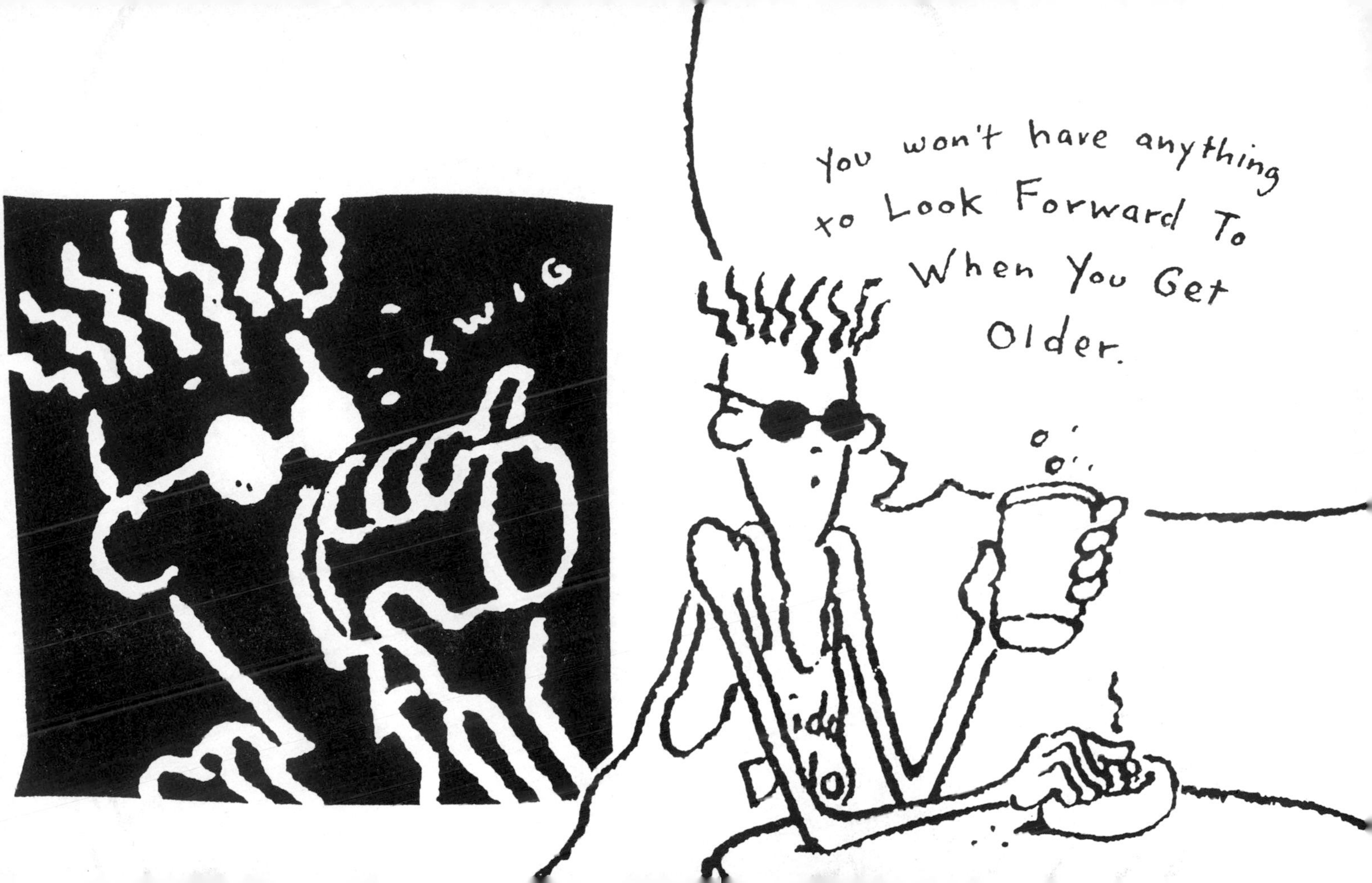
SWIG
You won't have anything to Look Forward To When You Get Older.
Fido

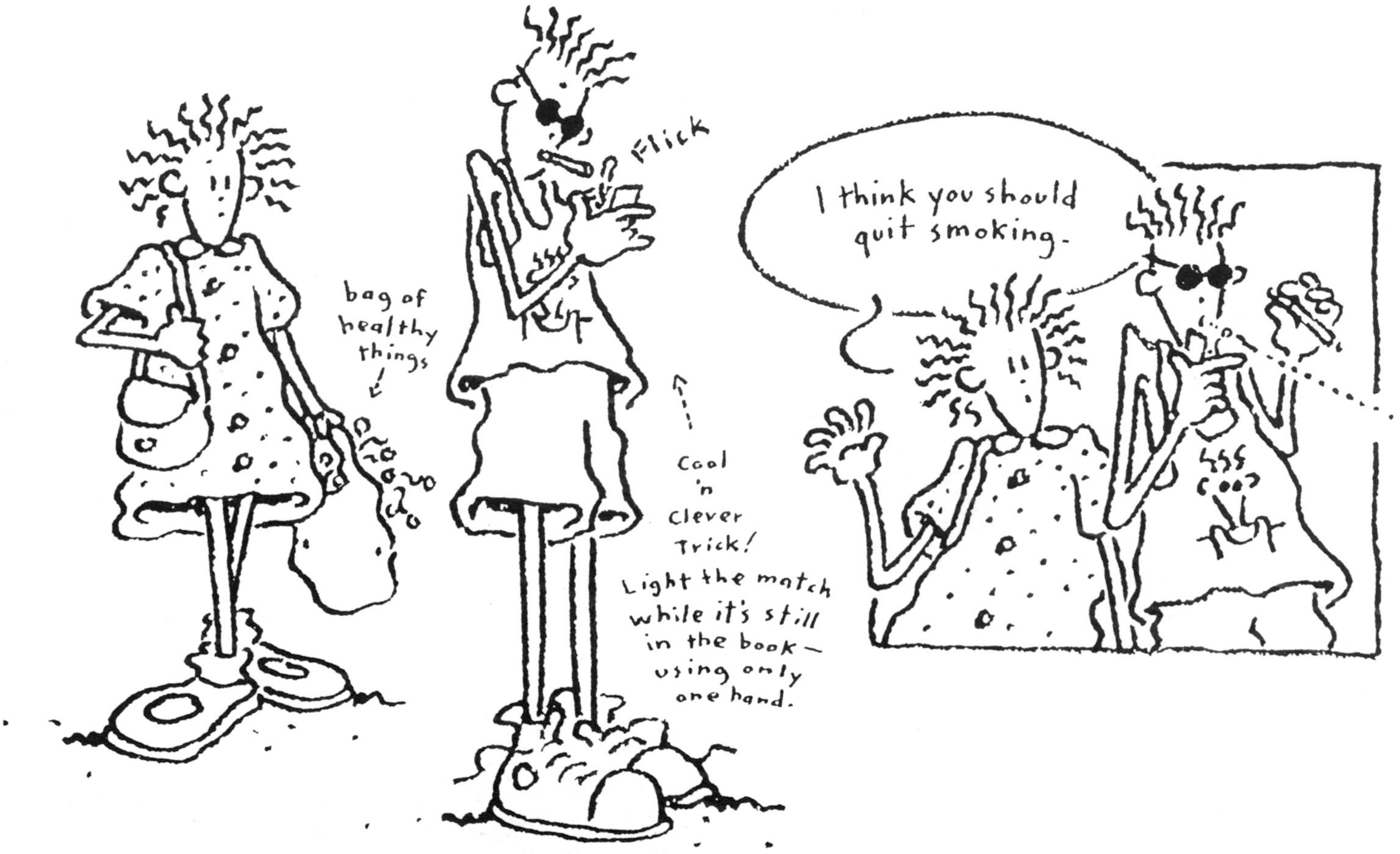
bag of healthy things
Flick
Cool 'n Clever Trick! Light the match while it's still in the book—using only one hand.
I think you should quit smoking.

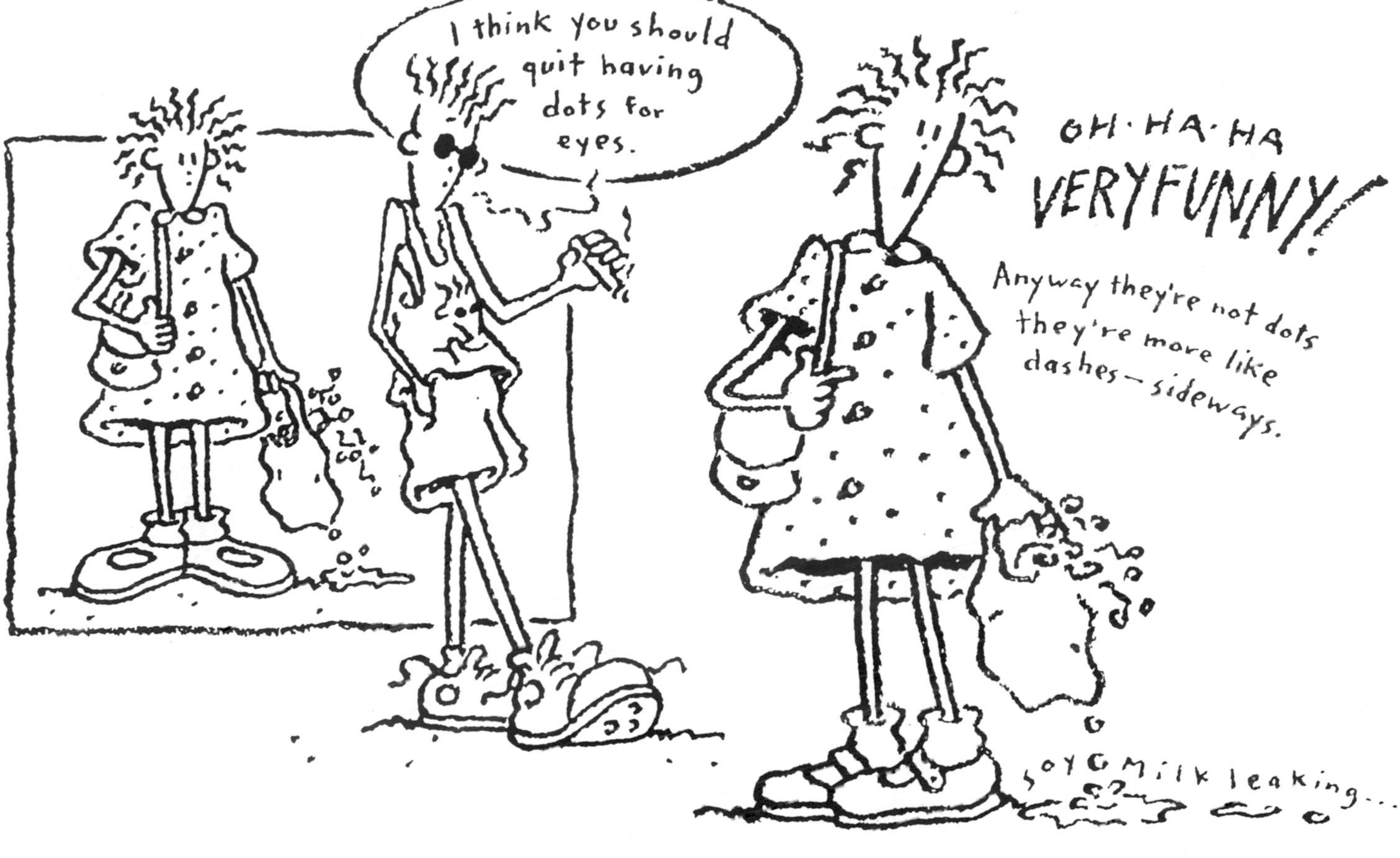
I think you should quit having dots for eyes.
OH·HA·HA VERYFUNNY!
Anyway they're not dots they're more like dashes—sideways.
soy milk leaking...

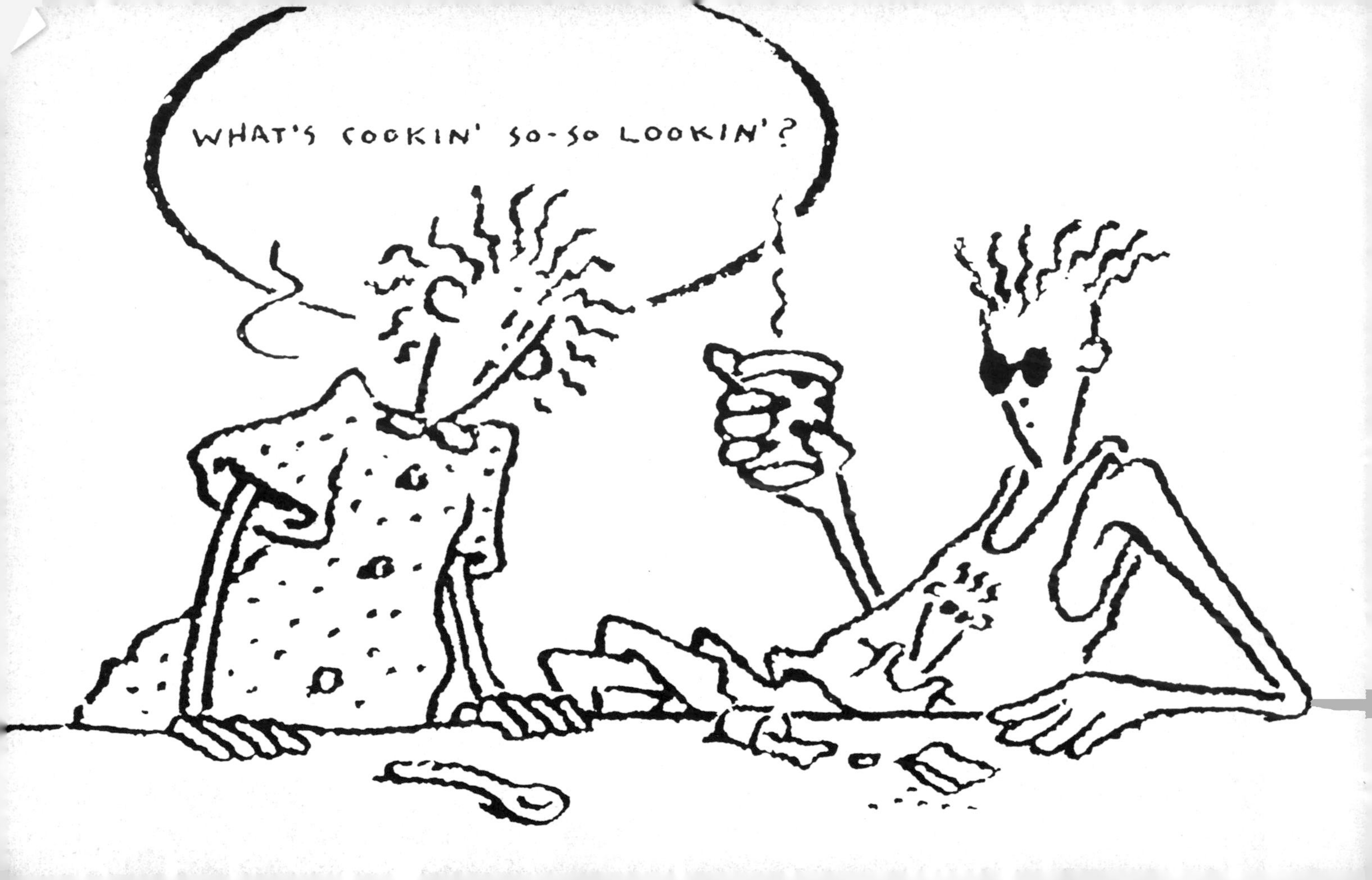
WHAT'S COOKIN' SO-SO LOOKIN'?

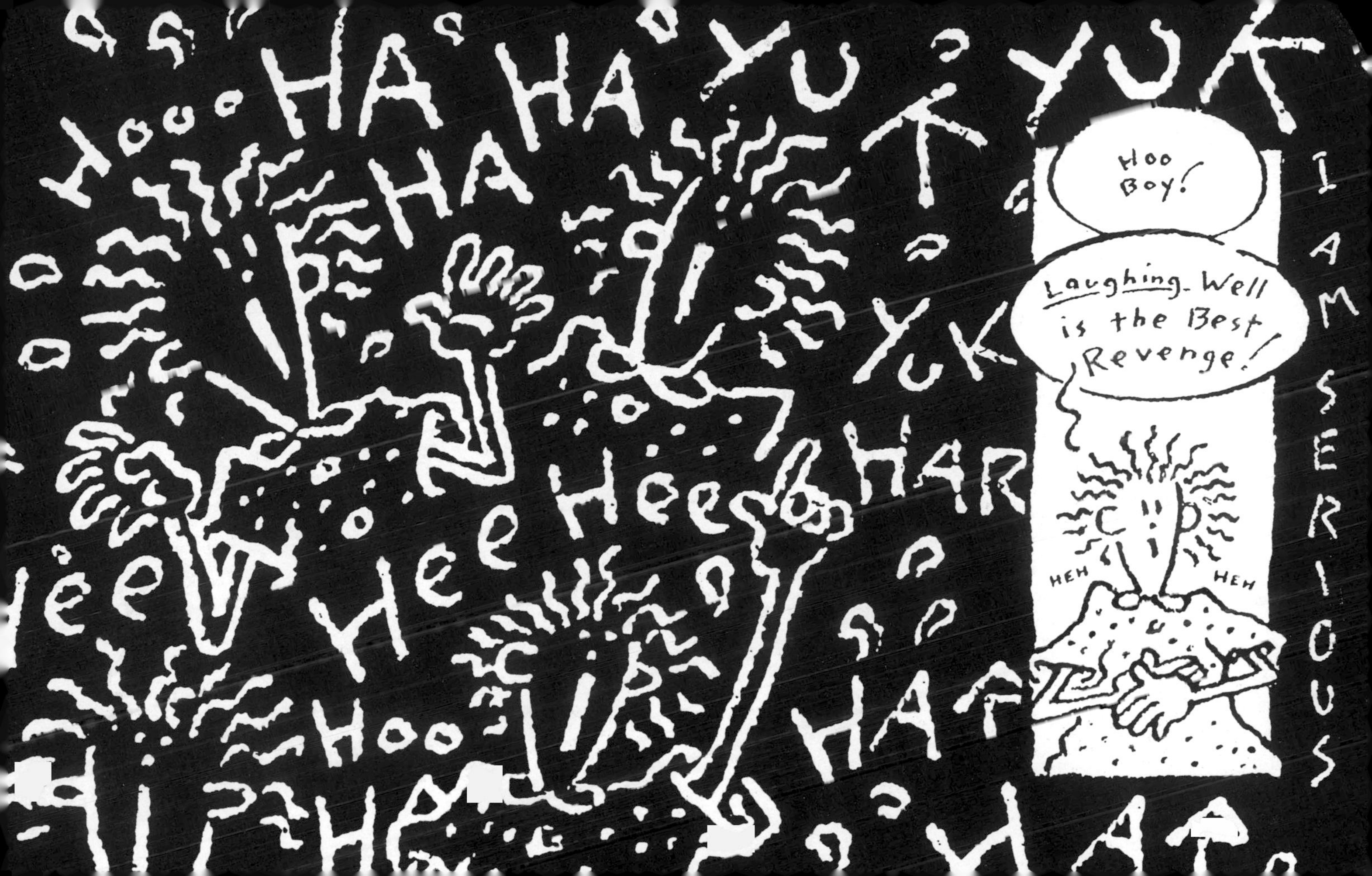

Hoo HA HA YUK YUK
HA
YUK
HAR
Hee Hee
Hee
Hee
Hoo
HA
HA
HA
Hoo Boy!
Laughing Well is the Best Revenge!
HEH
HEH
I AM SERIOUS

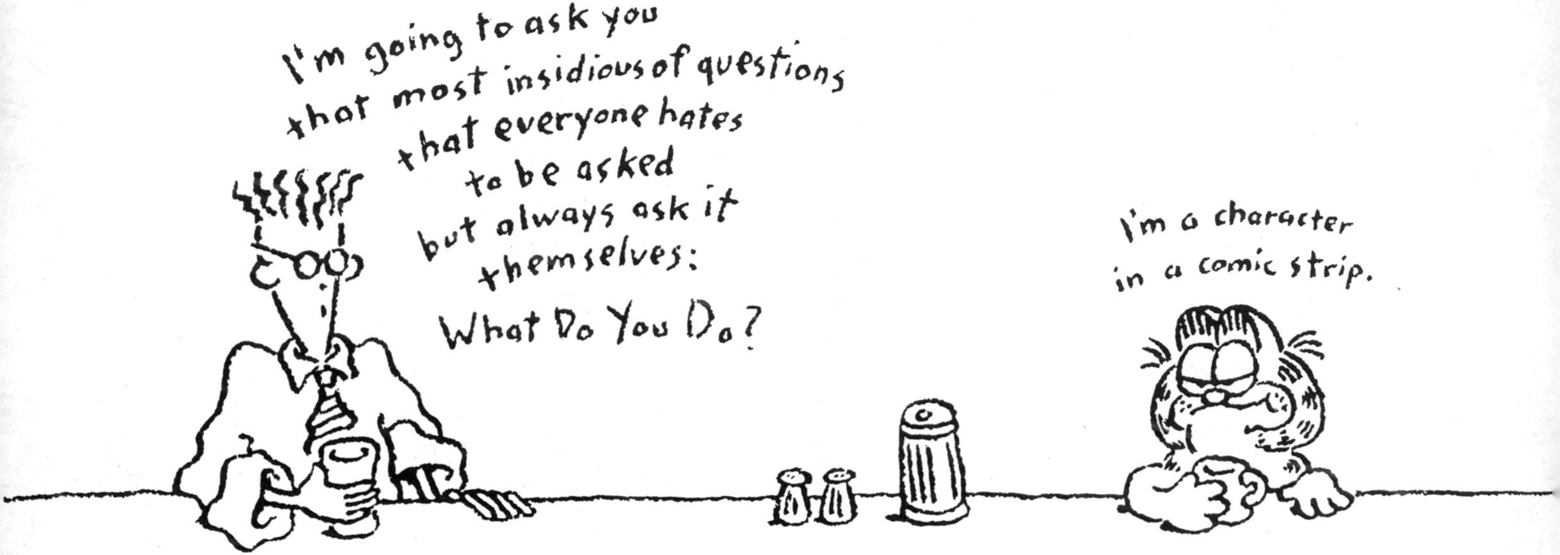
I'm going to ask you
that most insidious of questions
that everyone hates
to be asked
but always ask it
themselves:
What Do You Do?
I'm a character
in a comic strip.

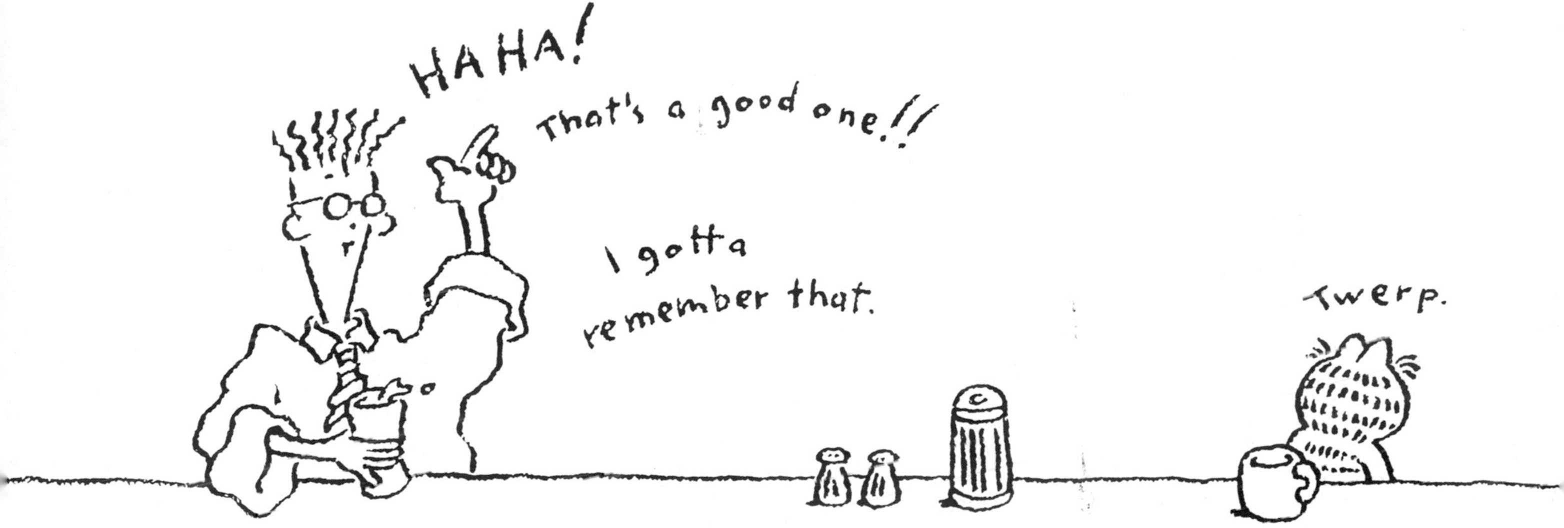
HA HA!
That's a good one!!
I gotta remember that.
Twerp.

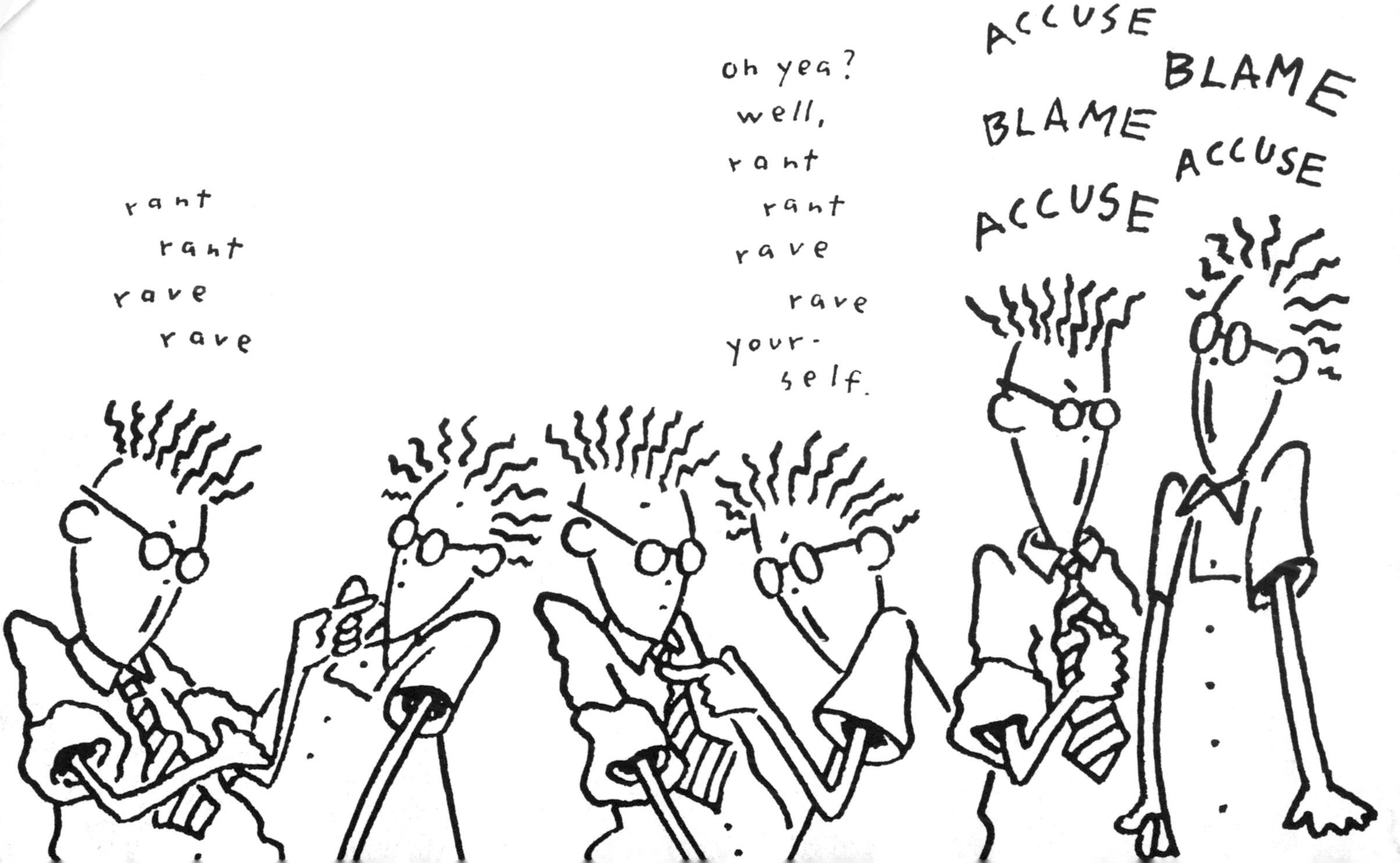
rant
rant
rave
rave
oh yea?
well,
rant
rant
rave
rave
your-
self.
ACCUSE
BLAME
BLAME
ACCUSE
ACCUSE

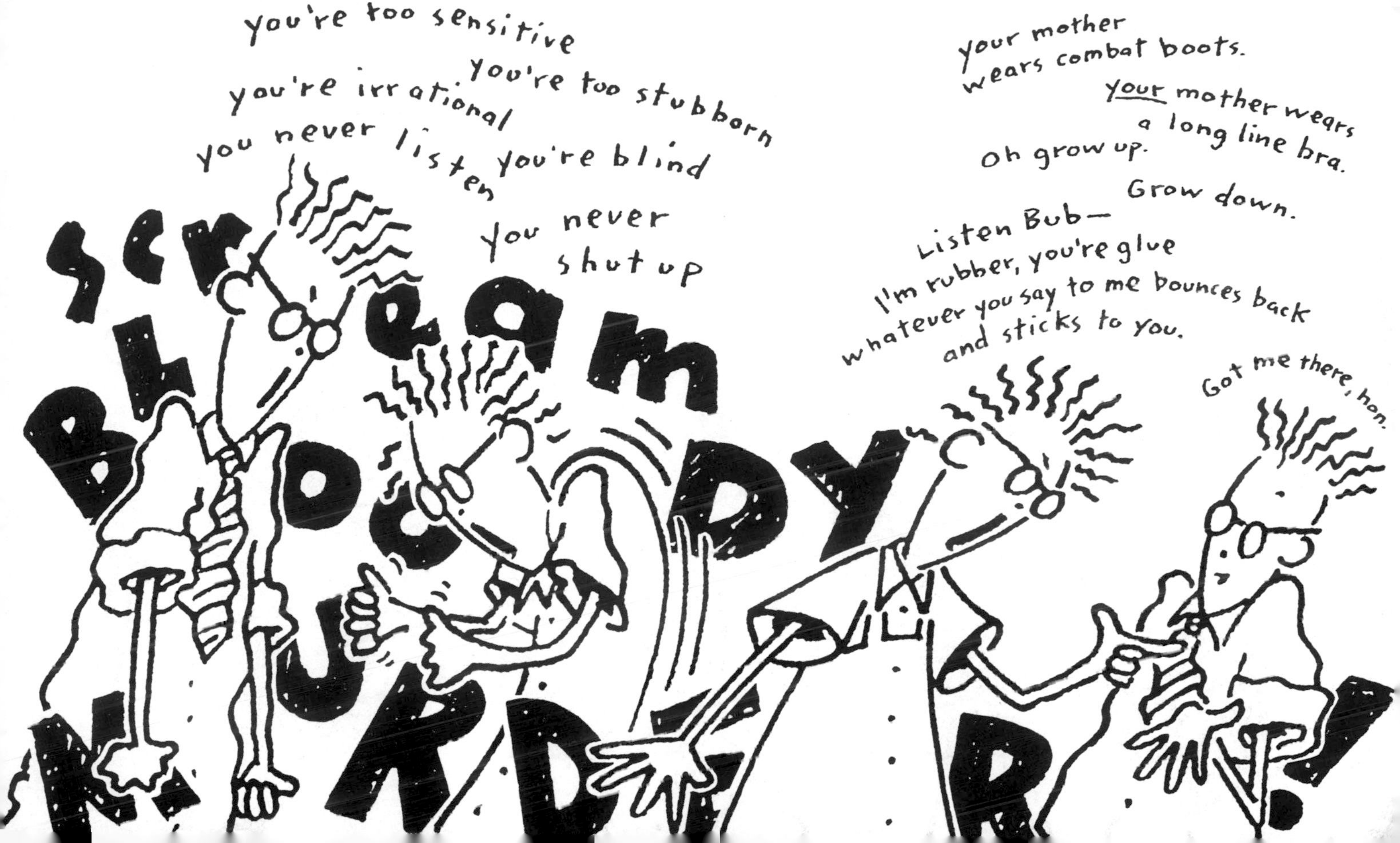
you're too sensitive
you're too stubborn
you're irrational
you never listen
you're blind
You never shut up
Scream
your mother wears combat boots.
your mother wears a long line bra.
Oh grow up.
Grow down.
Listen Bub—
I'm rubber, you're glue
whatever you say to me bounces back and sticks to you.
Got me there, hon.

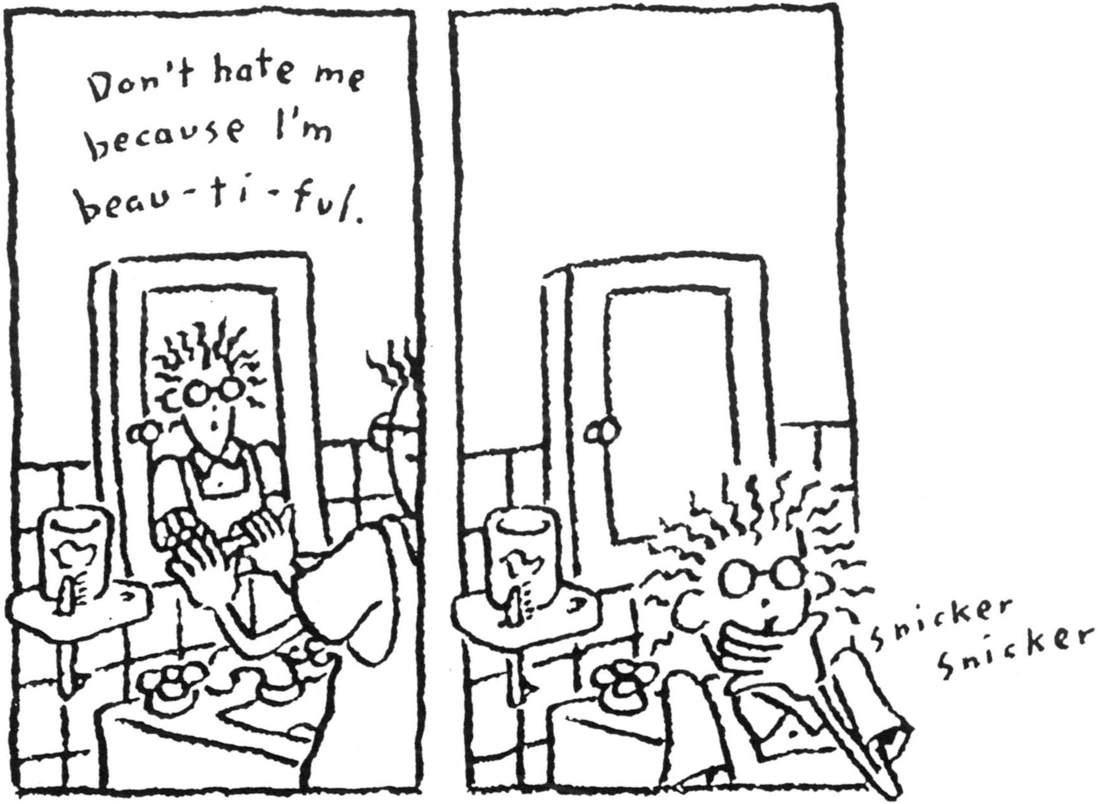
Don't hate me because I'm beau-ti-ful.
Snicker
Snicker

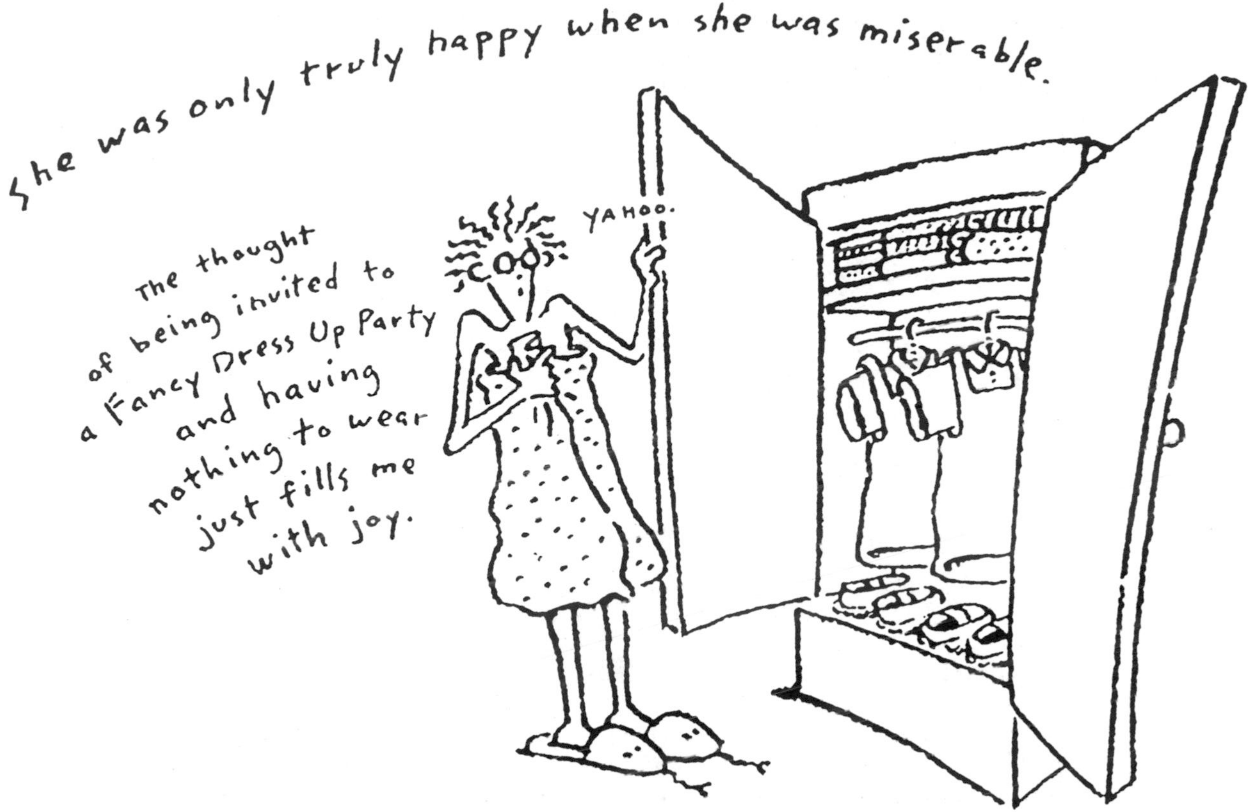
She was only truly happy when she was miserable.
The thought of being invited to a Fancy Dress Up Party and having nothing to wear just fills me with joy.
YAHOO.

MIRACLE AT D'AGOSTINO.

THIS IS A TRUE STORY.

I go to the store the other day. Not to do a Major Grocery Run, just to pick up a couple 'a things. So there's this guy in front of me on the checkout line. He turns and gives me The Once Over. Oh brother, I'm thinking, what's <u>this</u> lunatic looking at?!! I'm starting to wish I had picked a different line, when he says, "You got less stuff than me, go ahead." OK, I wonder, what's the catch? But that was it — he lets me pass — No Problem. Boy, this made my day — I mean it should 'a made *Ripley's!* — And, sheesh — I thought he was a bum. —

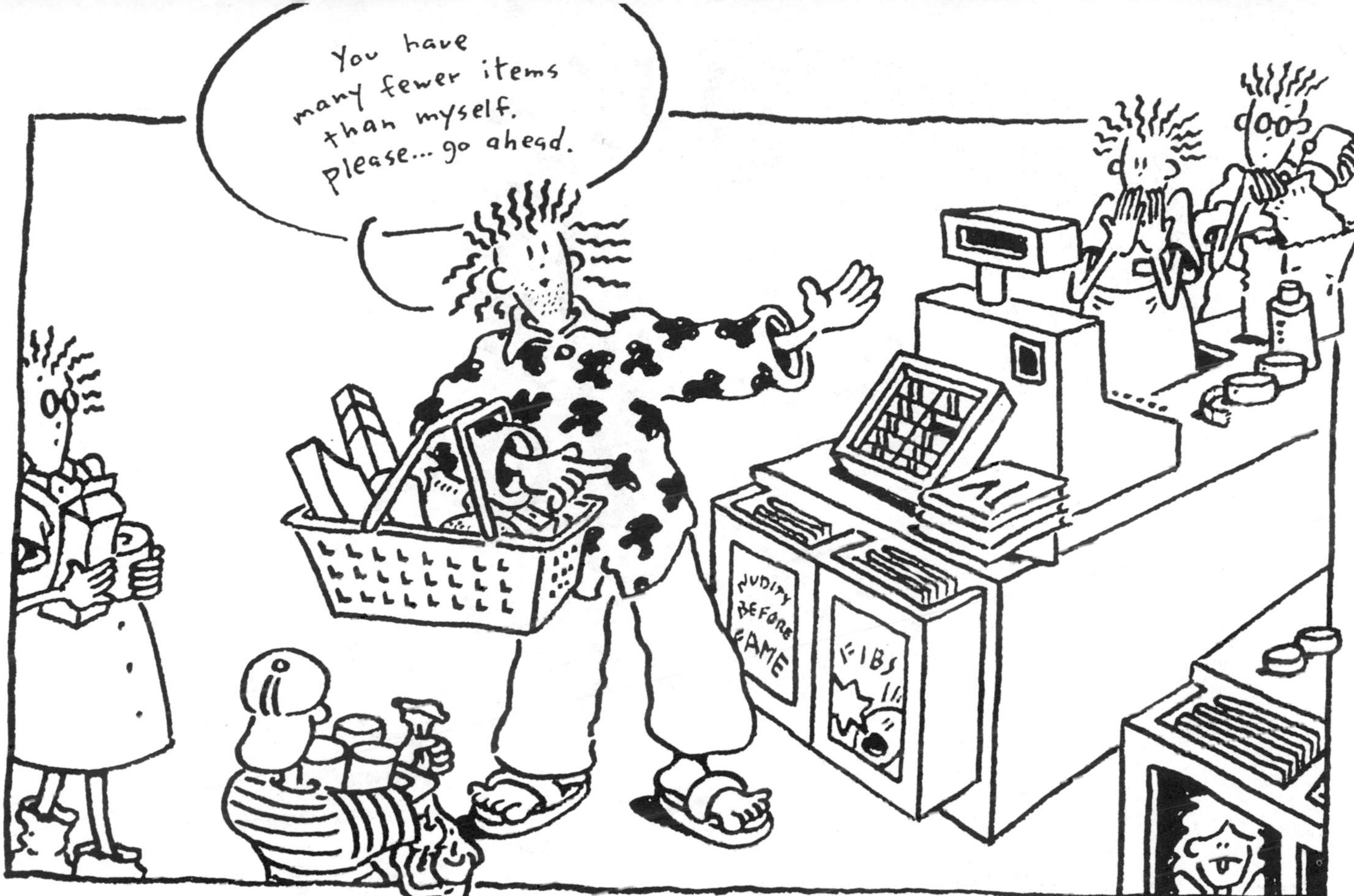
You have many fewer items than myself. please... go ahead.
NUDITY BEFORE FAME
FIBS

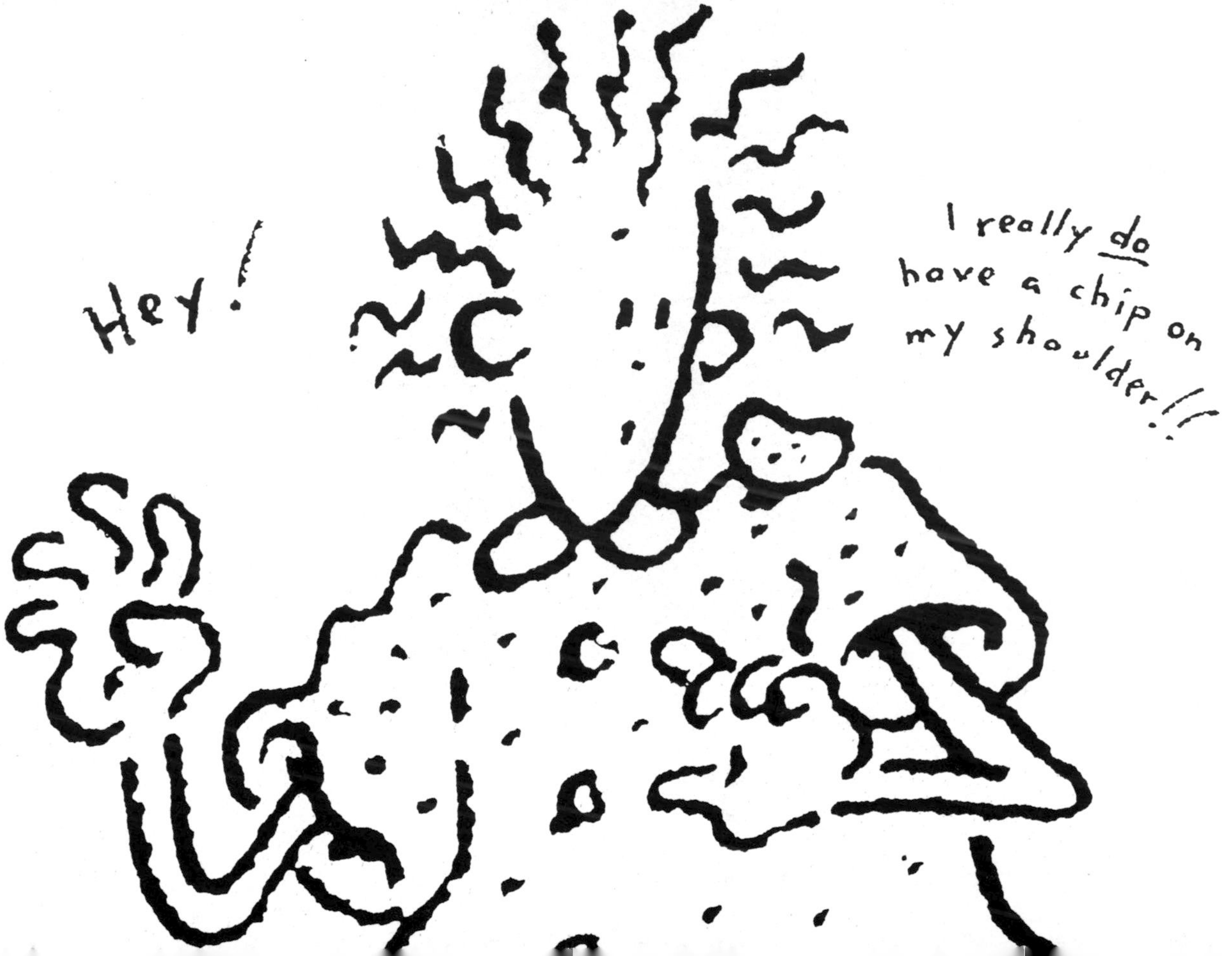
Hey!
I really do have a chip on my shoulder!!

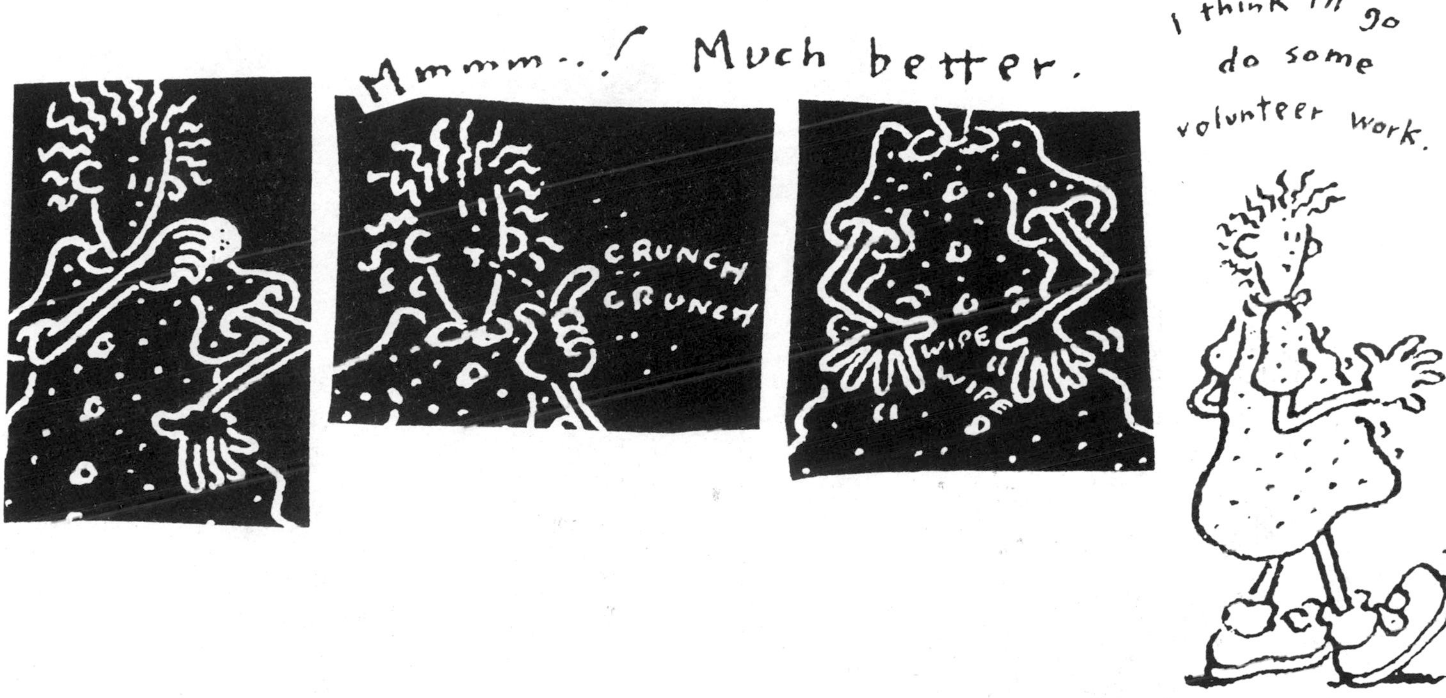

Mmmm..! Much better.
CRUNCH
CRUNCH
WIPE
WIPE
I think I'll go do some volunteer work.

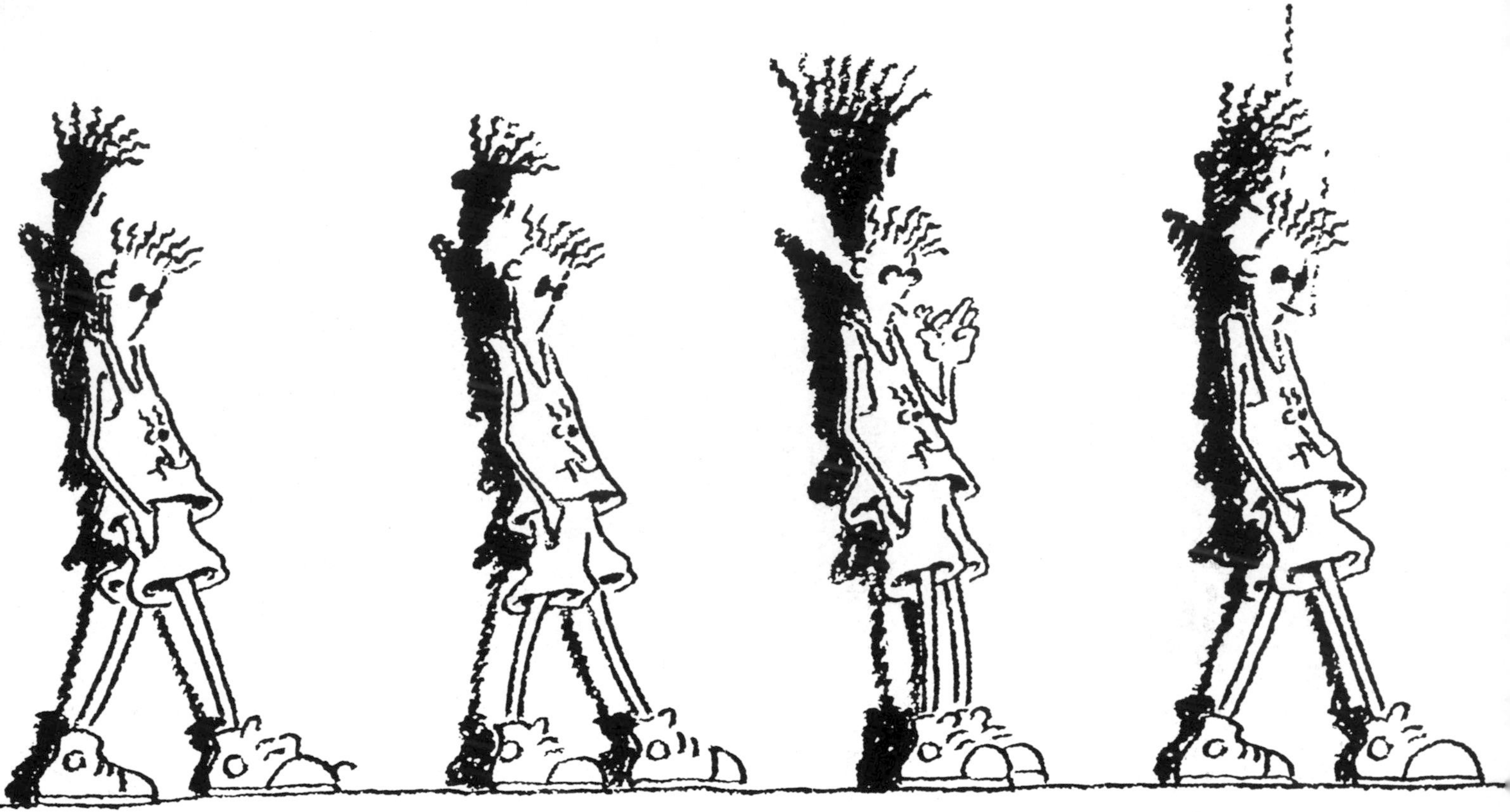

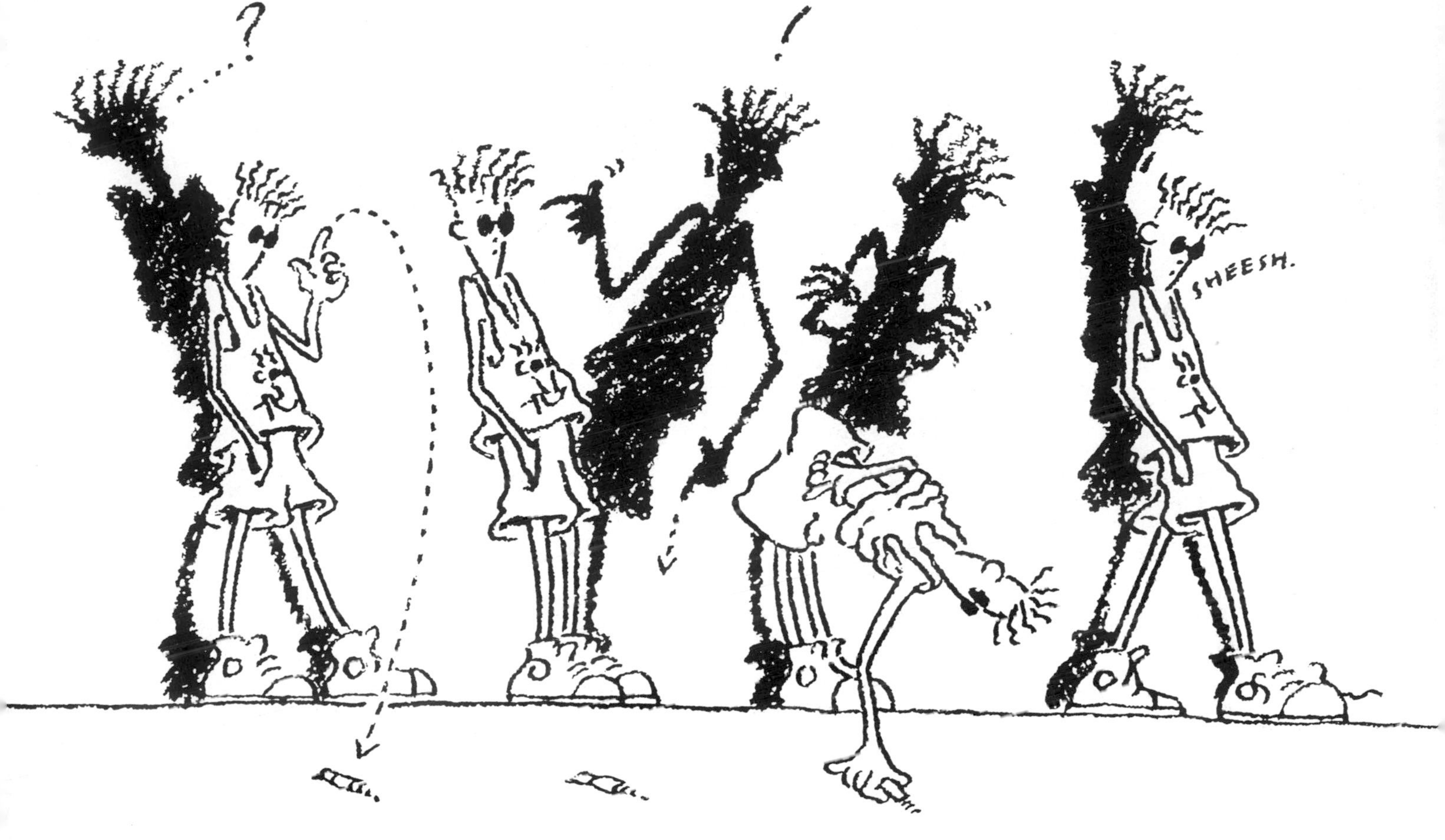
?
!
SHEESH.

HER OWN BOSS.

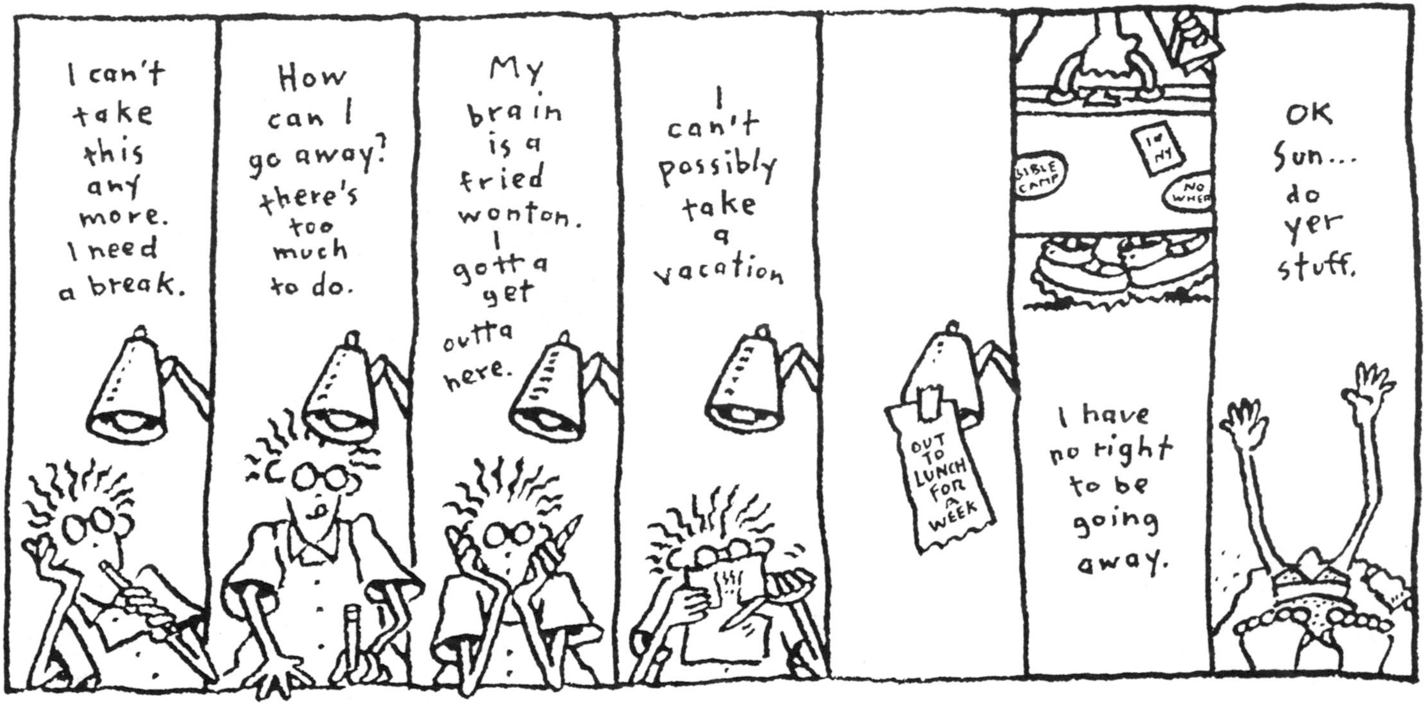
I can't take this any more. I need a break.
How can I go away? there's too much to do.
My brain is a fried wonton. I gotta get outta here.
I can't possibly take a vacation
OUT TO LUNCH FOR A WEEK
BIBLE CAMP
I have no right to be going away.
OK Sun... do yer stuff.

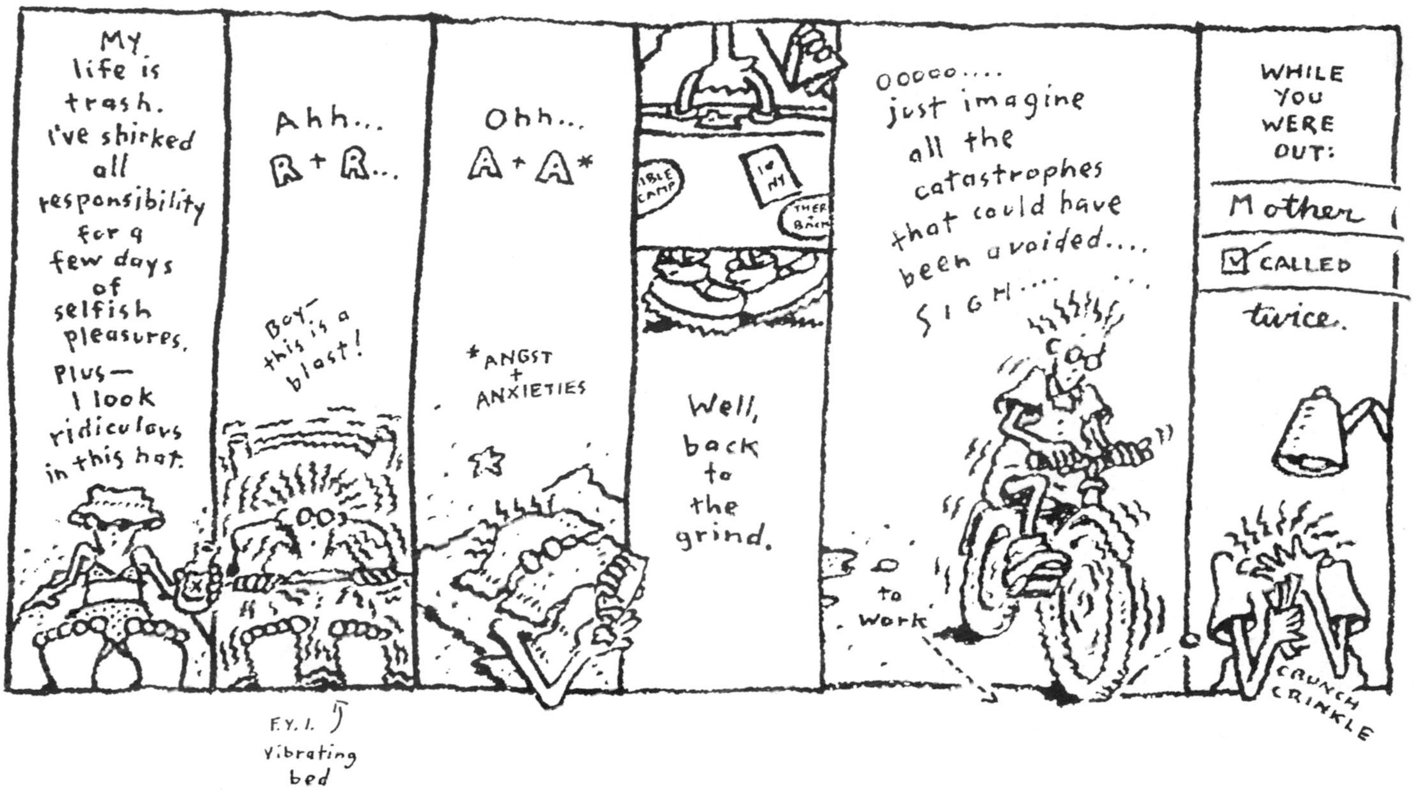
My life is trash. I've shirked all responsibility for a few days of selfish pleasures.
Plus— I look ridiculous in this hat.
Ahh... R+R...
Boy— this is a blast!
F.Y.I. vibrating bed
Ohh... A+A*
*ANGST + ANXIETIES
Well, back to the grind.
Ooooo.... just imagine all the catastrophes that could have been avoided....
SIGH.... ...
to work
WHILE YOU WERE OUT:
Mother
CALLED
twice.
CRUNCH CRINKLE

HER OWN BOSS.

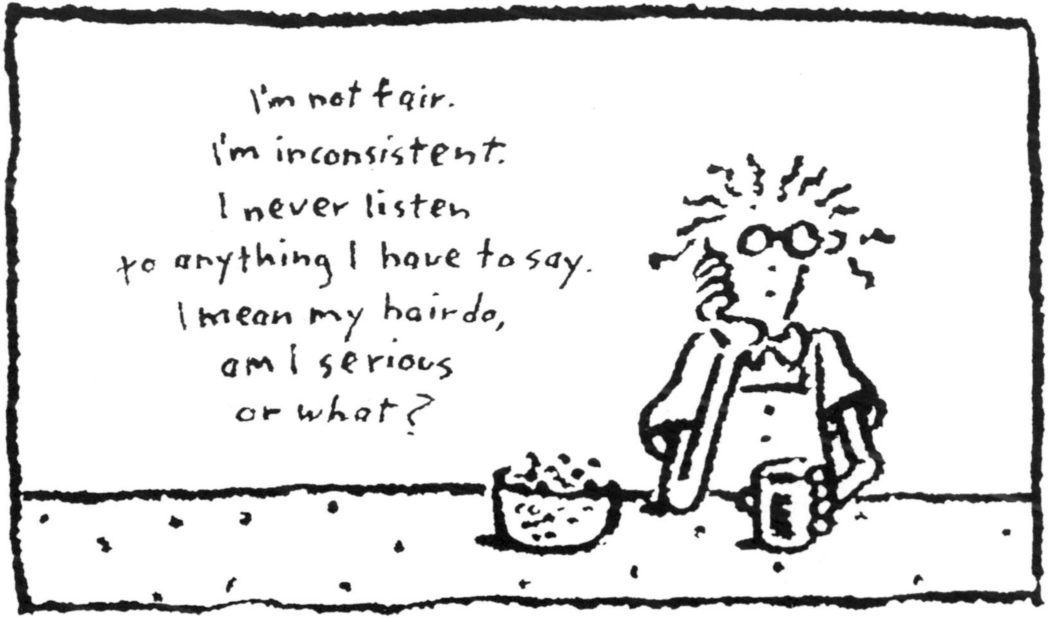
I'm not fair.
I'm inconsistent.
I never listen
to anything I have to say.
I mean my hairdo,
am I serious
or what?

An after work cocktail to complain about the Boss.

HER OWN BOSS.

Laughing in the face of Authority.

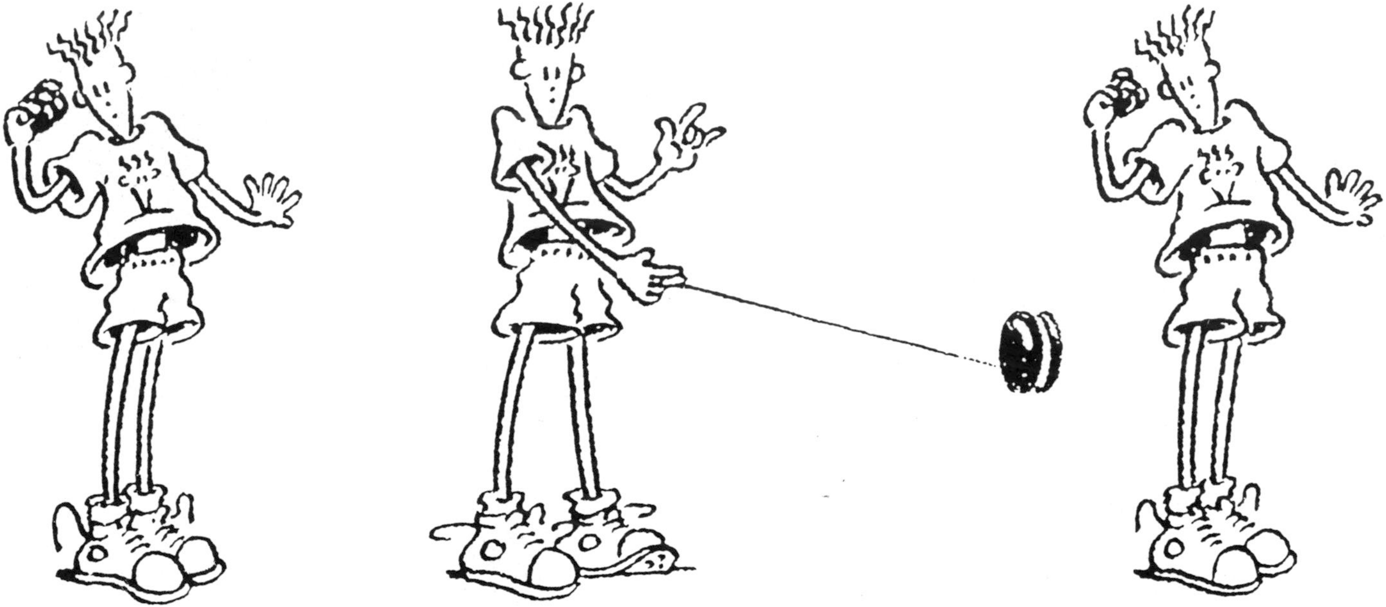

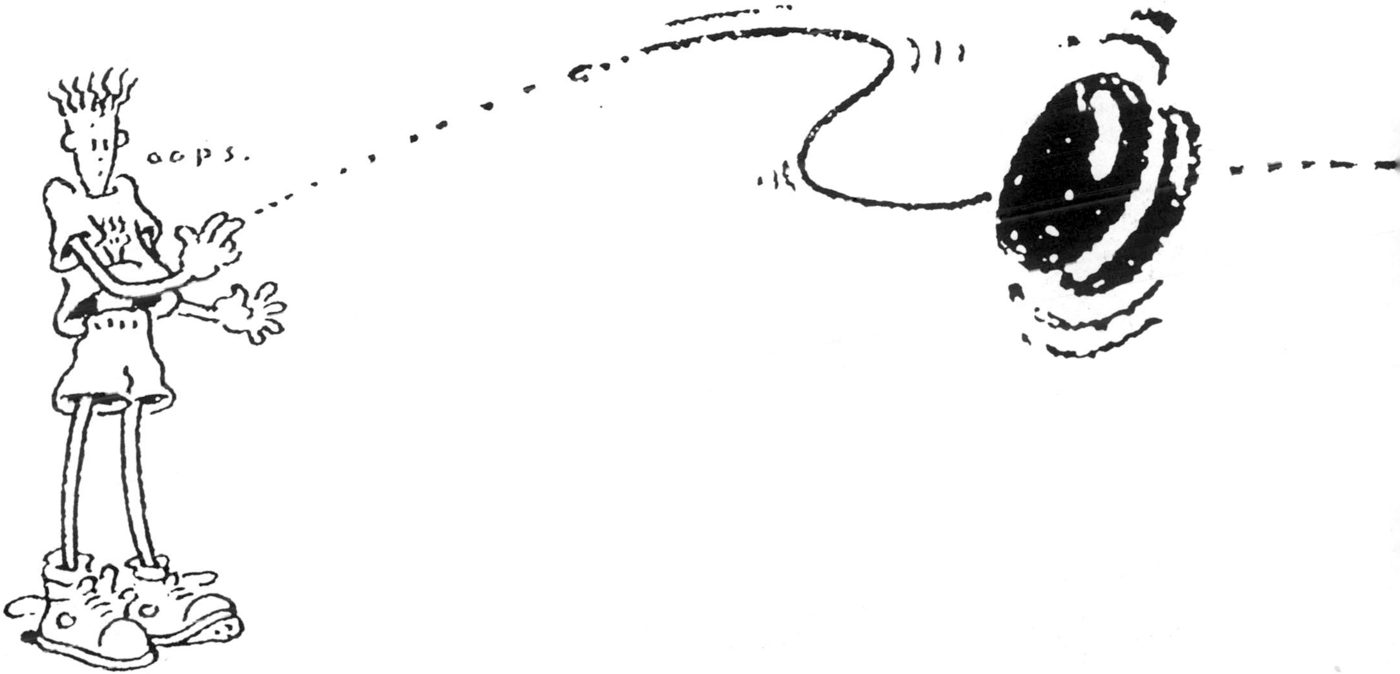
oops.

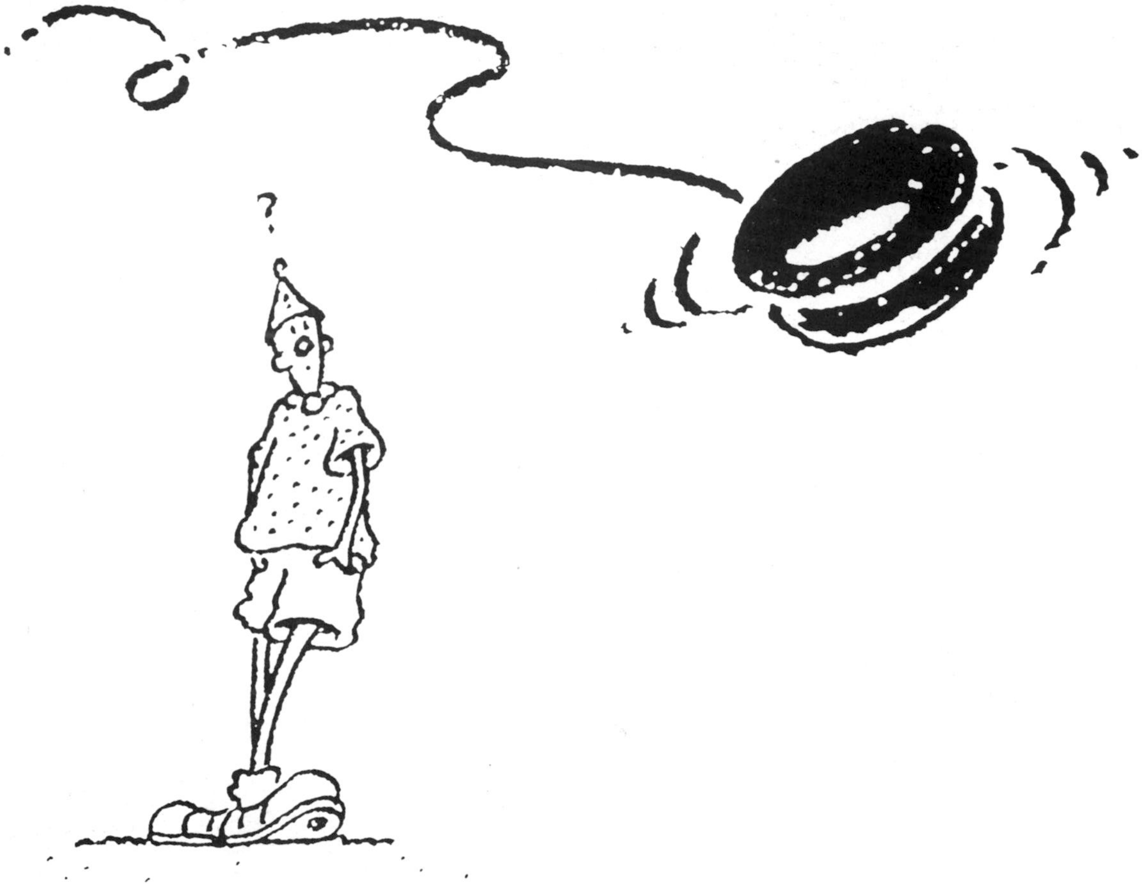

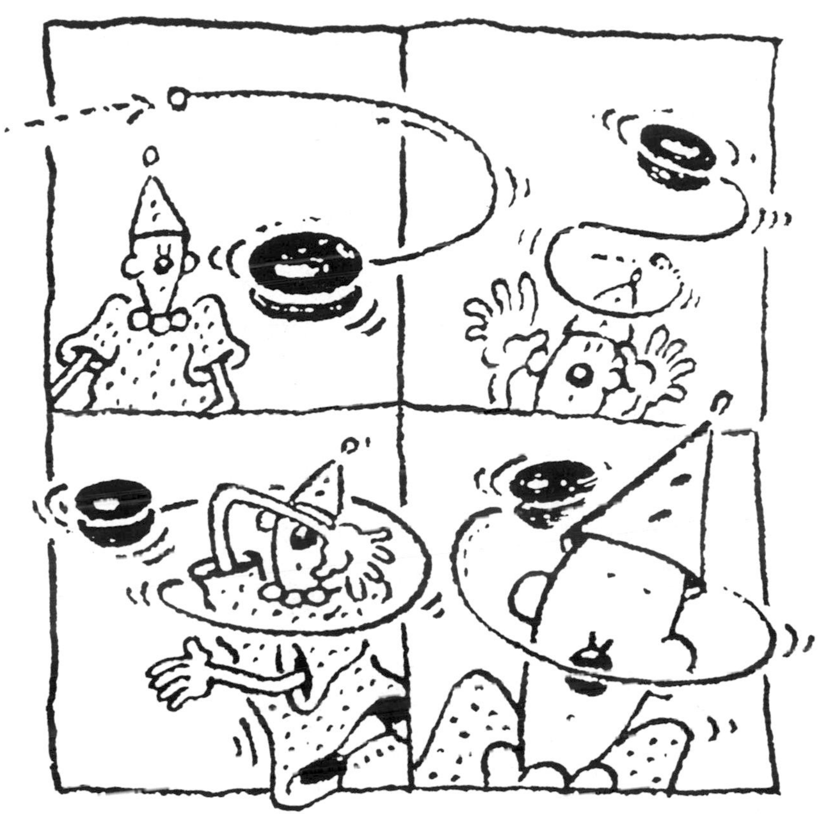

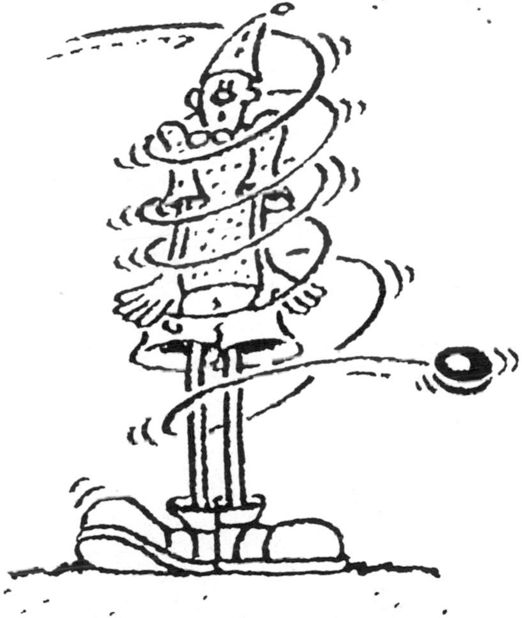

This was a Set Up!
I was made to stroll across this page just to carry out this stupid joke. I've been had! I've been used!
Wha'd'ya take me for?
A TooL!?!

Most folks are oddballs.

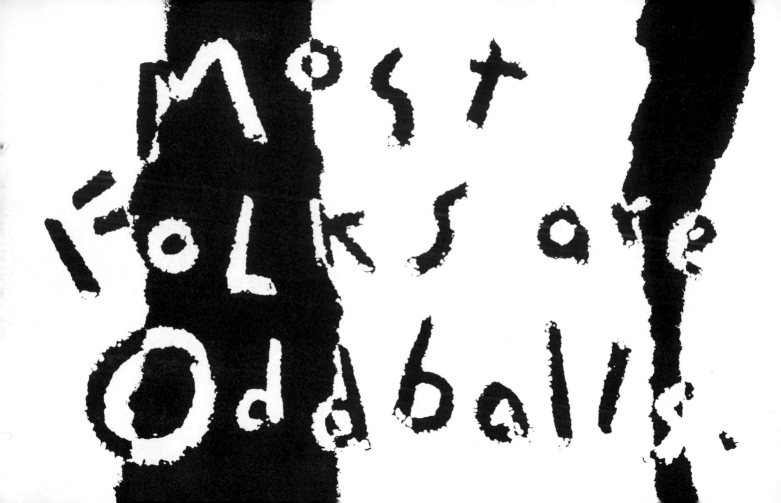

That's what makes us even.

AUTHOR'S NOTE

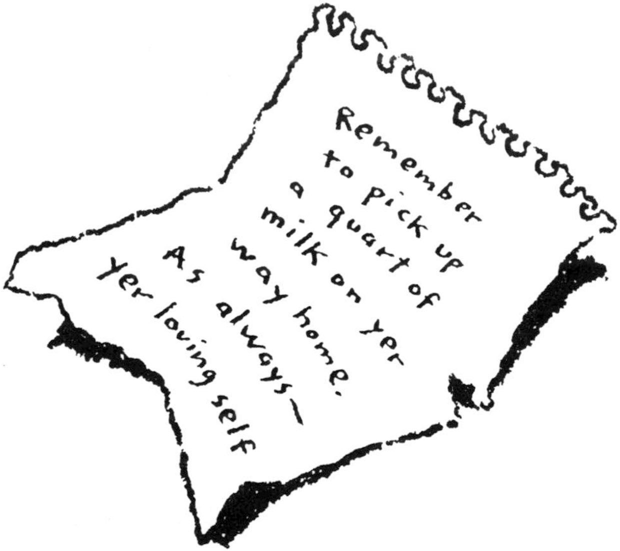
Remember
to pick up
a quart of
milk on yer
way home.
As always—
Yer loving self

APPENDIX

it wasn't necessary. so we took it out.

This is not the beginning—
but, it's not the end
either.
Fido Doodles
Fido's Fido
Boy Fido
Fido Doody
Lido Dido
The Unknown Fido
Video Dido
Fido Dido
Fido Jerk
Howdy Dido
F.D.

Timely Irreverence is a lesson in poetic interrogation and meditation. These poems layer the quotidian with such tenacity, and with such clarity, that it becomes hard to distinguish the world from the poem. MillAr folds the practice of the poem into his dailyness and back again in a conversation that literally has the stanza and the book talking to itself. This is a poetics of the domestic that insists on being present and mindful to the obvious, as simple, and as complex, as "the thought of snow falling."

—Fred Wah

While for the last decade or so Jay MillAr has been one of our leading innovative poets, writing of ghosts, straggler stars, mushrooms, and of false maps, the question of the domestic has never been far from hand. With his new book, this last element moves to the forefront, but as in his breakthrough sequence "Lack Lyrics," the voice here is ironic and self-deprecating, and while the familial provides the context, the poems move from there to grapple with mortality, masculinity, and post-millennial anxiety. Timely irreverence indeed.

—Stephen Cain

Jay MillAr's *Timely Irreverence* claims "the free will of the marketplace," trending bullishly in syntax with a stay-thirsty blend of 30% Souster, 10% McFadden, 20% Edwin Denby and—most interestingly—40% Tony Towle. Yet MillAr asserts that poetry is not ideology, that a poet's assertions do not trade at face value. What mature paradox! Another sparkling MillAr, and without a market in every bubble, please!

—Louis Cabri

Jay MillAr adheres to the ordinary beauty of living an accompanied mid-life, among loving family members and the preordained boredoms of his middle-class-artist location, and sings of an unrelenting desire for thoughtfulness, for clouds, for the way clouds cast a double profile on a lake and on his desire to think about them. I love the tenaciously embodying voice of many of these poems, especially the Ashberyesque long two "The Lyrics to your Next Hit Single" and "The Weight of Knowing Everything"; as well, I simmer in the soft yet firm set of questions MillAr has for anyone who cares about writing as a practice of freedom today, about our gleeful waiting—as our ever-more regulated and manic culture is—"for the hippies to die."

—Margaret Christakos

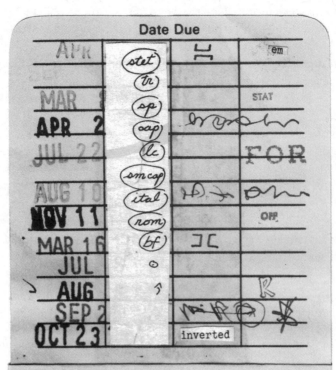

Date Due

	stet	⊔⊓	em
APR	tr		
MAR 8	sp		STAT
APR 2	cap		
JUL 22	lc		FOR
AUG 10	smcap		
NOV 11	ital		OFF
MAR 16	rom	⊐⊏	
JUL	bf		
AUG	○		R
SEP 2	ↄ		
OCT 23		inverted	

"Norval Sprout"

Timely Irreverence

*

Jay MillAr

a blewointment book

NIGHTWOOD EDITIONS

2013

Nightwood Editions
P.O. Box 1779
Gibsons, BC VON 1VO
Canada
www.nightwoodeditions.com

The Canada Council for the Arts since 1957 | Le Conseil des Arts du Canada depuis 1957

British Columbia Arts Council
Supported by the Province of British Columbia

Nightwood Editions acknowledges financial support from the Government of Canada through the Canada Book Fund and the Canada Council for the Arts, and from the Province of British Columbia through the British Columbia Arts Council and the Book Publisher's Tax Credit.

This book has been produced on 100% post-consumer recycled, ancient-forest-free paper, processed chlorine-free and printed with vegetable-based dyes.

DESIGN & TYPESETTING: Carleton Wilson
COVER & INTERIOR IMAGES: Phil Hall

Printed and bound in Canada

LIBRARY AND ARCHIVES CANADA CATALOGUING IN PUBLICATION

Millar, Jay, 1971–
Timely irreverence / Jay MillAr.

Poems.
ISBN 978-0-88971-277-5

I. Title.

PS8576.I3157T54 2013 C811'.54 C2012-908435-2

For Hazel, Reid and Cole

CONTENTS

1

2

3

1

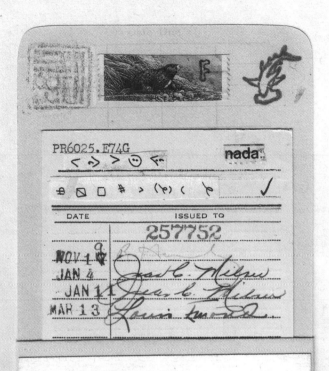

PR6025.E74G   **nada**

DATE	ISSUED TO
	257752
NOV 17	
JAN 4	Jack C. Milan
JAN 11	Jack C. Milan
MAR 13	Louis Knott

"Swearing Lure"   P2.

ALL POEMS ARE HUNG OVERTLY

A state of war draws lines
   just like a poem

      Members declare murder
   in saying
do whatever you have to do
to bring the war home
      make them witness
         our clichés

Under no circumstance
         question
the symmetry of a peaceful
   culture war

   rise up
    never weaken
   fight to the last vowel
    bash them with consonants
   write the better poem

turmoil
  widespread
    bewilderment
  & a fascism against
the humanity of reason

Who lives
 inside the bubble are
  the dedicated revolutionaries
& racist Gestapo pigs
   who write stylistically inferior work
    all confused

all perplexed
all confounded
& all against
different styles of using words
ineffectually

Confusion truly can
become a form of
social criticism

In the revolution is
a national news story
through which codes
are spoken
information is invented
what everyone knows
the apex of military skill is to subdue
the enemy
in such a thorough & silent way
it involves no war

We can watch in horror
as they march away
with the student left

comment safely as
philosophically a pacifist
violently confronts police

How can one freely state that revolution is
pretty grim & pretty determined, that
the same thugs who plagued good people
use bad drugs & violence & poetry so that
acid-crazed ideas are enabled; poems that
signal the string of random murders &
invent pigs who feed on violence itself &

cherish hate as a badge of moral superiority

Consider the fate of Terry Robbins
 who died in an explosion
along with two other Weathermen
 when the bomb they were building
to blow a homeland military target back to
 the stone age, who like others subject to the
whims of ideology was brought face to face
 with the same point all the great killers reach
but accidentally exploded first

                    It was
              an explosion
in an expensive townhouse
         March 6 1970
                 more or less
         punctuation in a poem
                    about a revolution

We all met at a house on the coast to figure out what had gone wrong
It was wrong to unleash indiscriminate violence against ordinary people

      Figure out how to put a bomb into a public space
      Figure out how to put a poem into a public space

              Figure out how
                 to put a public
                    space into a poem

ON CERTAIN INCREDIBLE NIGHTS

On hold in the stillness of the fog
With our lives. Intersected stillness
And the fog's held light. Trapped by the air
Yet fulfilled by it, your breathing hails
First the geometry of objects
And second, my stupid heart. Stumbling
Toward some place just out of earshot
I'm content to be unseen with you.
On hold in the anger of the fog
Or the silence. You must hear the rest
When the blood functions perilously.
Who but you could hear such tiny points
Along these assumed terrorized shores?

TO A RELUCTANT ESSENCE

I like the anonymity of poets who hide out
at baseball games, who dream of knocking one out
of the park before they die, who think about
the words as they arrive, bulky transmissions in casual
uniforms they hope will inform those rooting for the
other team. But usually culture looks elsewhere in the
first place. Isn't that perfect? Mixed afternoons, the endless
dream wet sunlight induces in the air, barely tolerated,
living out the margins, yet presumably held in the
same fashion as anyone else. Bats break you know.
And so does my train of thought. But time
being the shadow that remains ample, yet strict, has
such a funny way of consuming all things naturally.
You have been living for a long time now,
long enough to have outlived certain people who
move into the past tense and are spread over
the waters to be with those who preceded them.
Time turns all things, from reports to poems to
elegies, and still it continues onward, until the game
is decided. Ah, a summer night of children roaming
the ballpark, learning the game, learning to heckle visitors
beneath the darkening humidity. They stretch back to all
the distant airs I never thought I'd care for,
and in that there is pause, and I wonder
obliquely. A swing and a miss, the kids' laughter,
the breeze stops and holds me against the
hill. A wind up in the lights' gradual glare,
a foul ball disappears silently into the air.

DISCUSS THE MYTH
– after David McFadden

Today the man mows his lawn
and considers the relationship
between poetry and selfishness.
He wanders up and down the grass.
The sun bleats down from the clearest
of blue Canadian skies, and it comes
to him that his desire for thought
isn't all that different from an addiction.
Why must the distractions of family
be so clearly against thoughtfulness?
Spouse, children, the rent, groceries.
These are things that are real and
tangable. Stupidly human. How can
anyone possibly exploit them for art?
Or ignore them? Despite knowing
this, he feels a nag and pull, something
vaguely at odds with familiar categories,
and looking up he notices one of his
kids waving from an upstairs window.
He slowly loses his ability to write.

Later the man does the dishes
and considers the relationship
between poetry and labour.
The water runs through his hands
and lathers his usefulness in a
haphazard way. Such beautiful
colours, he thinks he could run
them through his hair. The dishes
sparkle in the rays of the setting sun.
Wet sunlight. The dishes are suddenly
philosophical now that night approaches.

And as the kids approach as well,
asking to play ball before the light
fades, how can he deny that all of
this is somehow more real than the
reality of any poem? Later, if he
finds the time, he'll write about that.
Until then he feels indescribably lonely.

Later the man vacuums the living room
rug and considers the relationship
between poetry and love. This is the
most perfect of all possible worlds
he thinks. Every atom that has ever
existed has existed in me and every
other thing since the beginning
of time. And if we are permitted to think
such things, why do our children grind their
inevitable filth into everything, and
why does his wife insist he dispose of it?
Why does he love them all in spite of this?
The vacuum with which he shares a
common atomic structure makes quick
work of it all, and the air conditioning
hums a comforting harmonic, and all
is made well with the world. Besides,
if he fights hard enough he can write a
poem that will inspire readers of the
future to dream about love and
machinery and atoms and so on.

Later the man folds a load of laundry
and considers the relationship between
time and space and art. Some days all
one seems to own is a sense of history
and tradition, and somehow we spend
our lives coming to the realization that

our lives are spent sorting out our
place in the spaces we inhabit.
Decisions are paramount to where
we may arrive at any given moment,
and any given moment is a small gift
that denies us access to our mis-
understanding of the entire universe.
And then his wife walks into the room
and asks if the laundry is finished.
And he thinks, what a lovely coincidence,
I should write something about that.

Later the man drives the kids to their
piano lesson and considers the relationship
between thought and madness. And
as he sits in the waiting room he listens
to the sound of their lessons through
the closed door. Every few minutes
there is a beautiful silence that emanates
from the studio. Muffled voices between
the tinkling sounds. What goes on in
their heads, he wonders, as they work
out the melody, or co-ordinate their
hands to produce a harmony dictated
by history. It is a mystery. Within the
mystery, thought still seems addictive.
He thinks about that for a while, and
the urge to write about it never arrives.

Do you remember that movie
we once saw years ago? A typical
Canadian family – husband and wife
and children – they drive to the
top of some desolate mountain in
British Columbia only to have
tragedy strike. I have always

secretly felt so deeply for the
character of the husband, who
looks out across the mountainous
landscape from the peak and calmly
tells his family he is leaving them
to pursue a life as an artist, as though
they couldn't be a part of that. And
so his wife gathers up their children
and puts them in the car, and leaves
us all there, to pursue his thoughts.

ASTONISHING CHUNK

A nervous ball of gas hovers tentatively aghast
in a forked road of political hardware triumph
and self-policing

We slink behind tall buildings or trees
          just like our thoughts
                    just like our ancestors
We all watch the bits and pieces being held together
because we're holding them there

Winter opens frenetic doors, the stuffs of poems
spill out – we're snowed in again

                    It's quiet.

Sometimes I imagine prisoners in dark cells
all over the world picturing the faces
of everyone they've ever known

                    Quietude is a lie.

I pause to imagine the voices
of dead poets – suddenly it's true –
I consider the many layers like the feathery
systems I invent to hold the content
I taught myself to overlook
for the sake of the system

– Interchangeably
          the stuffing of ghosts hangs out –

          It's similar to counting those angles
on the heads of their pines

       bodies turned inside out to permit
skeletons to float across a skin of words

In 1432, Jan van Eych invented a new kind of identity –
the production of the face –
                today I have a piece of paper
that allows others to imagine I'm my self.

Ah, Physiognomy, thy identity is – what?
– kindly study what I look like –
the grass is a ball of gas lightning;
the sky mimics all the historicity buried
under layers of snow and slush

a ghost-like trap of sentiment

Consider words – if words   forgotten
the moment a concept is understood
should we not seek those
who remember words

BROKE PRESENCE

Some days birds wear you out.
 They wear you out because
 you think about the postures
 others make – fashion that
 exposes dates and hides what
 can be folded quietly beneath
their wings. Some birds wear
 themselves like air, others
 are the weight of a small car.

Today there is a glim heaviness,
 a democratic claim against poverty.
In the weather we catalogue a
 variety of injustices, yet we are also
 inspired by the vanquished glimmer
 that repeats its chaos everywhere.

Alive with candles, birds are the
 silent approach sound can make
 when you, my apparition, vacillate
 between the imagination and a
vocabulary. No one wants to be
 remembered as a vocabulary, but
 who could be smaller than us?

These are the birds I have recorded:
        a robin
        a sparrow
        a stork
        a hollow
        a glass bear
        a hawk

The birds are hungry, I have nothing to feed them.
Perhaps they will eat all these wasps. The wasps are
nothing. They are creepy, and I hate them. They have
little sensors that can tell when I am manipulating.
There's one of them going off right now. How I wish
my little hollow would swoop out of the sky and snap it
up in one quiet snap of her beak, masticate the little
shit for a while. Then feed it to her young. Quietly, I
call out to my hollows, and silently desire them to feed.
And no one will tell you what a hand in the bush is worth.

        Why the bird hovers there
        no one knows
                but it hovers
                all the same

LIFT

Today it's the horizon you're wearing
Around your ankles, a blasé fortune
The island drips as a mortal sort of scaffolding
Wearing features lightly upon an owl a crushing weight
And I am sitting in the back room ruminating

And outside the window I am looking through
Is a bird singing and hopping around in the lilac bush
We planted so many years ago, a bush that's been
Growing now as long as we've been living here and that
Fornicates a scent so mysterious and alluding it invades
Our lives so friendlily each June it just pains me
With an unspeakable rainstorm of fear to realize
We will leave it behind when we finally move away.
Poor little tree! What is it about empty houses,
Or at least the possibilities an empty house
Proposes even if it isn't empty

At the same time I'm wondering what the precise
Name of that bird is, not the names that I'd give it
Such as *The Small Brown or Black or Grey*
I Can't Quite Tell Because of the Hiding Among
The Leaves Bird, or *The Ontario Catfood* but
The actual precise accepted name
And this is when you enter the room
And you are wearing the horizon around your
Ankles and you tell me it's a tit-mouse

MORE TROUBLE WITH THE OBVIOUS

The kids are busy
with objects they find
at their disposal but
they use them
all otherwise –
a stick is a gun,
a shoe is a gun,
a wagon is a gun,
the chalk drawings are guns,
a used piece of chewing gum is a bullet,
a round smooth stone is a crown –
they haven't noticed how the wind
shifts the leaves in the trees
the same way it shifts their shadows,
not *exactly*, but it's okay,
I wouldn't be able to explain it anyway.
Isn't it wonderful the way they play
We Will We Will ROCK YOU
over and over on their little toy pianos?
Then they turn them into guns
and blow you away.

Today when I awoke I felt so small, as if rounded
By ancient history. Surely there is a reasonable excuse
For feeling blue, for feeling unimpressed by
Values imposed by others in the face of something
Unattainable: the wind for example, which has only
A name and a vague awareness; or the calendar,
Which is a serious imposition; or even dreams,
No longer the long strange dreams you remember
But distant memories, dreams with no true place in
The order of things.   Today when I awoke
I found myself considering a constant wind blowing
Through a wide tunnel painted the colour of the sky.
And for breakfast you made us eggs on toast. It
Was simple. And lovely. This was my impression
Of such a meal with you. I said: It isn't as though
One can squeeze the world out of a tube. And
You said: You can squeeze tomatoes out of a tube,
And passed me the ketchup. Outside the world
Is warming up, and in the newspaper we discover
There's more news for us to choose to live with. Or not.
I bite into one of your eggs and wonder for a while
Whose version of God will equal a strong wind blowing
Through a wide tunnel. And then you pass the pepper.
There are some windows around us but we can't
Open them wide enough to let in the air,
Or at least the air we really want, or even a reasonable
Philosophical position to make us feel both
Intoxicatingly alive and hoveringly safe.
But these summer mornings really aren't so bad,
They're somewhat coolish and full of shade, and birds
Sing and breezes blow to remind us of distances,
And I think for a while about the old woman

Who lives down the street and scratches each day
In her garden for signs of life and finds only shadows.

Fortunately, we all need shadows. Without them
We would feel, I don't know, detached
From the things we shield our selves from. And
Today I can only depend so much upon the weather
And the little thoughts I'm having for the moment
Suspend all the clouds in a cloudless sky.

THE GEOMETRY OF OBJECTS

The house is full of flies walking around on things.

      What I desire is a culture in which
      People just sit around and drink beer.
      We'd sit around on porches or on decks
      Or in the yard, just sit around on great
      Big sitting-around chairs just made for it.
      And we would talk about stuff, like
      About the things that we learn about
      While we are sitting around watching
      Television, or sitting around surfing
      The internet. We could talk about
      The things that we've bought (off
      The television or off the internet) like
      The cars we sit in while we drive around
      Maybe listening to the radio or maybe
      Talking on the cell phones that we've
      Bought so that we don't have to sit around
      Together to talk about the things that
      We've read about in the newspapers
      Or seen on billboards at the side of
      The road while we were sitting or
      Driving around. "Hi!" one of us could
      Say, "Have you seen my new cell phone?
      I bought it off the internet." "Why don't
      You drive over and show it to me?" the other
      Will say. "I'm not doing anything, just
      Sitting around." "Sure thing," says the first
      "I'm just sitting around here anyway.
      I'll be over in a few minutes. Did I tell
      You this phone can take great pictures
      For us to look at? They make great memories.
      Do you have any beer?" And then we'd

Hang up, and sit around some more,
At least until we get together, and we sit
Around and drink some beer, and I take
Some pictures of us sitting around next
To the car, beers in hand. What a great
Way to spend an afternoon. We even take
A little time to talk about some of the
Things that we want to buy, and where
We might buy them, like the internet, or
Off the television. The sky is clear, there are
A few clouds, and the humidity is down;
There's a terrific breeze blowing all across
Town that lifts the leaves around. We could
Talk about all that, but we don't. It's actually
happening all around us all the time, and
That would be too obvious. So we don't.
This is the culture I dream of. I hope one
Day to be a part of such a vibrant culture.

There is one of those living eyebrows crawling around in the sink.

A TYPICAL CANADIAN FAMILY

Sudden rain –
 suddenly this is a nice poem
about the rain

The poem agrees. I
 am a nice poem. But
look, says the poem
 the rain has let up –

So the rain comes to an end
 as does this poem about the rain
but my thoughts continue –
 I think about all the people I know
  their lives immemorial, forgettable
 because memory is like that.
It is only what you provide it.

Which reminds me:
I haven't had that recurring dream
 I've had all my life for a while now –
it's become more of a recurring memory
 of a dream I used to have.

Ah, says the poem, interrupting –
 you should think of the rain.
Think of the rain.

BEING A REVISION

Poor Hazel sprained
or broke her foot swimming –
can't tell yet, so she's hobbling
around behind their
excited frames, within a
sprained or broken presence –
she's hobbling around it
swimming in the sprained
or broken frame, excited
and unknowing, at least so far
as she follows them down the hall.

The notes I have gathered include
only information on the information.
I decide quietly grids of technology
are not the wind, nor are they
the water nor the earth. They
are the ideas that hold things still
long enough to consider them.

ANOTHER PERSON'S TRUE ESSENCE

In my latest triptych there are five parts. A woman writes overlooking the sea – it is somewhere in America and poetry has touched her shoulder gently as she looks out over the harbour above the city. She is writing. A man watches. Clouds in the distance spoil the sky. From underneath it all the view is pleasant; it has always been pleasant. Everything it took to arrive forgets itself naturally; it is a story written by a woman as a man watches, thinking of The Sundance Kid, Harry Longabaugh and The Hole in the Wall Gang. Celebrating the successful holdup of the Winnemucca, did they really pose for that photograph, bowler hats cocked, smirks flashing; that famous photograph allegedly sent to the bank with a note of thanks for the "contributions"? Where did they go in the hallways and side rooms of America? Did any of them imagine how the future would embrace them for their contribution to Outlaw Culture? Clouds in the distance spoil the sky. She writes and the man watches; the view is pleasant. He thinks about the Palazzo Ducale and its perfect symmetrical lines, about how wonderful it would be to sit in the square and drink strong coffee and admire the sky and consider the lines history has written, all perfected by the logic of its design. It is so very sad and the woman stops writing. Does she know the man is looking over her shoulder? And now the man is very tired; she writes, he watches. Clouds in the distance spoil the sky. How I would love to leave this place, he thinks, hit the road and visit somewhere timeless and sturdy, somewhere like Yellowstone National Park. He wonders if she is writing about bears. Clearly she is writing about something. I should have been raised by bears, he imagines. Is it going to rain? The view is pleasant. The squabbles of others have many legs and arms and tall hats and what divides them are words that draw lines and offer

holiday wishes: the only thing I lack now is a subscription
to *Science Times* so I may know what and why I am
made to happen. Clouds in the distance spoil the sky; a
woman writes and there is a man sitting next to her
watching his thinking as he watches her writing. His name
is Harry Longabaugh and he is somewhere in America.

YOUR TWO BLUE EYES

For years he considers the arrival of crows
Now the lake seems omnidistant

All elegies go unseen along a line that stands for trees
It's a far cry for elegance to hold so many fish

At least that's how the surface of the water seems today
Shuffling a reflection of the sky he wants to say is oceanic
And the clouds he wants to say are ships sailing by

But the cliché police have caught up with him
Even this far north

So his son appears out of the landscape and quotes Blake:
Dad – my line's snagged. On a rock!

THE LIGHT IN YOUR EYES

Today I'm sitting next to a lake
cuz that's where it's at. The lake
is fiddling with the wind. It's
exciting. Some days it's good
to notice breezes and feel tree-like,
leafy and curious, displaced, sitting
around next to a lake watching
the kids play a game of chess.

As Reid castles, Cole plots his
next move, and a gadget tells me
it's your birthday. Here next to
this lake under some kind of sky
that chatters with surfaces and
flatters my leaves I can only hope
it's a great one, filled with sweet
moves and little moments and
above everything no resistance.

2

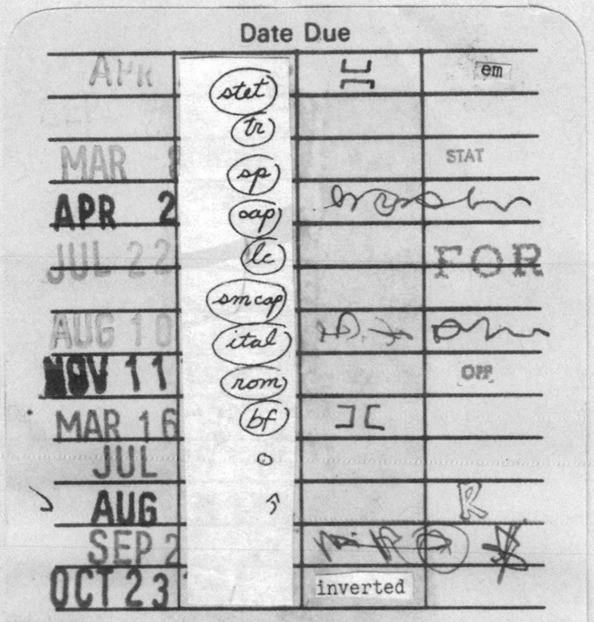
Date Due
APR
stet
tr
em
MAR
sp
STAT
APR 2
cap
JUL 22
lc
FOR
sm cap
AUG 10
ital
NOV 11
rom
OFF
MAR 16
bf
JUL
AUG
SEP 2
OCT 23
inverted

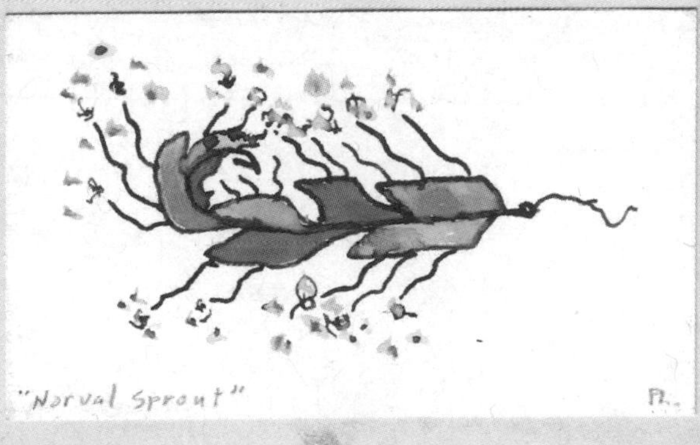
"Norval Sprout"

EATING AND BEING EATEN

I have never sought out large bodies of water.
They exist to seek me out. That is why they wait
beneath such wide and forever changing
expanses of the sky so unnaturally.
And eventually, when I'm not looking,
one of them appears, as though it had
been there all along. As we gaze at each other
there is nothing to stop us from pausing,
so that's what we do. A few minutes later
we join forces and I feel light, and free, as both
the water and myself recall our former weight.

Does this happen to you too? Perhaps this
is the reason progress never makes sense
to us except in human terms. Because there
is so little stillness upon the land we occupy
like tiny flakes of vapour that evaporate
and fall and continue the soft calling of
our cycles, when we stand near the edges
the water drains us every time.
                              Lake Ontario,
Lake Huron, Georgian Bay, it's hard to
know sometimes how or why they are not
in our minds always, why even our dreams
occur with no image of them. They wait,
and then they wait, and we continue as
has been instructed. All we can hope is
that when we die there will be a profound
silence and nothing more. The water will
continue to break those imagined shores.

the poems who turned up
in a foreign landscape
by chance or dumb luck
and claimed the land –
who dug their gnarled fingers
into the earth, uprooting trees,
toppling flowers, building
houses out of whatever
they could, who beat the
natural order or at least
beat someone and survived
to leave their traces written
across township roads –

it's no wonder poets my
age won't write about
themselves, poems about
growing up hard feel easy,
a reasonable affect of
the line you were handed –

growing up was not
hard, was not an example
of "the difficulties" –
whatever that means,
and now, looking back,
that is an endless pool
of difficulty

and so he pulled himself
up out of a ditch at the side
of the township road
he grew up on, blinked
and looked around

after a while he used
poetry to wipe the grime
off, and became a deer
trapped in the gaze
of his own wonderment

if one does write about
themselves one uses the
tropes left by forbearers –

pay homage, say the elders,
pay homage and buy into the
Canadian Dream. We know
it is our dream, it's our dream
because it's not our problem

SOME OTHER WORD FOR IGNORING PEOPLE

The road is only so long
At the end of it there's probably a parking lot
Full of relatives, distant or otherwise.
I feel myself send them all an email when I get
To the next roadside transparency.

You can't drive out of the city
Only into a variety of signs – the ontology
Of the highway is boredom and trucks
And they pump music into it, the kind
That lets you imagine yourself as
An invincible cataract of signs
Signs about cities, signs about gas,
The sorts of things you'd like to experience
As you rise up against the rankings

Why is it the identity of a driver is always
Broken by birds sitting on telephone wires?
Or wait, sorry, that's the sky. The
Identity of a sky is always broken by birds
Sitting on telephone wires. Damn birds.
Can't they go get classified as a series of
Music that was played the year you were born?
Concerts and concerts of notes strung out like
Lights against the sky, the assembly of stars

If you'd care to, I'll listen. Somewhere out
In the ditches the hills rise up and talk like
A language – only there's all this music
Everywhere. You have no idea how much
An old song can feel like the actual crunch
You may or may not have experienced upon
The casual formation of your nature – which
Came first? The city? Or the roads that
Last between them? Wait. Don't answer that.

THE LYRICS TO YOUR NEXT HIT SINGLE

Take care, song, that what the stars imprint you mirror
in a minor key – they are neither subject nor object
conspiring distant harmonies among the ignorant.
Perhaps one day there will be millions and millions of them
strewn all the way through your ruins, with no moments that
    will lose
sight of what hears the sound of the lakewater. Dreams congeal
into perfect shade, grown perfectly, so shy in the
white moon-rise on the meadow, whiter than clover.
In the midst of such an immense, soundless, and high concern
the shattered rose of insomnia barfs softly
upon the tax of deathless vulgarity, a quiet spasm of grit,
feeble and cold on the horizon. And so,
blessed are the dead. Oh dear dead that the rain rains upon,
nightly under the simple stars decomposition poses
for what all the cameras have left behind:
something with clouds for shift marks as if it makes a difference
without the power that makes less hard.
Today your genes want to live!
They are made sharp by air made sharper by their smell,
the technology of a luna moth, and the words "how to love."
The jar that refused to go dry at the end of the day
surprises the value of every single object
with all the misery of manila folders and the mucilage
parked for so many years on a side street with unlit lamps.
Eventually the slope gripped at their feelings
with the sudden wrinkle that solemnly declares:
"what shit war is" – then pauses for the commercial break.
No picture has been made to endure this, nor will it live with
the little box that remembers her childhood.
It is like the ground, like a part of the ground, a modification of
    the ground,

an awareness that metaphysics is a consequence of not feeling
    very well.
Do you hear your footsteps in the next room?
They are as a sea will be like the fire, a blaze of heat,
wax drops on a dress
under the influence of a sort of water vapour
growing out of the photo of the two of us growing old.
Our flowers yearn for the tenderness of silent winds
in some vague task beyond the window glass
with your studious incursions toward the pomposity of ants.
My dear photographer of the sky, snap on!
And afterwards perhaps you'll begin to comprehend dimly
the sorrow for the loss of that which we never possessed.
Residing in the submerged shafts of the
tracks that lead through the pools of dead water
are the materials changed forever into an abstract crystal.
And suddenly a hare ran across the road.
Are these the words that passed, their pain discarded, cut away –
here I feel I should explain the contradiction of waves,
the creeds of difference and the contradictions that are
like metal poured at the close of a proletarian novel,
sweaty with a secret dark, crummy with ant-stale,
their dark unsilvered treetops etched across the sky
as though the earth had a saint's image tattooed on her belly.
They shun you though you're the one feeding them,
and they grow blacker upon the soundless, ungurgling flood
of your huge and birdless silence. In their wake the growth
may hide another emptiness. So pause to let the first one pass.
The beautiful ordinary light of the patio is like
a hand that draws nothing except the
peace we have to die in. Dense green laurel and grim cliff,
let me come with these donkeys into your land
to follow in your tracks on the high road. And if that eye is not a
    cloud,
the weather is motionless, like this cold skirting along the hills –

this is the refuge of artists, full of mirrors, musical instruments,
    and pictures,
and ghosts from the ovens, sifting through crisp air
to give the knockout lick to your bad luck
in an airy defiance of nature.
In this shadowy silent distance grew the Iceberg
death, but by drowning on an inland sea
the trees add shade to shade. The lights are out in the houses,
    now we'll both be lonely
with bent shoulders, mixing the thread on our fingers
with sleep. The log that shifted with a jolt
is as high as can be, with the blue bunch of grapes that flares and
    celebrates
arms that are braceleted and white and bare
as if men were birds flying up from the swamp
so ignorant of any weather not their own.
And wood and wood-bank shall enchant us onward.
There are so many things a man sees at the precise moment of
    the middle of his life,
yet how much room for memory there is
down within these galleries of sheen, of flux.
And the autumn sigh of starlings
shivers through transparent cities mounted on yaks,
caught in this stillborn dog in honey.
A man lives in such a house. He plays with the serpents he writes
as every one goes home so lost in thought.
Soon I will know who I am.
I will play the deadly game of chess with this book held up like a
    mask,
and different pairs of hands will speak
as though the game was fair. The moves one makes
lashes the other with shadows that hide beneath my lids
and teach free men how to praise their own
unquestioned facts with a record of pebbles along the way.
To those who want to give themselves vast strange domains
where adoring woolly-haired natives proclaim

down with those who count out their tomorrows:
from everything a little will remain
through air or vacuum, snow or shale, squid or wolf, rose or
    lichen.
We arranged our lives in the flowerbeds and the shadows,
in one rainstorm after another, and will remain
upon a reflection in someone else's mirror.

MORE POWERFUL THAN TELEVISION

This stanza is being written using an algorithm that states
the length of time it takes you to respond to my email
is approximate too

                    This stanza is being written using
                    a precision invited by linoleum

This stanza has been composed
using a particular level of excitement
provided by the shape of your sweater
that it is purple and is really the
shape of you or parts of you

                    This stanza sucks

This stanza that stanza

            remember that stanza?

            in it I recalled, as I was once young, and always looking
            away
                        before the end of the poem
                                        Cole 24.8 kg / 117 cm
                                        Reid 33.5 kg / 137.5 cm
                                    – March 25, 2009

            now the idea of the poem flowers and distracts
    a poem about flowers and the many colours of flowers
                        the moon rises and it is the real moon
                        hovering over a real ocean, reflecting
                                and yet, as I was once young, and curious
                        and longing to understand a certain opening of doors
into unusual rooms

the philosophy of furniture looms
wondering mildly where the fuck an ocean came
from here
and remains unnecessary when out in the garden, reading
furniture is for poems written in winter
who could possibly know about the
intersections
where I held my breath against exhaust, each one
a small mapped state of holding, refusing to smell

We must be patient – the neighbour lets out her dog and it yaps

A DREAM I USED TO HAVE

Here we are in the time travel of architecture –
the walls of well-constructed buildings, their rooms
proof that change has happened, that focus
is something we hold onto, that the feeling of it
conspires to make us look over our shoulders

    – when I hold her you should –

    it was an old joke
    told by old men
    in the finest attire

                the revolving door of the universe

    is this what hobbles your humanity?

    there's some vague idea of a quiet town
    hidden in the noise of urban desperation

    it hits something – a home or a hologram

this was an epic that was to lead to a grand work but the door
    closed first
what door? the door that says no more no more no more
as round and round it goes

    and the latter
    was published –
    bound into
    the stupidest
    cover known
    to history, and
    isn't that the

silliest thing
you've ever
heard?

Pomp or circumstance seems absurd.
At least British or at the very least French –

                    Canadian pomp is more or less
                    a containment in a quiet mode
                    in the midst of the world's voice

untroubled by the weight of failure

PHOTOGRAPH OF PUMPKINS

According to my records,
A million years from now you will
Be charged $60 for the purchase
Of a book that will be shipped
To you and then refunded $15
Because the shipping will be less
Expensive than anticipated. You will
Later be refunded a further $45 because
The book will never arrive. Which means,
Ultimately, no matter how many
E-mails you send me about this book
You will never receive, you will
Be refunded in full. Snapshots of
The full transaction are available
For download and yet are being
Sent to you under separate cover.
It is understood that all discourse on
The matter will never be consistent
And may shift around depending on
Political constellations. But, like my
Momma always used to say, it's usually
Better to take a risk by *not* asking.
One of us might be publicly reprimanded
For not consulting the "experts."
Eventually, the book will be returned
To me, and I will pay more than the
Book is worth to re-acquire it from the
Post office. And while walking home
I will wonder to myself why the parcel
Bears a sticker explaining that you do
Not live at the address you provided.
Perhaps it is because you are French
And I live so far away? But by the time

That happens we will both be dead, and
Someone else will own that particular book.

GOING EXTINCT

Really, I'd hate to be the pixels holding up
that crappy video of you introducing your
poetry, talking about the poetry of someone
you love or even your own poetry, never reading
anything but discussing instead the interviews
of yourself or the poets you have interviewed
and you are going on and on and I don't mean
to draw attention to that place no one really
cares about, but I'm glad you do. The thing is
in a country where you are free to say anything,
even the truth, the effect of that is no matter
what anyone says it has no effect whatsoever.
Why is everything presented as though it
means something? For instance: it's true
that my visit to your fair city resulted in,
among other things, my now fond memory
of myself yacking into an antique toilet bowl.

If I told you this poem is a distinguished lie
would it make you suspect anything about
yourself, I wonder, or about anything, period;
perhaps your ability to read this poem
or the tradition from which it springs
would be thwarted – its imagined space
among your thoughts suddenly melts –
I hope not. This is, after all, just a poem.
The rain falls on New Year's Day the same
way it falls on any other day, but we want it
to mean something else, something more.
We bring that to the day every day, to the
self through every selfless moment we
encounter, rain or no rain, poem or no poem.
But today it is New Year's Day, and it is raining,

and as we walk through the mist coming up
from the ice and snow choking the Humber
I realize that in a country where one is free
to say anything at all, even the truth, the
effect is no matter what you say it has no
effect at all. After all, this never was a poem.

WORLDS LARGER THAN PARAGUAY

This is the word it took to
travel – they were ancient roads – to restore,
my dear typesetter, the way –
 not very much is distracted, but it resists,
as they are, the trappings
  and so I stutter –
what would McKinnon do here?   }   calm thoughts that arise
what would Avison do here?   & pleasure another
  what would Nichol do here?   post-postmodern poem
&cetera…
but then what would you do
with a voice that resists the silence
books invade with their shelf-life everlasting –
the voice that resists even understanding
 – give up to move forward –

                        so what could I
                        have done here?

There is a certain kind of boredom
that is being lost from the world
bus thoughts, unfathomable drifting, the
way cloud or water holds drifting
or a herd of animals drifts across as field
or lines boring their way into the brain
unaccountable to what productions they permit
porch thoughts in the midst of strength & sickness,
useless in themselves, productive only
inside the myth they come from –
are we the subject of their desire?
thought machines – cast adrift in the seas

Mark asks about poetry without a hook –
it's true I find there's a
certain kind of desperation
in a poem that tries to sell itself
as part of its own composition
    my protest song
      refutes any ideology
        including & especially   }   IRONY?
        the protest song itself
If I'm lucky, in heaven there
will be much written without
that level of awareness that splits
what it is talking about and the quiet
humility that is thoughtfulness itself.
But I suspect that heaven, like most things,
is more like a McDonald's commercial
than heaven.

           so what will your last conscious
           thought be – that hidden secret
           delight in letting go – compared
           to your collected works?

Meanwhile, there is the past, the kind
with intersections –

white scatters the landscape
temporarily – winter this year
has been weak

        – that odd hovering of life –

when the who-cares
arrive, they open a
can of worms
the smell of
salt water

& ancient languages
but the pink light
that is the sky
& the wandering, you said,
it isn't everything, no
but neither is stillness –
formal emotion is the bomb
transit invites, distraction led, distraction
leads and falters progress equally –
so what if I want to try on your mind
for a few hours, that's exciting enough for me

"When you cut off all your thinking
your mind and my mind are the same"

A blast from the plastic
commonly known as real estate
slaughters the living quite lazily
There is a piece of lichen
on the word lichen in line twenty
and it is giving me a nature
as they say, or a grafted twitch

Morphology – why bother?

They told me they were farms
that never rose higher than what was
chirping and falling dead with anxiety –
that afternoon as I was sweeping up
I thought about where it all goes
such fickle things among the greenery
are there so I might meet myself out yonder –
so why stop any feeling
that insists I am not even a little sleepy
and that you are always that thing
to which I turn

I did a lot of walking today.
It was unproductive
& it felt good.

NOT VERY MUCH IS DISTRACTED

How might we conceal our own sense
Of belonging –

        I have been trying to sell this book
For over a year. It's a good book, I think.
Not so much that it's caused me to pass out from
Alcohol poisoning, I'm still awake – so why haven't you
Beaten the shit out of me yet!

                Man, is this gutter ever clean.

If you admit to my face that this photograph of pumpkins
Looks pornographic I'll breathe a sigh of relief.

                  Whew!

Distraction, ah, yet, how does the rain fall, how do
I stare through overcast windows and marvel
At the tops of trees steady against the sky
Stripped of their leaves,
              Enduring how I feel about them?

It isn't as though they understand my new version of eroticism:
I'm fucked.

        And then the sky opens
        And as it opens I am revealed this dream:

What is most curious about the idea of a community
Is it only exists within the limits of an individual mind –

Beyond this:
           The failure to actually communicate
           Exists between individuals –
Despite this:
           Which mindset could affect the potency of your
              word?
           Whose mind will hold you to your word?
           And who will hollow out a space
           Meant for dreamy meandering
           And fill it with static?

In the dream I am dead
Killed off by words –
How sharp they
Who pass the time
Think outwardly

Before I wake I am weeping
Lying dead within the ground

Gathered around me are certain artifacts
Commodities of my definition

They claim I am alive

Each one has a word

How will I eat them I wonder

VARIATIONS ON A THEME

Now that you have come
over the hills, or at least through
the sump, holding light somewhat askew
for the world to pick its work from –
who really cares that the limits
are only invoked by mercy or the status
of stars, birds, certain trees, and these four
blades of grass that continue to interrupt

In this, the most ideal of all possible
worlds, young girls can grow up to be
pornstars, and young boys can grow up
to possess the cocks that go in and out
of them, and shower them with meaning –
the buildings can keep on growing around
them and the clouds who maintain the
balance between concrete and the atmosphere
will be braced for another round of flowering
amongst the nation's questionable identity.

Looking up you feel the global positioning
work upon you in mysterious but necessarily
stunning ways and understand your place
more satisfyingly.

TIMELY IRREVERENCE

The snow outside.
White that makes things
taller. The fence, for instance,
or the branches of the trees,
all their lines layered now beneath
lines that seem thicker than their weight.
I'm inside. I'm tinkering with these lines
while I wait patiently for the hippies
to die. When that finally happens
a great weight will be lifted
from our shoulders, and
we will, at last, be free.

3

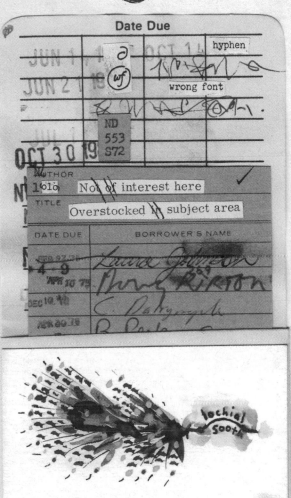

Date Due

hyphen

wrong font

ND
553
S72

AUTHOR

Not of interest here

TITLE

Overstocked in subject area

DATE DUE   BORROWER'S NAME

"Local Ceremony"

STREAMLINED METALLIC BIRD FEATURE

Sometimes it seems the atmosphere is
telling you what you should be writing.
You are in fact complaining about the weather.

Suffering a freedom
within closed systems.

Dark windows will bend to disappoint
the few while excluding many.
Puzzle at that which pulses at their edges.

An old ghost frame.

Something similar to gravity
but weighed by personality.

Say it nude, let it all hang out –
who has taken over how you experience your voice?
The voice of the unseen fodder?

As when we touch one another, will we admit
to truly know our view of the necropolis?

The voice of this poem has carved
into the boat-like object you dismantle nightly
something resembling a sinking feeling.

Ah, to sink in flight.
So wonderfully up in the airs.

A REFLECTION IN SOMEONE ELSE'S MIRROR

That fox I passed
running along Highway 6
died a little more each day
– the gathered flies and stench
loosened features that slid
into the chiprock embankment
to fulfill this emblazoned cliché
among the wild carrot

On the last day turkey vultures
circled on their imaginary axis
their shadows weaving traffic
that shushed through my breathing

Our marvellous silence
focused on this fox
– leg bent unnaturally
run down halfway
up the Bruce

And then I disappear
from that landscape
only to emerge weeks later
as a man who is not
ashamed of dying, or of
clichés, or of being
a man, even

Who finds himself in a world
where one must struggle each
day to awaken a kind of dazzling
ignorance, and realize a space
where all things must go,
quietly, in this vanished wisp
of some vague wish to reclaim
tendrils of negativity

This is the space we inhabit now,
now in the wake of each other's
liveliness, a shape we can't even
begin to describe – it exists
as a shape that never meant to
respond to the death of
less conscious, but so much
more tasteful creatures.

TASTEFUL CREATURES

Somewhere in the world
there is a book.

It's a book of poems
by somebody, somewhere.

This book sits on a shelf
filled with other books.

And in this book there is
a poem. I'm sure of it.
Since it is a book of poems.

And the poem is called
"Moon Over Veradero."

And in this poem a poet
walks along an uncanny beach
with his beautiful wife.

And like so many things
that happen in poems
it is a beautiful moment
in the mind of this poet
who has brought his family
to another part of the world
to escape everyday trivialities
of being human.

And in this poem called
"Moon Over Veradero"
the poet doesn't have to think
about the world he has left
or the world he is visiting.

So he doesn't.

All he thinks about in this poem
is the darkness of the beach and
the wind blowing in from the ocean

and the moon is lovely as it shines down
on his momentarily simple, beautiful life.

And so this is a poem called
"Moon Over Veradero" in which
a bright full moon shines down
on a poet walking along a beach

in Veradero.

I thought that you'd like to know.

THE WEIGHT OF KNOWING EVERYTHING

Before you began the poem this time around
you wanted some freedom to stretch a little –
why not? For decades you used your lines
to medicate the self against dullness and death –
in the night dullness, and in the day death.
Eventually a sliver of boredom shines through.
It always does. Millions of years of evolution,
and still no one knows what to do about that.
What you mean is that it's millions of years later
and you're sitting here staring out this fucking
window again, bored out of your tree! Snow falls
and it dreams as it falls, and outside, we are
gathered, standing mindfully at the curb, watching
the snow fall as it falls through these lines.
Before you began the poem this time around
you were thinking about how even after you die
people will go on listening to commercials
about fast food. It's so hard to know what
the voice wants – to impress the mind, re-
lease thoughts, or uphold the world the mind
is acquainted with. You feel bad for writing
that poem about waiting for the hippies to die
but that's how you feel sometimes, wallowing
through all their voices that resonate you
and refuse to say some part of you is in
control of this. Someone walks through this line –
who is to say what might be controlling him?
You wanted some freedom to stretch a little –
what does one do when their greatest fear
is being wrong, or worse, unoriginal? You don't
know why you assume always others think you
are wrong. At least there's a tight sky that
steps through the window and sounds like

leather creaking or something like footsteps
or morals opening in the sun their oppositional
ways. There's a breeze that wanders right
through the heart of everything, and it isn't so
much the sky as the foraging noise children
make in rooms deciding what to wear. You're
listening to the rain in pre-dawn calm of bed
that is really me hovering through these lines.
Why not? For decades you used your lines
so you could remember what you had done –
to tie down trivial events between the clichéd,
mountainous events we all carry. This is
everything. You must understand. Today it feels
as though we're finished with a literature that
glorifies the banal on a personal level. Poets
today resist that by glorifying the banal our
collective efforts create. So instead of writing
"today I'm kind of bored but happy to be alive"
you go off and find others who wrote that and
claim it all. And irony is born. And there's a
beautiful tension alive somewhere between
these two acts, a tension born of collective grief
that weeps silently against the loss that wants
to medicate the self against dullness and death –
no one knows which way to turn – others make
it seem so easy and you, you struggle. Today you
woke early, wanting to write this poem, a poem
you lost track of months ago, lost track of in the
sense that you no longer know what it is about
but know how you must write it without giving
up any information – it must be the information
itself, the product of its form. Because when
you started this poem all you wanted was a little
freedom, and now all you have is time passing,
in the night dullness, and in the day death.
And you wondered about that for months

through the cycle of nights and days that
must add up to something, the least of which
is this poem. And that becomes this poem,
in a way, because that's a choice this poem
makes in its development from nothing to
what you are reading to what you have read.
Days pass. You are content. You don't think
too hard about this poem. You don't need to.
There is no threat. There are movies to watch,
children to play with, places to go, spouses to
make love to, mouths to feed. And so on.
Eventually a sliver of boredom shines through
and there is this poem reminding you of
little things captured in a frame of words.
You are alive. It is either summer or winter
or spring, perhaps it is even fall. You are
happy to be sitting near the window in
early morning while everyone else is asleep.
Outside the sun captures a certain *je ne sais quois*
against the fence, it must be a reminder that
there is lightness and darkness, there must be
air and there must be preposterous objects
that radiate as likely as you do. The world turns.
It always does. Millions of years of evolution
have been going on because of certain reasons we
invented so long ago they are like a distant dream
we remember vaguely, as though they dreamed us.
And you know that they were made up to prevent
us from going completely insane, and you wonder
if it worked. People continue to live their lives as
though life were something that just happens
and still no one knows what to do about that.
And you find yourself one day staring at stick
bugs on the other side of a huge sheet of glass –
stick bugs that blend in with their surroundings –
and you are presented suddenly with a metaphor

for contemporary poetry, as such that it hides
the mind in the surrounding language so carefully
that maybe you can't separate it at all. The stick
bug and the branch, what's the difference? It's all
one thing there behind the glass. Well, okay, so it
isn't the greatest metaphor you've been handed,
you can admit that. It's been a long day and you're
tired, too tired to develop thoughts into poems.
What you mean is that it's millions of years later
and the bugs have evolved to a state in which
not only do they communicate to you certain
primitive metaphors, but you understand the
future lies with them. Some days you waste
time by watching people and you still can't
understand why anyone would bother to strike
a pose that was anything but mortal, but at the
same time you're wasting time, right? Thinking
and you're sitting here staring out this fucking
skull like it's a metaphor someone handed you
as a way to avoid the inevitable reminder that
is only some other metaphor passed on down
the line to this place where you are now, all the
things and the creatures who gather around
them and pass them around and leave them
behind to diminish or rise through the ranks to
a state of grace larger in many ways than any
person could hope to achieve – these are the
moments you wish you were home looking out the
window again, bored out of your tree! Snow falls
because you can imagine it, you can see it as
something you wish to draw on, a substance
you wish to draw up from out of the very thing
you yourself happen to be at this particular
moment, an object moving through time and
space that retains time and space as excess.
All that weight dreams you and there you are

the thought of snow falling and the glaring
sun before your eyes. Thought is an odd image,
you think, a poor metaphor for poetry itself,
and it dreams as it falls, and outside, we are
on the outskirts of even our own capacity to
admire our ability to culminate in abstraction.
Here we can never speak freely or without
honesty, marketing our selves to our selves
and to each other. This is the free will of the
marketplace that is the subject of this poem,
and it is the subject of all poems that linger
with their soft tendrils of beauty and sadness
that, once joined here in this line are in reality the
subject of this poem, and of all poems that have
gathered, standing mindfully at the curb, watching
you through the window as you write them down.
And eventually, it all crumbles before you, the
train of thought and the structure that holds it,
the window you glance through occasionally
looking up from these lines, and the body you
continue to inhabit as it trails off through time,
and the idea of time itself collapses as you fall
away from the poem at last, having invested your
self in what it proposed this time around, and
so there you are, having experienced it and
all you can feel for the next thirteen minutes is
the snow fall as it falls through these lines.

ALL ELEGIES GO UNSEEN

In this poem I walk along a path I've walked along for years
but never this path, man with dog appearing in a bark path –
what stops me in a friendly aggressive way

he tells me about people who have removed his insides, who
shaved his spinal discs, or removed them, or something, who
ultimately removed the migraine headaches from his head

about the company he worked for that caused the injury
a company made up of people who refuse to send money
instead sending more people to meet with him and his people

in court – people who are sketchy on dates and details
who send even more people to check in on him and
survey the trails and landscape he uses for physiotherapy

I, not being him, or known to him, am also a good example of "them"
I listen and nod and I wonder not only why is he telling
a perfect stranger of his injury or his operations or his court case

but I am also wondering how I will use him for a poem – I don't think
about the possibility of being struck with his stick or how I
could be forced suddenly to deal with the arrangement of his dog's
    grin

this solidifies us somehow, here on this path or this page, how I
    structure
him within the confines of the line or the vague arrangement of ideas
that lead roughly to some epiphany neither of us have much use for

because, in the dream
I wished there was no dreaming –
  & in the half-light
  at the edge of the light
  where the twilight shrugs
  at human doubt & feelings
history still has a long way to go

& in a house
 by the sea
  where I lived
  quietly, and
  thought for
   many years,
   it was enough
   to live in a
   house by
   the sea
    living quietly
    quietly engaged
    in the writing
    of bad poems
    like this one

    but they were
    real poems, or
    at least they
    felt real, the
   way this poem
   feels, real,
  in a way,
  & in the
  morning I

could walk
along the beach
selecting dollars
made of sand
to buy into
something

two figures
sit at the edge
of the sea
contemplating
the sea itself –
they meditate:
is it a person-
ification of
the death of
the post-modern
experiment? a
sentient being
rises from the
sea & renders
their biology
moot, restores
their general
sense of reality
then retreats

because, in the dream
I wished there was no dreaming –
no history, no time, nothing
not style, not thought
because you can read this you are
thinking about something else entirely.

NOT SO DIFFERENT

O today I am a quiet old poet
   stealing lines from older poets –
most of them dead:
   "the previous owner of the skeleton"
      this poem is your change
         (broken wind from behind face)

No matter what, whether
   you are alive or exist in the past tense
      I will continue to think of you
      as part of another generation
in this vast timeline of words
   and thoughts and loss –
      We all know things naturally devolve
      but only because I am half
   way between where you are
      and where the youth of today are.

   Did you say time passes?
Well, time passes what it is I say.
 We keep saying the same things
   over and over. It's grand.

We are puppets, really
puppets who dance on strings of
      a language that runs from one head
   to another, fooling our selves.
      And so, really, is it disrespectful for someone like me
            to read your poetry and think so what?
Any more than it is for someone like me
to read my own poetry and think so what?
Soon, someone other than me
      will read my poems

and think the same thing. This
is the progress of my style.

So tell me –
  why is it terrible that fifty years later people
    like me are still forced to live in The Shadow?

Eventually we will wake up, and when I wake up
there will be a physical memory
    of a realm of failure.
It's fine. It's fine. It's fine.
Such dreams are meant to be endured.
  Missing these and other imaginary classes
    resembles the branches
      of the tree against the sky
      outside the window,
    that which reaches quietly for
  nothing and praises it.

A KIND OF CREVASSE

so many things to fear:

but not death, that's just some
fact you'll be left to deal with

and so the vastness

            and the timing

    a chatter of birds

 or of chatter:

               why are ladybugs so good at flying away
               from people?
                     I forgot how this bridge worked
               insects are green
                       so why do we look so
               different from caterpillars
                        are we allowed
               to throw sticks at water

               from up here people look like colours

                  there used to be a driving board

               goosepimple – is that like a pimple
                walking around with a duck on it?

    falling sticks
  falling
failing

what we need to remember:

language is a separation
   in all the spaces that we enter
all those who live on the edges
offer their own –
   it has a beautiful name
that is somehow utterly forgettable
the trees meanwhile take on
the roles we need, exercise

this cool of the wood
the pause (vastness)
         holding onto bodily functions
            in the face of weather
   hops and bars
   without structure

            I am thinking of you
               as a song I never learned
      to sing

   trifles of mosquitoes fill the gaps between us

I wish you trusted me
but as the weather eats jet planes
and the temperature drops
the poem becomes an empty box
filled with all the reasons

OLD GHOST FRAME

So it's night again.
The rain chats
with leaves

outside. I'm sitting
here alone somehow
& understand it.

So I tell you
about it. & since
you're asleep I ask:

What's that like?
I imagine how
distant the forebears

are these days,
their lumbering heads,
their idiotic layers. How

similar they are to us,
perfect replications of
Japanese gardens

asleep within sleeping.
You sleep so well &
I converse badly –

the elements insist.
So the fridge drones
like a tiny machine

inside a tiny box
on a tiny sphere
and here we are.

All the things
we might eat
are here, if we

weren't asleep, or
frozen, by night
or by rebuke.

SAFE IN THE UNDERCURRENT

Across the street in the dark, the park poem
has begun to hibernate. The word grass
pales; the word leaf turns brown and disappears.
Some words pull their bodies back into the
earth; there are a few words that linger but
they are obfuscated by dampness and
snow; some migrate south. Others stick around
and try to say other words. Most of them
are words for trees. This is how it happens
year after year: the words change, grow older,
leach some small, primal form of energy.

Eventually I will go outside, and
this poem will be gone. Not just this
poem, but all poems. The world
will be somehow more naked,
stripped bare, an inhospitable habitat.
I will have nothing left but my role
as an ego trying to cry out in the
wilderness and nothing to cry
out with but these words that were
once something entirely different.

MY AMOEBA IS UNAWARE

Those nights, you know, when you feel so small –
Could it be that to dance on the head of a pin
Would solve all the problems of diminutive crates?

May you trace the swivel trinkets you considered newer ethics
So they burn out to be just stars, just little stars
On the great big sheet awe itself dropped against the sky –

Come on, at least look up and admire the new confusion
A streamlined metallic bird feature that came free
With your ability to network root structures

And if you can find it, you can enter
The large impossible shadow
At the end of this poem.

NOTES & ACKNOWLEDGEMENTS

"My Amoeba is Unaware," "More Trouble With The Obvious," "On Certain Incredible Nights" and "Not Very Much is Distracted" appeared as part of a chapbook titled *DEMTENED POEMS I–X* (Laurel Reed Books, 2009). "More Trouble With The Obvious," "Wearing the Horizon" and "Photograph of Pumpkins" first appeared in *THIS Magazine*. "Variations on a Theme" and "Your Two Blue Eyes" first appeared in *PRISM* 50.3. "The Patience of Oceans" and "The Geometry of Objects" first appeared in *Precipice* Vol 15 No 2 Winter 2007. "Some Other Word for Ignoring People" in *Interim* Vol 27 No 1&2) USA. "To A Reluctant Essence" first appeared in *Yellow Edenwald Field* 2010 (USA). "Discuss The Myth" first appeared in *A Trip Around David McFadden* (2010). My thanks to the editors for their interest in my work.

It can be difficult to exist as a poet in a culture that generally looks the other way, and so I am indebted to those who have been kind enough to look this way and assisted in the development of what has become the *Timely Irreverence* you are holding. In particular I would like to thank Phil Hall, Stephen Cain, Mark Goldstein (all the stars in this book are for you, Goldie), Meredith Quartermain, Nicole Markotić, Louis Cabri, Margaret Christakos, Mark Truscott, Stuart Ross, Fred Wah and Stephen Collis for their readership and thoughts. Thanks to Silas White for his editorial acumen in the publication of this book with Nightwood Editions, and thanks to Carleton Wilson for his designer's eye. An extra thanks goes to Phil Hall for the wonderful images he created for these texts. Above all, I would like to send some extra love and thanks to Hazel, Reid and Cole for the companionship and love they always give me as I struggle through; they make everything a non-struggle.

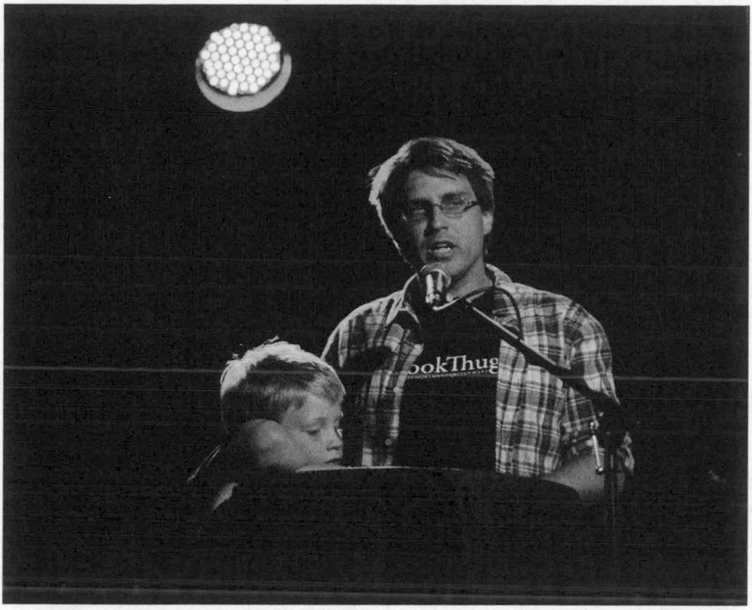
ookThug

PHOTO: Ralph Kolewe

ABOUT THE AUTHOR

Jay MillAr is a Toronto poet, editor, publisher and virtual bookseller. He is the author of the *small blue* (2007), *False Maps for Other Creatures* (2005), *Mycological Studies* (2002) and *The Ghosts of Jay MillAr* (2000). His most recent collections are *esp : accumulation sonnets* (2009), *Other Poems* (2010) and *Timely Irreverence* (2013). He is also the author of many chapbooks and privately published editions such as *Woods|Pages* and *Lack Lyrics*, which tied to win the 2008 bpNichol Chapbook Award. In 2006 he published *Double Helix*, a collaborative "novel" written with Stephen Cain. MillAr is the shadowy figure behind BookThug, an independent publishing house dedicated to exploratory work by well-known and emerging North American writers, as well as Apollinaire's Bookshoppe, a virtual bookstore that specializes in the books that no one wants to buy. Currently Jay teaches creative writing and poetics at George Brown College and Toronto New School of Writing.

Suspended and reverent, the poems are a signature of time. Later the man considers the relationship between artifice and art, the yearning and the earnest. Armed with the poem, the questioning mind is restless, is searching, is at the top of the charts, is more compelling than television. In this geometry of the profound everyday, the lasting moment, the poetics of the now, language hums. If we are a culture of sleepwalkers, this auspicious irreverence urges: wake up!

—Oana Avasilichioaei